BLACK POLITICAL ATTITUDES

IMPLICATIONS FOR POLITICAL SUPPORT

edited by

CHARLES S. BULLOCK, III
HARRELL R. RODGERS, JR.

Black Political Attitudes

BLACK
POLITICAL ATTITUDES
Implications for Political Support

edited by
CHARLES S. BULLOCK, III
University of Georgia

HARRELL R. RODGERS, JR.
University of Missouri — St. Louis

MARKHAM PUBLISHING COMPANY/Chicago

MARKHAM POLITICAL SCIENCE SERIES
Aaron Wildavsky, Editor

To Robert D. Bullock and Pat Williams

ACKNOWLEDGMENTS

We would like to thank our research assistants Jack Bob Ethredge and Robert Nielson who acted with dispatch in xeroxing copies of the articles included herein. Seleta Braziel and Teresa Epps performed the secretarial duties associated with securing permissions. Fran Bullock, Susan Harrington, Diane Ferneau, and Linda Woodward calmly and expertly transformed the editors' headnotes from near illegible scribblings into typed sheets. Charles Bullock is particularly appreciative of the kindness of the Brookings Institution in granting him office space as a Guest Scholar during the hectic time when the final work on the book was completed. As usual, we enjoyed the patience and moral support of our wives, Fran and Judy, for which we are particularly grateful.

CONTRIBUTORS

JOEL D. ABERBACH is Assistant Professor of Political Science and Research Associate in the Institute of Public Policy Studies at the University of Michigan. He is co-author of the forthcoming book, *Race and the Urban Political Community,* and is author of articles in scholarly publications. He is currently engaged (with Jack L. Walker) in a longitudinal study of urban unrest, political alienation, and administrative response in Detroit, and (with several colleagues in the department) in a crossnational study of political ideologies of high-level bureaucrats and politicians.

BONNIE BULLOUGH has been a productive scholar in both sociology and nursing, holding advanced degrees in both fields. She has received a PhD in sociology as well as an MS in Nursing from UCLA. Professor Bullough is currently Assistant Professor of Nursing at her alma mater. She is co-author of two books: one on poverty and health care and the other on educational achievement in eighteenth century Scotland.

RICHARD L. ENGSTROM, a recent recipient of a PhD from the University of Kentucky, is an Assistant Professor of Political Science at the New Orleans campus of Louisiana State University. His current research efforts are in urban politics and legislative behavior.

JOE R. FEAGIN received his PhD from Harvard University and is currently Associate Professor of Sociology at the University of Texas at Austin. His research interests fall in the areas of urban sociology and race and ethnic relations. He is preparing a book on the ghetto riots of the 1960s.

EDWARD S. GREENBERG, Assistant Professor of Political Science at Stanford University, received his doctorate from the University of Wisconsin. He has been recognized for his teaching skills at both institutions. Professor Greenberg is presently working on a book dealing with the meaning of democracy in a technological-bureaucratic society.

HARLAN HAHN is Associate Professor of Political Science at the Riverside campus of the University of California. He received his doctorate from Harvard and has taught at the University of Michigan. He has published articles in a number of political science journals.

M. KENT JENNINGS is Professor of Political Science at the University of Michigan and Survey Research Archives Director at the Inter-University Consortium for Political Research. Since receiving his doctorate from the University of North Carolina, he has done extensive research in political socialization, the politics of education, and the electoral process. He is co-author with Richard G. Niemi of the forthcoming *Families, Schools, and Political Learning*.

KENNETH P. LANGTON is Associate Professor of Political Science at the University of Michigan where he has been since completing his PhD at the University of Oregon. He has published several articles and a book, *Political Socialization,* in the area of comparative political socialization. His current research efforts are directed toward the study of organizational socialization and political mobilization in South America.

SCHLEY R. LYONS is Associate Professor and Chairman of the Department of Political Science at the University of North Carolina at Charlotte. He received his PhD from American University and has taught at the University of Toledo and Ithaca College. Currently he is preparing a monograph on the politics of metropolitan reform.

JEFFERY M. PAIGE is Assistant Professor of Sociology at the University of California, Berkeley, and a Research Associate in its Survey Research Center. While completing work for his PhD at the University of Michigan, he served as a consultant to the National Advisory Commission on Civil Disorders. He is currently engaged in a crossnational study of rural class structure and agrarian radicalism in emerging nations.

HARRELL R. RODGERS, JR., is Associate Professor of Political Science at the University of Missouri–St. Louis. After receiving a doctorate from the University of Iowa he taught at the University of Georgia. He is the author of *Community Conflict, Public Opinion, and the Law,* is co-author of *Law and Social Change,* and is currently involved in studies of censorship and political socialization.

DAVID O. SEARS, Professor at the University of California at Los Angeles, holds a joint appointment to the departments of Psychology and Political Science. His PhD is in Psychology from Yale

University. His books include *Public Opinion, Social Psychology,* and *The Politics of Violence.* He has done research on attitude change, race relations, urban riots, and political socialization.

GEORGE TAYLOR is a doctoral candidate in Political Science at the University of Georgia. He is co-author or author of articles in a number of journals and in *The Dilemmas of Political Participation.*

NORMAN C. THOMAS is Professor and Chairman of the Department of Political Science at the University of Cincinnati. His PhD was conferred by Princeton University. Professor Thomas has served on the faculties of Duke University and the University of Michigan. He has published widely in a number of political science and public administration journals.

JACK L. WALKER is Associate Professor of Political Science and Research Associate in the Institute of Public Policy Studies at the University of Michigan. He is currently engaged, with Joel D. Aberbach, in a study of urban unrest, political alienation, and administrative response in Detroit, and is also engaged in a study of the origins and diffusion of political innovations. He is co-author of the forthcoming *Race and Urban Political Community* and of articles in several scholarly journals.

HAROLD L. WOLMAN, Legislative Assistant to Senator Adlai Stevenson III (D—Ill.), is Professorial Lecturer at American University. He has served as Associate Director, National Priorities Project of the National Urban Coalition. Before that he was an Assistant Professor of Political Science at the University of Pennsylvania. His book, *Politics of Federal Housing Policy,* was published in 1971.

CONTENTS

INTRODUCTION

As political scientists, we know no more about the political attitudes of black Americans than we do about those of other subcultures. Stimulated, perhaps, by the struggle over civil rights and by the attendant violence, some notable recent efforts have been made by researchers to fill this void in our knowledge. This volume is a collection of some of the better empirical research that focuses on black political attitudes and their implications for the American polity.

The research pieces gathered are best analyzed, and frequently cast, within a systems analysis framework[1] which we can briefly summarize. Systems analysis conceptualized the polity as an open entity subject to stimuli from its environment (see the figure on page xvi). Stimuli are communicated to political authorities (public officials) by two types of inputs, demands and supports. Demands are wants communicated to political authorities by a variety of means such as voting, personal communication, lobbying, or even violent acts such as riots. Political authorities may respond to demands by converting them into binding outputs such as legislation, executive orders, or court decisions. The citizens of a polity may perceive an output as a reward or a deprivation according to how they are affected by it. The system is dynamic because feedback from outputs influences future demands and supports. For example, an output such as a civil rights act may stimulate racists' demands for its repeal as well as activists' requests for a stronger bill or more vigilant enforcement.

The second type of input, support, implies acceptance or tolerance of the various aspects of the polity. David Easton, discussing the role of support, observes that

> If the authorities are to be able to make decisions, to get them accepted as binding, and to put them into effect without the extensive use of coercion, solidarity must be developed not only around some set of authorities, but around the major aspects of the system within which the authorities operate.[2]

A Systems Approach to the Polity

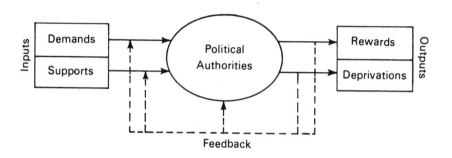

Two types of support, specific and diffuse, have been distinguished. The former results when an individual perceives that an output of the system benefits him personally; for example, many black citizens gained the ballot through passage of the Voting Rights Act of 1965. As a result of federal action ensuring his right to vote, a black might hold a more favorable evaluation of the government or of one of its components – the President or Congress. Diffuse support, on the other hand, can be seen as a bank account of good will that an individual has for the political system; only in the long run is it affected by outputs. Diffuse support is important to the maintenance of a polity because it allows the system to draw on a reservoir of good will when outputs do not satisfy demands or when citizens do not perceive benefits from certain outputs.

Loss of political support results from output failure of several kinds. Support may be undermined if political authorities fail to respond to demands, such as those by blacks for racial equality, or if their response to demands is in the form of outputs that are perceived as inappropriate or ineffectual. Obviously, citizens and authorities make judgments about the quality of outputs and their value in meeting some need or want. For example, many blacks have seen civil rights acts as inadequate and insincere efforts promoting only token changes. The failure of responsible policy makers to anticipate conditions that may cause discontent may also result in a loss of support. An example might be a sudden economic slump that produces high levels of unemployment.

Without some minimal level of support, of course, a political system could not survive. Without support for specific political authorities there would be no one to convert demands into outputs. Demands could not be processed without support for a reasonably stable set of structures and rules (a regime) employed for conversion. Without support there would be no cohesive group of persons bound together by a mutual feeling to form a political community.

In this volume our primary concern is black support for the political system. We center attention on four major questions:

1. What are black attitudes toward the political regime, the political community, and political authorities?

2. What factors are important in shaping black political attitudes? For altering them?

3. What are the implications of black political attitudes for system support and stability?

4. What impact do black desires and demands have on policy outputs? What implications for support lie herein?

In Part One we compare the political attitudes of black pre-adults to those of white pre-adults in an attempt to assess the implications of the observed differences for political support. In Part Two we consider several aspects of black adult attitudes. Articles deal with (1) the impact of segregation on black alienation, (2) changes in blacks' attitudes toward whites, and (3) black attitudes in riot areas. We consider some of the implications of these attitudes and some of the factors associated with attitude change. In Part Three we analyze the potential as well as the actual impact of black political influence on the shaping of public policy, with delineation of potential implications for system support of the ease or difficulty encountered by blacks seeking to participate in shaping public policy.

NOTES

[1] See especially these works of David Easton: "An Approach to the Analysis of Political Systems," *World Politics,* 9 (1956–57): 383–400; *A Framework for Political Analysis* (Englewood Cliffs, N.J.: Prentice-Hall, 1965); and *A Systems Analysis of Political Life* (New York: Wiley, 1965).

[2] Easton, *A Systems Analysis,* p. 158.

PART ONE

The Political Attitudes of Black Pre-adults

The study of political socialization—how individuals learn political values—is a relatively new area in political science. Most of our current knowledge is derived from a few major studies based almost entirely on white middle class respondents.[1] Although this knowledge is increasing, we still know very little about the attitudes of subculture members in American society. We do know that in all cultures a great deal of political learning takes place during the school years; it is generally believed that these early cognitions play an important role in shaping adult political behavior. This is not to say that one's earliest learned beliefs are immutable, but only that they contribute to the formation of later beliefs and are sometimes very stable over the life cycle.[2]

The first four articles in this part reflect on the support of pre-adult blacks for the political system by scrutinizing their attitudes toward political authority figures, legal compliance, and political efficacy and cynicism. The final selection investigates the effect of civics courses on some of these items. Although space limitations prevent our including articles on the attitudes of black students toward the regime and the political community, findings in these areas are discussed.

Two fundamental questions link the selections: (1) Are the attitudes of black students substantially different from those of white students? (2) If so, what are the implications for the political system; that is, can we anticipate that maturing blacks will be alienated from the system or that they will be active and happy partisans? The first question can be answered with some certainty. Research discloses that black students manifest many political attitudes substantially different from those of whites. The consequences of these differences for political behavior have yet to be fully delineated but the boundaries of educated speculation can be defined.

1

AUTHORITY FIGURES

The first two selections focus on attitudes of youth toward selected authority figures. Scholars generally agree that children first become cognizant of the political system through awareness of familiar public officials such as the nation's President and local policemen.[3] With rare exception researchers have found that young whites tend to idealize these figures, especially the President, whom they see as a benevolent protector.[4] The child's attachment to authority figures tends to decline with age but his support for the offices and institutions of government intensifies.[5] Easton and Dennis have argued that the child's early attachment to authority figures leads to the development of positive attitudes toward political institutions through the transfer of this early-acquired affect.[6] Whether this is the case or not, we know that the average white student is a strong supporter of the system throughout his school years.

In the first selection, Edward Greenberg provides evidence on the attitudes of black students toward authority figures. He reports that both black and white students respond positively to authority figures in the earliest grades with black third graders slightly more supportive of the President and the police than their white peers. Both groups experience a decline in attachment as they mature but black affect dissipates more rapidly during the middle grades. By the ninth grade, however, white youth manifest lower affect for the President because of a slight recovery of attachment among black students. How can the more rapid decline of attachment among blacks and the subsequent recovery for the President but not the police be explained? Greenberg answers that the black child's support drops rapidly as he perceives the deprivation around him but a reverse occurs when he becomes aware of the effort of the national government and the President to expand the civil rights enjoyed by blacks. This speculation is buttressed by Greenberg's discovery that the most perceptive blacks show the most rapid decline and recovery, and by Sigel's finding that black children were very much aware of the civil rights efforts of President Kennedy.[7]

An interesting anomaly in the Greenberg data is that although by the ninth grade black youngsters display greater affect for the President, they give a poor evaluation to the President's role performance. Black freshmen did not think the President worked very hard or was very helpful or powerful. Perhaps the absence of greater progress in civil rights triggers these judgments.

The selection by Harrell Rodgers and George Taylor reports that black children have significantly more negative attitudes toward the police than white children do. Existing theory would lead us to believe that this attitude could have severe implications for black political support. In a major study Easton and Dennis speculated that the policeman is important in imbuing children with a sense of the legitimacy of external authority and that the policeman remains an important symbol of the legitimacy of the political system throughout the pre-adult years.[8] Easton and Dennis hypothesize that if the maturing child developed negative attitudes toward the police it would probably affect his acceptance of all political authority, unless some compensatory mechanisms come into play. Rodgers and Taylor test this hypothesis and find that attitude toward the police is not an important correlate of authority acceptance for black students, although it is for the whites. Black students are not less compliant or less trusting of the political system despite their more negative attitudes toward the police. Clearly, blacks' attitudes toward this particular political agent do not color their attachment to the larger political system.

The authors speculate that black children might be socialized to regard the policeman as an enemy and that confirmation of their expectations does not undermine their system support. Further, black support might be maintained despite negative attitudes toward the police by a transfer of affect to other aspects of the political system, such as the national government or the President. Since there are numerous points to which a citizen can direct his support, this may be an important means by which citizen loyalty is maintained. When one agent or part of the regime (local government, Congress, Supreme Court, or President) does not live up to expectations, support can still be maintained if another aspect of the government has attraction. Greenberg's speculations about the positive attraction of the President and national government because of civil rights activities take on new dimensions when viewed in this light.

GOVERNMENT

Although it is not reprinted here, we will discuss other research by Greenberg (based on the same data as the above selection) that is useful in understanding the attitudes of young blacks toward the political system. The first involves a comparison of black and white students' attitudes toward the government.[9] Greenberg finds that the distribution of attitudes toward the government parallels the pattern observed when authority figures were the object of affect, being high for third graders of both races, declining for both groups—although more markedly among blacks—and being followed by a slight recovery by black freshmen.

Greenberg's analysis is divided into three parts. In terms of the good will of the government and its role performance, he finds little divergence by race with evaluations of the good will of the government declining with maturation in both groups. Also, both groups are inclined to believe that the government performs its tasks competently—this is stable over the grade span. In terms of paternalism-benevolence, however, distinct differences develop between the races. At the earliest grade levels students perceive the government as trustworthy, helpful, and caring. The incidence of such evaluations declines with age, but declines more rapidly for blacks. By the ninth grade blacks have recovered some of their affect but still fall below the average for white children. As in the case of authority figures, the most perceptive black children account for most of the serious decline and recovery. Most of the renewed confidence of the blacks is in the national government. This fact leads Greenberg to conclude that "attitudes favorable toward the national level of government by older children appear only when they become aware of the activities of that government beneficial to black people."[10]

Greenberg also concludes that black students are more likely than whites to adopt a subject orientation toward the government, as opposed to a participant orientation. In response to the question: "How do we pick our leaders?" fewer blacks at all grade levels chose "whoever the most people want." Also, when asked to select the sentence that best tells what democracy is, blacks were more inclined to select "where leaders do what they think is best for the people."[11] Thus black children are less likely to see government leaders as responsive to citizen demands, and are more likely to perceive themselves as powerless to control the government.

The slight recovery of the black children on the paternalism and benevolence scales is interpreted by Greenberg as based on specific support.[12] That is, awareness of specific beneficent acts by the national government or the President accounts for the recovery. If this conclusion is correct, the sustained support of blacks is based on perceptions of continued social progress and therefore is much more tenuous than if it were based on diffuse support. Halting progress in civil rights or a serious economic slump could have very negative implications for black attitudes.

POLITICAL COMMUNITY

White children have normally been found to be highly identified with and supportive of the American political community.[13] Greenberg finds identification with and attachment to symbols of the American political community somewhat lower among black students.[14] In terms of being able to name one's country (a first step to identification), blacks fall below whites at the third grade and do not catch up until the ninth grade. Both blacks and whites have no trouble choosing the American flag and the Statue of Liberty as American symbols, but black attachment to the flag drops with age. At the third grade 96.3 percent of the black pre-adolescents chose the American flag as the best, but in the seventh and ninth grades the number had dropped to 76 percent; white support for the flag was much more constant. The most perceptive blacks are the most likely to reject the flag. Greenberg concludes that "as Negroes acquire increased political information, sophistication, and consciousness, they will demonstrate an increasing tendency to reject the national political community."[15]

COMPLIANCE

One of the most dramatic indications of support for the system is willingness to comply with laws and public authority figures, a topic studied by Richard Engstrom. Using a sample of 288 children from Lexington, Kentucky, Engstrom analyzes differences in black and white children's willingness to accept the commands of policemen. Since black children normally evaluate the police more critically, Engstrom's expectation (derived from a three variable model) is that blacks will be less compliant. In fact, he finds no difference between the races, although compliance seems to be prompted by different considerations. While the compliance of white students stems from benevolent perceptions of the policeman, that of the black students is conditioned by fears of the policeman's punitive powers. Engstrom sees need for concern in these findings:

> The absence of . . . affective motivations to comply with the authority figure may forewarn a weaker attachment to the regime for the adult black. The power-punishment basis for black compliance to police may indeed be relatively fragile. Our own data suggest that older black children see the policeman as possessing less power and less punishing ability than their younger counterparts. If the age trend continues, even this coercive base might be expected to dissolve.

Another article on the same topic by Rodgers and Taylor (not reprinted here) reaches similar conclusions.[16] In terms of a general orientation to obey laws (as opposed to obeying a specific authority figure), blacks were as compliant as whites. However, black compliance seemed to hinge upon trust in the political system. Black students alienated from the political system were much more unwilling than alienated whites to comply with disagreeable laws. Maintaining the trust of blacks in the political system would seem essential to their continued compliance.

POLITICAL EFFICACY AND CYNICISM

A child's evaluation of his ability to influence the government (political efficacy) and his trust of government provide a barometer of his general attachment to a political system. In "The Political Socialization of Ghetto Children" Schley Lyons examines the level of efficacy and cynicism among black and white students in Toledo. He finds that children living in inner city slums (especially blacks) were much less politically efficacious and much more cynical (low political trust) toward the political system. "Negroes felt less efficacious in high school than whites felt in junior high, and Negroes were about as cynical toward politics at the elementary school level as white children were in senior high." Several studies based on northern samples have found that black students are less trusting and efficacious than whites,[17] and a study based largely on southern blacks found them to be less efficacious although not more cynical.[18] An obvious implication of such findings is that young blacks may be less likely to participate in the political process, which would reduce their ability to improve their conditions through the ballot. Low participation by blacks contributes to continued deprivation, which in turn leads to lower levels of efficacy and trust. The process, in other words, is circular and nasty.

THE CIVICS CURRICULUM

In the final article in Part One Langton and Jennings investigate the impact of high school civics courses on students' political interest, political knowledge, civic tolerance, political efficacy, and cynicism. In general they find that the civics curriculum has little effect on white students because the information is redundant. For blacks, the material is sufficiently new that their political knowledge level seems to rise with civics courses as does political efficacy. Also, though blacks score lower on civic tolerance than whites, their tolerance increases slightly following course exposure.

Not all of Langton and Jennings' findings are positive. Exposure to civics courses tends to increase the loyalty of blacks but lowers their participant orientation. "It appears to inculcate in Negroes the role expectation that a good citizen is above all a loyal citizen rather than an active one." Also, in the South civics courses seemed to raise cynicism levels, while in the North they had the opposite effect. Perhaps southern students were most influenced by increased information about the racist behavior of their local and state governments while northern students were impressed most by information about the efforts of the national government in broadening civil rights.

SUMMARY

Too few studies have been conducted on black students for us to draw final conclusions about the implication of their support for the political system, but some areas of speculation have been opened. The profile of the black student, as compared to the average white pre-adult, is one of lower attachment to the American political community, less faith in the government (in terms of paternalism-benevolence), lower efficacy and political trust, a subject as opposed to a participant orientation, and compliance based on perceptions of power to punish and trust in the political system. Attachment to the presidency (except for role performance) and the national government seems to be relatively high, but we do not know if this changes by administration. Do blacks perceive Nixon and his Administration as positively as they did Kennedy and Johnson and their Administrations? Indications are that they do not. On a number of occasions the Harris poll has asked blacks: "Can the federal government be depended on to help blacks a great deal?" For the 1960–68 Kennedy-Johnson period, 72 percent of those polled answered in the affirmative. For the Nixon years, this has dropped to 3 percent.[19]

One conclusion seems obvious: black students are less supportive of the political system than white students are. If this lower support is specific, as Greenberg suggests, the dangers are multiplied and the participation of blacks in riots is more easily understood. The lower support of pre-adult blacks also makes it difficult to believe that the current generation of young blacks will be as tolerant of failures in alleviating black inequality as were their elders.[20]

NOTES

[1]See David Easton and Jack Dennis, *Children in the Political System* (New York: McGraw-Hill, 1969); Robert D. Hess and Judith V. Torney, *The Development of Political Attitudes in Children* (Chicago: Aldine, 1967); Kenneth P. Langton, *Political Socialization* (New York: Oxford University Press, 1969).

[2]M. Kent Jennings and Richard G. Niemi, "Patterns of Political Learning," *Harvard Educational Review*, 37 (August, 1968): 443-67.

[3]Easton and Dennis, *Children*, chapters 8-11.

[4]Easton and Dennis, *Children*.

[5]Easton and Dennis, *Children*.

[6]Easton and Dennis, *Children*.

[7]Roberta Sigel, "Image of a President: Some Insights into the Political Views of School Children," *American Political Science Review*, 62 (March, 1968): 216-26.

[8]Easton and Dennis, *Children*, p. 213.

[9]Edward S. Greenberg, "Children and Government: A Comparison Across Racial Lines," *Midwest Journal of Political Science*, 14 (May, 1970): 249-75.

[10]Greenberg, "Children and Government": 267.

[11]Greenberg, "Children and Government": 271.

[12]Greenberg, "Children and Government": 275.

[13]Hess and Torney, *Development of Political Attitude*, pp. 23-31.

[14]Edward S. Greenberg, "Children and the Political Community: A Comparison Across Racial Lines," *Canadian Journal of Political Science*, 2 (December, 1969): 471-92.

[15]Greenberg, "Children and the Political Community": 487.

[16]Harrell R. Rodgers, Jr. and George Taylor, "Pre-Adult Attitudes Toward Legal Compliance: Notes Toward a Theory," *Social Science Quarterly*, 51 (December, 1970): 539-51.

[17]Greenberg, "Children and the Political Community": 267; J. E. Laurence, "White Socialization: Black Reality," *Psychiatry* 33 (May, 1970): 174-94; Jack Dennis, *Political Learning in Childhood and Adolescence: A Study of Fifth, Eighth, and Eleventh Graders in Milwaukee, Wisconsin* (Madison: Wisconsin Research and Development Center for Cognitive Learning, 1969).

[18]Kenneth P. Langton and M. Kent Jennings, "Political Socialization and the High School Civics Curriculum in the United States," *American Political Science Review*, 62 (September, 1968): 852-67.

[19]Clayton Fritchey, "Court Must Be Beyond Reproach," *Washington Post* (October 9, 1971), p. A-15.

[20]See Harrell R. Rodgers, Jr., "Toward Explanation of the Political Efficacy and Political Cynicism of Black Schoolchildren," mimeo.

Chapter 1

ORIENTATIONS OF BLACK AND WHITE CHILDREN TO POLITICAL AUTHORITY FIGURES

Edward S. Greenberg

METHODOLOGY

The study was conducted in Philadelphia in the spring of 1963, utilizing 980 children. Children from grades three, five, seven and nine were included in the sample. Previous research has demonstrated the importance of the elementary school years in the political socialization of the child. Therefore it was deemed important that all children with the ability to understand a paper and pencil test be included. Pre-testing suggested that the effective lower range of such abilities was the third grade.

Given the high probability that the political socialization of black children changes as they become older and gain new life experiences, older children were also included in the sample. However, given the high dropout rate of black youth during the high school years, it was felt that the ninth grade would be the effective upper limit.

One of the central independent variables in this study is social class, but sampling for social class among the black population presents certain difficulties. One of the most widely used indicators for the assignment of respondents to a social class is occupation. However, in a society with unequal opportunities for economic and social advancement, the occupational structures of the black and white communities

Reprinted from the *Social Science Quarterly*, 51 (December, 1970), pp. 562–71, by permission of the author and publisher. Footnotes have been renumbered; some footnotes have been deleted.

This research was made possible by a grant from the Institute for Research on Poverty, University of Wisconsin, and the Russell Sage Foundation.

are not congruent. Black people tend to concentrate at the bottom of the occupational structure, whereas whites dominate the middle ranges.[1] Consequently, occupation does not have the same meaning in the black community as it does in the larger society. Occupations such as clerk, mailman, or redcap may be seen by the white community as distinctly lower class yet they often afford the perquisites for a middle class life style within the segregated community.[2] Objective occupational data, therefore, are inadequate for assignment of black respondents to social class.

Because of this non-comparability across race lines using occupational data, and given the inability of younger children to report accurately the income of their parents, neighborhood was selected as the basic indicator of social class. This was done with full appreciation of the limitations of the method, no alternative procedure being available. It remains the case that within the segregated black community, neighborhoods differ sharply with respect of quality of housing, schools and city services. In short, black neighborhoods are stratified.

Thus, Philadelphia was divided into relatively homogeneous race and class districts (based on home valuations, opinions of school officials, etc.). One elementary school was randomly selected within each district type, and the allied junior high school was added. Two classes were randomly selected at each grade level used in the study. Children were assigned to the modal social class of their school, unless the occupation of the father was clearly atypical of the neighborhood (e.g., such as a doctor or lawyer in the "core" ghetto area).[3]

The sampling procedure appears to have quite successfully distinguished between social class neighborhoods within each racial group. The evidence appears below (Table 1). Since access to school records was denied, data were drawn from the census tracts that school officials estimate most closely correspond to areas feeding children into each school.

The items in the questionnaire related to children's orientations

Table 1
Characteristics of Sampled Neighborhoods

	Black				White			
	Lower Class		Middle Class		Lower Class		Middle Class	
	Elem. school	Jr. high school	Elem. school	Jr. high school	Elem. school	Jr. high school	Elem. school	Jr. high school
% of housing deteriorating	5.5	5.1	0.9	0.5	2.2	3.2	0.2	0.03
Ave. value of dwelling	$6,000	$5,570	$9,750	$8,500	$6,750	$6,350	$11,500	$14,500

toward authority figures were subjected to McQuitty's "elementary factor analysis," a crude but effective method for isolating highly interrelated items.[4] The analysis was done separately for white and black children, and similarly clusters were apparent in the seventh and ninth grades. For younger children, factors are not in evidence; all of the items merge into one or two clusters. The movement thus appears to be from diffuseness to distinctiveness; a movement from confusion to a more sharply defined and sophisticated perspective.

Each cluster of questions is formed into an index by giving one point for every positive response.[5] Thus, the highest score for both positive affect and role competence would be three and the lowest would be zero.[6]

POSITIVE AFFECT[7]

The patterns of affective response to the President and the policeman reveal some very interesting findings, some expected and some entirely unexpected (Table 2). Consistent with previous research, it is evident that both groups of children are likely to be highly supportive of authority figures in the lower grades, but to suffer serious erosion in the upper grades. Young children tend to idealize authority, but eventually come to more realistic terms with those figures as they grow older.

Especially striking, and somewhat unexpected, is the strong position of the policeman relative to the President among younger children. Note that even black children, participants in a community that is characteristically hostile to police,[8] are more supportive of the policeman than the President, and at levels equal to that of whites. Surely, this is powerful confirmation of the idealization thesis. Most clues received by black children point in a direction away from charitable assessments of the police, yet they are no less likely to idealize than are white children.

Table 2
Percent by Race and Grade Scoring High (3) on Presidential and
Police Affect Indices

| | President | | | | Police | |
	Black		White		Black	White
Grade 3	57	(209)[a]	50	(111)	75	72
Grade 5	23	(255)	46	(114)	43	66
Grade 7	13	(121)	20	(119)	27	54
Grade 9	18	(196)	8	(118)	23	40

[a] Ns for Tables 2 and 4.

For both groups of children, then, the policeman seems to represent a more powerful and salient authority figure than the President. At second glance, this should not seem overly surprising. The President is a distant figure, mediated through third parties, whereas the policeman is immediate and visible.

Equally important as the general similarities among younger groups of children is the rather sharp divergence of black and white children in grades above the third. While both groups experience a fall in affect for the President, the particular patterns are interesting. Black children decline in affect much more quickly than white children but by the ninth grade they are overtaken by their white peers. The oldest white children demonstrate rather low assessments of the President. Indeed, interviews with white children were rather shocking in the frequency of expressed hostility towards President Johnson.[9] Comments ranged from "ich" and "I hate his guts" among the less articulate students to more coherent (but equally hostile) remarks from the more articulate.

Black children, on the other hand, show a very slight tendency to recovery in their regard for the President. This can probably be traced to an awareness that the federal government and the President have been active in the field of civil rights. This awareness became clear in discussions with these junior high school children.

Entirely expected, given the hostility towards police in the black community, is the decline in positive feelings towards the police among black students, and the growing divergence from white students. It seems that as children become more aware of the relationship between the community and the police, they experience an erosion of their initial support.

Social class does not prove to be a very powerful variable with one exception.[10] Black lower class children show a rather precipitous decline with respect to police, a phenomenon that is not too surprising. It is lower class black children, to be sure, who are most likely to become members of a street, peer culture and to "get in trouble" with the agents of social control.[11] Their contact with the police is not likely to be pleasant.

Political communities are stratified on dimensions other than economic well being. They are also stratified by level of political sophistication and information.[12] We crudely tap such a dimension, by asking the children "whether Negroes and whites are treated the same in this country."[13] Children who respond in the affirmative were coded "less perceptive," children responding in the negative were designated "more perceptive."[14] The patterns are very clear (Table 3). The most serious decline in positive support is found among the most perceptive children.

This suggests that the most aware and perceptive children may be least supportive of some elements of the political system. Without further evidence such a statement is tentative, but it is a question that ought to be pursued further. Note, however, that the "President's Advisory Commission on Civil Disorders" found that riot participants had higher levels of political information and knowledge than the general community.[15]

Table 3
Presidential and Police Affect Index: Percent Scoring High
(black children only) by Grade and Perception

	President				Police			
	Blacks and whites are treated the same		*Blacks and whites not treated the same*		*Blacks and whites are treated the same*	*Blacks and whites not treated the same*
Grade 3	59	(117)	57	(49)	73	72
Grade 5	25	(137)	20	(66)	45	55
Grade 7	26	(48)	5	(66)	33	26
Grade 9	29	(52)	12	(122)	38	15

ROLE ATTRIBUTES

Children are also able to make judgments about the ability of an authority figure to perform the tasks of his position. The second index taps children's assessments of the qualities authorities bring to their respective duties. Are they more intelligent than other people? Do they work harder? Do they possess and exercise power?

Several interesting patterns are evident in children's assessment of role attributes (Table 4). As was true of the "positive affect" dimension, young children tend to react quite positively to authority figures, to be perhaps overly generous in their assessments. This adds further weight to the idealization thesis raised previously. Also of interest is the fact that the younger black children are more prone to be supportive than are whites.

Table 4
Presidential and Police Role Performance Index:
Percent Scoring High by Race and Grade

	Black	*White*	*Black*	*White*
Grade 3	81	70	75	68
Grade 5	33	68	35	65
Grade 7	35	50	30	45
Grade 9	23	51	26	36

The developmental pattern for black children beyond the third grade is unambiguous. That is, with respect to both the President and the policeman, they manifest serious declines in role related judgments. White students, relative to black students, maintain a substantial appreciation for the role attributes of the President. Indeed, it is interesting to note that older white children come to opposite judgments about the President on the two dimensions under consideration. That is, they tend to be quite low on the positive affect measures yet relatively high on the role dimension. Black children tend to remain low on both.

One might conceivably trace this state of affairs to two factors, the nature of the schooling provided for black and white children[16] and to feelings of affect. It must be concluded that despite sometimes vigorous legislative and judicial activities, schooling for black children in the United States remains separate and unequal. It has been found that such schools reflect adversely upon school achievement and cognitive development. In this context, it will be argued that the assessment of role performance and qualities of political authorities is largely a cognitive consideration, and as such, the nature of schooling becomes of central importance. Surely, role assessment is, in good part, a cognitive activity. No matter how one feels about a particular President, it is obvious that the chores of the office are backbreaking and unending, and that moreover, he exercises enormous power. This is the type of information that is usually transmitted in classroom work. The quality of the school must surely be a factor in the child's incorporation of the information.

There must as well be some carry-over from the positive affect dimension, a dimension along which black and white children diverged with maturation. In assessing role performance, children probably allow their feelings of affect towards authority to color their judgments about role performance. Few people have such a structured view of the world that each compartment of their cognitive and affective reservoir remains isolated and unaffected by other compartments.

In the case of the role attributes dimension, children's assessments are not, by and large, differentiated by either racial class or accuracy of perception. The only exception is the slight tendency for lower class children to show higher levels of support. With respect to this dimension, race remains the critical variable.[17]

THE VULNERABILITY-IDEALIZATION HYPOTHESIS

The data in this paper speak to another important issue in the literature, that being the vulnerability-idealization hypothesis raised by a number of scholars.[18] Those arguing for such a vulnerability-idealization hypothesis are affirmed to the extent that all groups of children in this study show marked "idealization" of political authority figures in the third grade. No matter the race or social status, children tend to display high "positive affect" and "role attribute" orientations in the lower grades. Vulnerability, the sense of powerlessness among young children, may well be a factor.

Yet as Jaros so perceptively points out in his critique of the universal vulnerability-idealization hypothesis,[19] not all groups of children hold exactly the same view of authority nor do they feel equally vulnerable. Our data support Jaros. Despite the prevalence of early idealization, the data show rather distinct race and slight class differences. That is, black children tend to idealize authority more than do whites and lower class children do so more than middle class children. Not all children, therefore, hold similar views of authority.

A DIFFERENTIAL VULNERABILITY HYPOTHESIS

The two seemingly opposite hypotheses may be combined by suggesting that children differ in their conceptions of political authority figures and that such differences can, in some measure, be explained by differences in feelings of vulnerability. That is, both black children and lower class children feel more vulnerable than do other children and tend to more readily idealize political authority (see Table 5). The data show that blacks are more fearful than whites, and lower class children are more fearful than middle class children. This becomes especially significant in

Table 5
Percent of Third Grade Children Responding:

Black (N = 108)		White (N = 111)	
(1) I'm often afraid of Government			
27.8		16.2	
Middle class	Lower class	Middle class	Lower class
23.1	32.1	16.4	16.1
(2) I'm afraid of the President			
20.4		15.3	
Middle class	Lower class	Middle class	Lower class
13.5	26.8	10.9	19.6
(3) I'm afraid of the Policeman			
18.5		10.8	
Middle class	Lower class	Middle class	Lower class
11.5	25.0	1.8	19.6

light of the fact that black and lower class children are most likely to idealize authority in the early grades. Differential levels of idealization, then, may be logically traced to differential feelings of anxiety or vulnerability.

EARLY LEARNING AND ATTACHMENT

Returning now to consideration of the "positive affect" and the "role attribute" clusters, we are led to a number of conclusions. Of special interest is the fact that older black students demonstrate rather high positive affect for the President but low appreciation of his role, whereas white students are reversed. Thus while white children are not particularly enamored of the President, they seem to at least gain an appreciation of what his job entails.

The data suggest that maturing black children come to perceive the President as a kind of benign grandfather figure. While among the oldest black children there is an inclination to see him as friendly and to express "I like him," he is not seen as particularly hard working, helpful or powerful. To the extent that a grandfather image may be defined as warm but ineffectual, the image would seem to fit.

The evidence also suggests that the policeman is a more potent and relevant authority figure than the President for young children. This should not be too surprising. The only contact with the President for a young child is through the media and through his parents. Given the low saliency of politics in most American family conversations and the child's limited contact with politically relevant material in the media, the President must remain a rather distant figure.

The policeman on the other hand must be very salient to the young child. The child experiences the policeman in a rather immediate sense; his reality is not filtered or mediated through any third party or institution. He visibly directs things, he gives orders, he wears a uniform and carries a gun. To the third grade child he must be an awesome character indeed.

However, this high attachment in the third grade fails to hold back the growing disaffection for police among black children. It apparently takes little time for black children to bring their attitudes toward the police into line with the realities of their everyday lives.[20] Early attachment is thus quickly eroded by personal experience with the police and by absorption of community attitudes with maturation.

Thus, later experience serves to seriously undermine the initial attachment of the black child to the police. Early attachment does not persist against the overwhelming array of personal and community experiences with the forces of social control and order. While we are dealing with an extreme case, it is at least a basis for calling into question the prevalent hypothesis that early attachment to authority figures is transferred to the remainder of the political system. Only longitudinal analysis can give us reliable evidence, but it appears that early attachment to the President and the policeman does not prevent an eventual decline in positive affect for both of these figures. If positive affect is not maintained for these figures, it is not easy to see how that affect is transferred to other political institutions as some scholars suggest.[21]

In the final analysis, this controversy cannot be settled without longitudinal data. Without such data, there exists no way to reject the possibility that those who are not attached to political authorities do become attached to the political system at some later point in time, or conversely, that those who are initially attached to political authorities later become alienated from the system.

NOTES

[1]For a number of excellent articles which highlight the relative economic positions of black and white see the following collections: Talcott Parsons and Kenneth Clark, *The Negro American* (Boston: Beacon Press, 1965); and Louis A. Ferman, Joyce L. Kornbluh, and Alan Haber, *Poverty in America* (Ann Arbor: University of Michigan Press, 1969).

[2]An excellent discussion of this phenomenon may be found in St. Clair Drake and Horace Cayton, *Black Metropolis: A Study of Negro Life in a Southern City* (New York: Harper and Row, 1945).

[3]Since we shall make statements of the type, "black children think so and so . . . ," and "white children think so and so . . . ," it was necessary to weight the black lower class sample. Census data reveals that the ratio between white collar and blue collar in metropolitan areas for whites is 1:1 and for blacks is 1:2.5. (Skilled labor was included in the white collar group for blacks given the different interpretation of the meaning of occupation in the black community discussed above.) Since approximately equal numbers of children were sampled in each group, the black lower class sample was weighted by a factor of 2.5 to allow for general statements about black children in Philadelphia. Failure to weight the sample would have seriously overrepresented the black middle class.

[4]Louis McQuitty, "Elementary Factor Analysis," *Psychological Reports,* 9 (1961), pp. 71–78.

[5]The items are as follows:

		Factor Loading
Positive Affect	The President (Policeman) is/ isn't very friendly	.66
	The President (Policeman) is/ isn't very helpful	1.00
	I like/don't like the President (Policeman) very much	.44
Role Attributes		
	The President (Policeman) knows/doesn't know very much	.32
	The President (Policeman) works/doesn't work very hard	.25
	The President (Policeman) can/can't make people do what he wants them to do	1.00

[6]In dealing with children and the development of political orientations, one faces certain intractable problems not faced in normal opinion research. That is, the problem of changing orientations with maturation makes the use of indices more precarious. In adult populations, it is usually the case that one finds consistent factors over most age groups and indices are easily built. With children, one has the case where a situation of no structure in world view evolves into a structured one as the child grows older. In short, one does not have the luxury of consistency. And yet, we will persist in the use of these indices. We do so because we face a similar problem using item analysis. The meaning of items changes for children with maturation, so as researchers we are always faced with inconsistency when dealing with children. Logically, the problem of consistency is not eliminated by moving from index analysis to item analysis.

Thus, indices are constructed with the full realization that they are based upon item clusters that do not appear until the upper grades. We must proceed on the assumption that latent structure exists in the lower grades and becomes apparent in the upper grades. This is not so far fetched as it sounds. If we compare the graphs of development of each item, items within clusters are almost identical to each other and differ significantly from items in the other clusters.

[7]Negative responses are not reported nor are "don't knows" because our central concern is the pattern of development of *positive* affect and support.

[8]In every poll (of which I am aware) that taps the attitudes of black people toward public and private officials, police invariably fare the worst. For summaries see *The Report of the President's Commission on Civil Disorders* (New York: Bantam, 1968); William Brink and Louis Harris, *Black and White: A Study of U.S. Racial Attitudes Today* (New York: Simon and Schuster, 1966); and Jerome Skolnick, *The Politics of Protest* (New York: Ballantine Books, Inc., 1969).

[9]Among older children, man and office become clearly distinguishable. From conversations with these children, it becomes evident that responses to items were based on perceptions of President Johnson, a most unpopular president at the time of the study.

[10]To conserve space, these data are not reported. The reader may refer to Greenberg, *Political Socialization to Support the System.*

[11]An excellent discussion of this point may be found in David A. Schulz, *Coming Up Black* (Englewood Cliffs, N.J.: Prentice-Hall, 1969).

[12]For the best exposition of this theme, see V. O. Key, *Public Opinion and American Democracy* (New York: Knopf, 1961).

[13]In this instance, we are concerned with black children alone. That is, how does a socially disadvantaged group transfer its experience into political terms.

[14]This item, accuracy of perception, would seem to be a potentially powerful variable. In the first place, as mentioned in the text, political communities are stratified by levels of political information and sophistication, a phenomenon which is closely tied to significant differences in political behavior. Second, the various riot commission reports of recent years have all pointed out that riot participants tend to be more politically aware. That is, disaffection seems to be tied to knowledge. It would be interesting, therefore, to examine at what point in the socialization process such a linkage is made.

While only a single item is used to assess accuracy of perception, it is highly correlated with other information items in the test instrument, thus reinforcing confidence in its use.

[15]See *Report of the President's Advisory Commision on Civil Disorders* (New York: Bantam, 1968), pp. 128–129.

[16]The crisis in black education is documented comprehensively and devastatingly in both *The President's Advisory Commision on Civil Disorders* and in *Equality of Educational Opportunity* (U.S. Office of Education, 1966), better known as the "Coleman Report"; and in *Racial Isolation in the Public School* (A Report of the United States Commission on Civil Rights, 1967).

[17]Again, to conserve space, the data are not reported. Please refer to Greenberg, *Political Socialization to Support of the System.*

[18]See Note 6.

[19]Dean Jaros, "Children's Orientations toward the President: Some Additional Theoretical Considerations," *Journal of Politics,* 29 (May, 1967), pp. 368–387.

[20]The police have a history of brutalizing black people. See Skolnick, *The Politics of Protest.*

[21]The notion that later life experiences may override early learning is consistent with the formulations of Gabriel Almond and Sidney Verba, *The Civic Culture* (Princeton: Princeton University Press, 1963), Chap. 12; and K. Prewitt, H. Eulau and B. Zisk, "Political Socialization and Political Roles," *Public Opinion Quarterly,* 30 (Winter, 1967), pp. 569–582.

Chapter 2

THE POLICEMAN AS AN AGENT OF REGIME LEGITIMATION

Harrell R. Rodgers, Jr.
George Taylor

An important condition or regime stability is acceptance by citizens of the legitimacy of the political system and its agents.[1] This study approaches this meta-hypothesis via an integrative focus on policemen as agents of regime legitimation and on children as new recruits for the political system. The rationale for the paired emphasis on police and students is direct. A recent study of the civic attitudes of children concluded that the policeman is an especially important representative of the American polity because he is one of the earliest governmental figures perceived by children being introduced into the political system.[2] Easton and Dennis believe that the policeman's visibility gives him strong theoretical importance for the socialization process because it makes him a convenient link between the child and the political world.[3] The policeman likewise performs a critical function for the political system, Easton and Dennis hypothesize, by imbuing the young child with a sense of the legitimacy of external authority.[4] Through the physical symbol of the policeman the child learns there are legitimate sources of authority he must obey outside his family. The authors surmise that since most young children respect and feel positively about the policeman, they readily accept the legitimacy of the political order he repre-

Reprinted from "The Policeman as an Agent of Regime Legitimation," *Midwest Journal of Political Science,* 15 (February, 1971), pp. 72–86, by permission of the authors and Wayne State University Press. Copyright 1971 by Wayne State University Press.

This research was made possible by a grant from the Social Science Research Institute of the University of Georgia. The authors would like to thank their colleagues Charles Bullock, Robert Clute, and Brett W. Hawkins for advice and criticism on an earlier draft of the paper.

sents.[5] The child's acceptance of external authority as legitimate is believed to be critical in the development of a moral obligation to comply.

THE HYPOTHESIS AND THE DATA

Easton and Dennis further speculate on the importance of the policeman by hypothesizing that:

> If as children mature they come to despise, distrust, scorn, or reject the police, the probabilities would be considerable (assuming no compensatory mechanisms came into operation in later years) that acceptance of the whole structure of authority at all levels would suffer.[6]

This is an interesting and important hypothesis. Easton and Dennis are elevating a largely-ignored civil servant to an important role in the political system. The policeman becomes an agent of the system who initially cues and awakens sentiments in the child that are vital for a stable political system (i.e., a sense of the legitimacy of external authority). Additionally, the child's image of the policeman may have important consequences for the political system even as he matures. The purpose of this paper is to test this latter conclusion by examining the association between attitudes toward the police and acceptance of political authority. By testing this hypothesis we hope to expand the generality of support theory.

The data for analysis consist of responses by secondary school students. Unlike the Easton and Dennis sample, which had a white-urban focus, our sample contains a large number of black students. The data were gathered by surveying ninth- through twelfth-grade students from seven high schools in a southern urban area. Two of the seven schools were segregated (1 white, 1 black), two were integrated (42 percent to 51 percent white), and three were partially integrated (15 percent to 35 percent mixed). The sample was stratified by grade and three classrooms were randomly selected from each. Paper-and-pencil questionnaires were administered to all students in each classroom selected. The interviewers were graduate students trained by the authors. If the class was segregated an interviewer of the same race administered the questionnaire. Three hundred and two usable questionnaires were obtained. One hundred and ninety-six of the students were white, and one hundred and six were black. The whole sample will be examined first and then the data will be broken down by race.[7]

ATTITUDES TOWARD THE POLICE

Each student was asked five questions concerning attitudes toward the police (See Table 3). The responses to the questions were weighted and added to produce a Police Attitude index for each student, which ranged from 5 (most positive) to 24 (most negative).[8] In the following statistical analysis this score serves as the major independent variable. For descriptive purposes the students' responses to the above mentioned questions can be classified into three categories: positive (N = 62), ambivalent (N = 178), or negative (N = 62).[9] This classification indicates that the majority of the students have some positive and some negative attitudes toward the police, with about 40 percent of the students manifesting either strongly positive or strongly negative attitudes.

The Police Attitude index is related to two types of authority-acceptance: (1) willingness to abide by authoritative decisions (compliance with laws) and (2) reported confidence or trust in the political system (diffuse support).

The propensity of the student to comply with laws is the most dramatic test of Easton and Dennis' hypothesis. We approached this topic by asking each student: "Do you think people should always obey laws? Two hundred and two answered "yes," 94 answered "no." If the respondent answered "yes," he was asked, "Why would you obey a law you disagree with?" If he answered "no," he was asked "Why not?" The responses the students gave for their compliance disposition were classified by an adaptation of Kohlberg's typology of moral development,[10] creating a five-point compliance variable.[11]

The correlation between Compliance and Police Attitude is .33 [*Note:* The measure of association used throughout the paper is Gamma.], indicating a significant (p < .01) relationship between the student's attitude toward the police, and his attitude toward obedience of the law. The more negative the student's attitude toward the police, the more likely he is to accept disobedience of the law. For example, 87 percent of the students with a positive attitude toward the police believe that one should always obey laws, while only 51 percent of the students with a negative attitude toward the police respond thusly.

The second type of authority-acceptance was measured by five questions concerning the honesty, efficiency, representativeness, and trustworthiness of political officials and institutions.[12] Factor analysis revealed that the five questions measured a single dimension which was labeled Political Trust. Responses were weighted and added to produce a Political Trust index (or support index) on each student, ranging from 5 (very high trust) to 25 (very low trust). This raw score for each student is utilized in the analysis below. Again for descriptive purposes we can classify each student's score on the Political Trust index as: high (N = 60), medium (N = 169), or low (N = 73).[13] All but some 24 percent of the students manifest medium or high trust for the political system.

The correlation between Political Trust and Police Attitude is .36. As with Compliance, the relationship is significant (p < .01). The more negative the student's attitude toward the police, the more inclined he is to manifest low political trust. For example, only 14 percent of the students with a negative attitude toward the police evince high political trust, whereas 37 percent of the students with a positive attitude toward the police are in the high trust category.

Attitude toward the police, then, seems to be significantly related to both political trust and compliance disposition. We might consider the possibility, however, that the relationships are spurious. For example, it could be that a student's political trust determines both his attitude toward the police and his compliance disposition. Spuriousness is usually determined by using a partialling technique which indicates the association between the dependent and independent variable while controlling for the effect of all other independent variables. The partialling technique used in this work is straight multiple regression.[14] The beta coefficient produced by regression analysis evidences the amount of change in the dependent variable for every unit of change in the independent variable, while holding all other variables constant.[15] As may be seen in Tables 1 and 2, the relationship between Police Attitude and both Political Trust and Compliance holds up even when a number of other variables are entered into the equation.[16] In both cases only a nominal amount of the variance is accounted for by all the variables. This indicates that authority-acceptance can be understood only as a product of multivariate causation. This does not mean that Easton and Dennis' hypothesis is incorrect; no doubt they understood that attitude toward the police is only one of a number of variables which determine authority-acceptance.

Additionally, one might consider the possibility that there is a developmental relationship between Police Attitude, Political Trust, and Compliance (i.e., Police Attitude causes Political Trust which in turn causes Compliance, or vice versa). Tables 1 and 2 reveal that Political Trust and Compliance are significant correlates of one another. Unfortunately the data do not satisfy the conditions necessary for testing three-variable causal models.[17] However, we do know that when Police Attitude is regressed on either dependent variable (Political Trust or Compliance), and the other held constant, the beta coefficient is reduced in both cases, but not substantially. If a developmental relationship were present we would expect the coefficient to disappear, as with a spurious relationship.[18] The stability of the coefficients suggest that there is no strong developmental relationship between the three variables.

Table 1
Correlates of Compliance Disposition

Independent Variables	Beta*
1. Grade Average	−.21
2. Political Trust	.20
3. Police Attitude	.14
4. Personal Trust	.13
5. Laws Are Just	.10
*p<.01	R = .41

Table 2
Correlates of Political Trust

Independent Variables	Beta*
1. Political Efficacy	.32
2. Personal Trust	.27
3. Compliance Disposition	.16
4. Police Attitude	.13
5. Laws Are Just	.10
6. Grade Average	−.10
*p<.01	R = .60

DIFFERENCES BETWEEN BLACK AND WHITE STUDENTS

As Jaros has noted, "studies in political socialization which differentiate their findings by race are rare."[19] From a limited but growing number of studies, however, we are led to suspect that during the elementary school years black children probably manifest as much affect for agents of the political system as white children. Greenstein noted that lower status children tend to have a more positive image of the President than higher status children,[20] and Jaros found that black children manifest as much affect for the President as white children.[21] A study by Greenberg expands these findings to the police. During the elementary school years, Greenberg found that black students evince as much affect for the police as their white peers.[22] By high school, however, Greenberg found that black students manifest significantly more negative attitudes toward the police than white students. The expectation, then, is that black students in our sample will have significantly more negative attitudes toward the police than white students, and that these more negative attitudes represent a decline from earlier more positive attitudes.

Table 3 depicts the five items asked of the students concerning attitude toward the police. The table is broken down by race; and the association between race and agree-disagree responses is reported. The table indicates clearly that the black students have persistently and significantly more negative attitudes toward the police than their white peers. The black students are significantly more inclined to question the honesty, fairness, and objectivity of the police. The descriptive classification of police attitudes reveals that 33 percent of the black students, as opposed to 15 percent of the white students, can be classified as having negative attitudes toward the police. Easton and Dennis' hypothesis leads us to suspect that the black students will be less compliant and less trusting of the political system than the white students.

For Compliance, however, the data reveal that whereas 64 percent ($N = 125$) of the white students can be classified as compliant, 75 percent ($N = 79$), of the black students also fall into this category. The white students, then, are less compliant than the black students, although the difference between the two groups is not significant. Easton and Dennis left open the possibility that compensatory mechanisms might ameliorate the impact of negative attitudes toward the police. We assume that compensatory mechanisms would be positive political attitudes that are more important than negative attitudes held by the respondent in predicting support for the system. Multiple regression will be used below to determine if compensatory mechanisms can be isolated to explain why the black students' more negative attitudes toward the police seem to have so little impact on their compliance disposition. The size of the correlation between Police Attitude and Compliance for both groups suggests that compensatory mechanisms might be found. The correlation between Police Attitude and Compliance is .42 for the black students, and .33 for the white students. In both cases, as with the total sample, attitude toward the police is significantly related to compliance ($p < .01$). The relationship is strong in both cases, but somewhat stronger for the black than the white students. The relationship is particularly strong for the black students on the positive end of the continuum. Every black student who rated a positive attitude toward the police is compliant ($N = 12$). However, only 46 percent of the black students, as opposed to 57 percent of the white students who reported negative attitudes toward the police are non-compliant.

Turning to Political Trust we find that there is no significant difference between black and white students on this variable.[23] Black students

Table 3
Association Between Attitude Toward the Police and Race

		Total Sample %	Blacks %	Whites %
1) Generally speaking, most policemen like to give someone like me a "hard time."				
*5. Strongly Agreed		10	18	6
4. Agree	$X^2 = 32.48$ p < .001	15	25	10
2. Disagree		43	36	47
1. Strongly Disagree	Gamma = .52	24	11	30
3. D.K.		8	10	7
2) How honest do you think the police are compared to most men?				
1. More honest		17	11	19
2. As honest	$X^2 = 25.45$ p < .001	44	42	62
4. Less honest		13	25	8
3. D.K.	Gamma = −.40	15	22	11
3) If I were in trouble with the police, I would feel most confident in being treated fairly.				
1. Strongly Agree		25	26	25
2. Agree	$X^2 = 9.12$ p < .05	46	35	51
4. Disagree		13	18	10
5. Strongly Disagree	Gamma = .09	4	7	4
3. D.K.		12	14	10
4) A police officer is only following orders when he is carrying out his duties, and cannot be blamed for what he does.				
1. Strongly Agree		12	9	14
2. Agree	$X^2 = 10.17$ p < .02	34	25	38
4. Disagree		33	42	28
5. Strongly Disagree	Gamma = .25	17	21	15
3. D.K.		4	3	5
5) If I need help, I can rely on the police to come to my aid.				
1. Strongly Agree		15	8	19
2. Agree	$X^2 = 7.47$ p > .05	42	42	43
4. Disagree		21	26	18
5. Strongly Disagree	Gamma = .21	10	8	10
3. D.K.		12	16	10
		100%	100%	100%
		N = 302	N = 106	N = 196

*Designates the weight assigned each response in generating the police attitude index.

are somewhat lower in their trust of the system than whites (29 percent to 21 percent low trust), but the difference is not statistically significant. The correlation between Police Attitude and Political Trust is .28 for black students, and .39 for white students. The relationship is significant for both groups (p < .01). On the positive end of the continuum the relationship seems to be stronger for the white students. Of those white students rated high on political trust only 7 percent (N = 3) expressed negative attitudes toward the police, whereas 33 percent (N = 6) of the black students rated high on trust reported negative attitudes about the police. On the negative side, 45 percent (N = 14) of the black students who expressed low political trust reported negative attitudes toward the police, as opposed to 24 percent (N = 10) of the white students in this category. As with Compliance, there seem to be additional factors which need to be taken into consideration for the black students.

Tables 4 and 5 show the results of regression analysis on Compliance and Political Trust for both groups. Analysis reveals that the relationship between Police Attitude and authority-acceptance holds up only for the white students. When a number of variables are regressed on Political Trust and Compliance for black students, Police Attitude is completely partialled out of the equation. In both cases where Police Attitude makes a significant contribution to the equation for white students, it accounts for very little of the total variance.

The variables which are the best predictors of authority-acceptance for black students seem to be compensatory in nature. For example, Political Trust (one of our two dependent variables) is the best predictor of Compliance for the black students. Thirty-three percent of the black students, compared to 7 percent of the white students, manifest high political trust despite reporting negative attitudes toward the police. Similarly, Political and Personal Efficacy scores are more often high for black students despite negative attitudes toward the police than for white students. For example, 33 percent of the black students who reported high Political Efficacy rated a negative attitude toward the police, compared to 3 percent of the white students. The results of these compensatory variables is that the black students' Police Attitude (especially negative attitudes) do not, in many cases, affect their authority-acceptance.

The interesting question is why does Police Attitude play a different role for the white than for the black students? Two seemingly logical explanations may be discounted. First, it may seem reasonable that the difference is caused by the fact that the blacks in our sample are from the South and may still be rather obsequious.[24] This explanation lacks attraction, however, because the black students do not seem to be at all reluctant to criticize the system and its agents (especially the police). Secondly, we thought the difference might be explained by the variance in regime support by the students. The black students manifest the greatest attachment for the national government, and the white students evince highest affect for their local governments.[25] The black students

Table 4
Correlates of Compliance Disposition

Independent Variables	Beta*
Black Students	
1. Political Trust	.49
2. Personal Trust	.23
3. Sex	.19
4. Political Efficacy	.14
5. Intent to Continue Education	.12
*p<.01 R = .46	
White Students	
1. Grade Average	−.29
2. Laws Are Just	.29
3. Police Attitude	.18
4. Family Structure	.14
*p<.01 R = .49	

Table 5
Correlates of Political Trust

Independent Variables	Beta*
Black Students	
1. Personal Trust	.39
2. Political Efficacy	.35
3. Compliance	.27
4. Grade Average	−.20
5. Personal Efficacy	.16
6. Sex	.11
*p<.01 R = .68	
White Students	
1. Political Efficacy	.29
2. Personal Trust	.21
3. Police Attitude	.19
4. Laws Are Just	.15
5. Integration Index	.11
*p<.01 R = .58	

might be less affected by perceiving an agent of the local government to be an enemy than white students who are most attached to that level of government and who do not perceive an attractive alternative government to which they can transfer their support. This explanation does not hold up, however, because the association between regime support and Police Attitude is inconsequential for both groups (white students, .05; black students, .00).

Since these explanations do not seem viable we can only speculate about the difference. Greenberg's research leads us to believe that most children regardless of race manifest positive attitudes toward the police during their early school years.[26] As the black child matures and starts to take a larger part in his environment, however, his affect for the policeman declines. This decline could result from his experiences with the police and/or the treatment his elders socialize him to expect from the police. If this process is almost universal for black citizens, they may come to accept hostile police as being part of the nature of things and not allow their attitudes toward the police to influence their support for the larger political system. On the other hand, it is generally alien to white culture for the policeman to be perceived as an enemy. Consequently, when the white student develops negative attitudes toward the police it may bode a more drastic effect on this attitude toward the whole political system.

CONCLUSIONS

For the sample as a whole our analysis supports Easton and Dennis' speculation that individual attitudes toward the police are significantly and independently related to acceptance of political authority (compliance with laws and Political Trust). When we divided the sample by race and utilized regression analysis, however, we found that Police Attitude is an important determinant of authority-acceptance for the white students, but not for the black students. For example, although black students manifest significantly more negative attitudes toward the police than their white peers, they are not less compliant with or trustful of the political system, because their negative attitudes toward the police are often compensated for by other positive political attitudes. For many black students, in other words, their negative attitudes toward the police are an exception to their generally positive attitudes toward the larger political system. The extent to which these findings are culture bound, if any, will have to await broader research. On the basis of our finding, one might speculate that in many instances when the black student manifests negative attitudes toward the police it means that he sees the policeman as an irresponsible agent of an otherwise viable system. Conversely, our guess is that it is the white student who most often sees the policeman as a symbol of the larger political system, and links his opinion of the one to the other.

Police Attitude might play a different role for black and white students as a result of their typical and expected experiences with the police. The black high school student may be socialized by his environment to expect the policeman to be an enemy. If this expectation is fulfilled, it may not have much impact on his attitude toward the larger political system. The white high school student, however, typically expects the policeman to be a friend. A disappointing experience which produces negative attitudes toward the police, may have a more significant effect on the white students' support for the larger political system.

Last, we should note that even though Police Attitude is a significant predictor of the white students' authority-acceptance, it is only one of a number of determinants, and not the most important, of that attitude. An obvious conclusion is that authority-acceptance is a complex phenomenon which is the product of multiple causation.

NOTES

[1]This belief has become a maxim in the literature. See for example David Easton and Jack Dennis, *Children In The Political System* (New York: McGraw-Hill Book Co., 1969), p. 221; and Walter Murphy and Joseph Tanenhaus, "Public Opinion and the United States Supreme Court: Mapping of Some Prerequisites for Court Legitimation of Regime Changes," *Law and Society Review,* II (May, 1968), 359; Richard Merelman, "Learning and Legitimacy," *American Political Science Review,* LX (September, 1966), 548–561; Ted Gurr, "A Causal Model of Civil Strife: A Comparative Analysis Using New Indices," *American Political Science Review,* LXII (December, 1968), 1106.

[2]Easton and Dennis, p. 209. See also Robert D. Hess and Judith V. Torney, *The Development of Political Attitudes in Children* (Chicago: Aldine Publishing Co., 1967), pp. 50–59.

[3]Easton and Dennis, p. 212.

[4]*Ibid.,* p. 213.

[5]*Ibid.,* p. 239. See also the contradictory conclusions of Robert D. Hess and Judith V. Torney, pp. 57, 214.

[6]*Ibid.,* p. 240.

[7]The need for this type of analysis has been stressed by Jack Dennis, "Major Problems of Political Socialization Research," *Midwest Journal of Political Science,* XII (February, 1968), 85–114; and Roberta Sigel, Review of *The Development of Political Attitudes in Children* in *Public Opinion Quarterly,* XXXII (Spring, 1968), 534–536.

[8]Factor analysis revealed that the five questions on Table 3 measured a single dimension which we labeled Police Attitude. The factor analysis technique was Kaiser's varimax solution, with SMCs in the diagonals, orthogonally rotated. The cutoff point for the factor loadings was set at .50.

[9]The division was: 5 to 10, positive; 11 to 17, ambivalent; 18 to 24,

negative. The divisions were based on the logic of the test instrument (based on a pretest in which respondents were allowed to rank themselves), and the normal curve. See Oliver Benson, *Political Science Laboratory* (Columbus, Ohio: Charles E. Merrill Publishing Co., 1969), p. 238.

[10]L. Kohlberg, "Moral Development and Identification," in *Review of Child Development Research,* ed. by M. L. Hoffman and Lois W. Hoffman (New York: Russell Sage Foundation, 1964), pp. 383–432. The adaptation of the typology is explained in Harrell Rodgers and George Taylor, "Pre-Adult Attitudes Toward Legal Compliance," *Social Science Quarterly* (forthcoming).

[11]The variable is based on whether the student believed the law should always be obeyed, and the reasons he gave for his attitude:

(1) Yes, Avoid-Punishment

(2) Yes, Rule-Conformity

(3) Yes, Self-Accepted Moral Principles

(4) No, Rule-Conformity Tempered by Personal Judgment

(5) No, Self-Accepted Moral Principles

[12]The Survey items used to construct the Political Trust index are those usually included in Survey Research Center questionnaires. See footnote 8 for an explanation of the factor analysis technique used to check for unidimensionality. The questions were:

(1) Do you think quite a few of the people running the government are a little crooked, not very many are, or do you think hardly any of them are?

(2) Do you think people in the government waste a lot of the money we pay in taxes, waste some of it, or don't waste very much of it?

(3) How much of the time do you think you can trust the government in Washington to do what is right, just about always, most of the time, or only some of the time?

(4) Do you think that almost all of the people running the government are smart people who usually know what they are doing, or do you think quite a few of them don't seem to know what they are doing?

(5) Would you say the government is pretty much run by a few big interests looking out for themselves or it is run for the benefit of all the people?

[13]The division (determined by the method described in footnote 9) was: 5 to 11, high; 12 to 16, medium; 17 to 25, low.

[14]We are using an interval technique because it best describes our data, and provides us with the most sound partialling technique. On this point Richard P. Boyle has recently pointed out that "empirical dangers of assuming equal intervals are not great." See "Path Analysis and Ordinal Data," *American Journal of Sociology,* LXXV (January, 1970), 461.

[15]See Hubert Blalock, "Causal Inference, Closed Populations, and Measures of Association," *American Political Science Review,* LXI (March, 1967), 130–136.

[16]The additional independent variables to be added to the equations were selected because the literature suggests that they are correlates of the dependent variables. Eleven additional variables were chosen and included in each run. Three of the variables—personal efficacy, political interest, and social position—as measured by Hollingsheads' two factor index of social position, did not correlate significantly in any of the runs. See A. B. Hollingshead, *Social Class and Mental Illness* (New York: John Wiley & Sons, Inc., 1958), pp. 390–391.

Three of the new independent variables – personal trust, political efficacy, and personal efficacy – were indices constructed from the familiar Survey Research Center items. Factor analysis was used to check for unidimensionality (See footnote 8). The survey items can be found in Joel D. Aberbach, "Alienation and Political Behavior," *American Political Science Review,* LXIII (March, 1969), 92. The literature on the correlates of various measures of systems support is small and frequently contradictory. See for example: G. R. Boynton, Samuel Patterson, and Ronald Hedlund, "The Structure of Public Support for Legislative Institutions," *Midwest Journal of Political Science,* XII (May, 1968), 163- 180; David Sears, "Black Attitudes Toward the Political System in the Aftermath of the Watts Insurrection," *Midwest Journal of Political Science,* XI (November, 1969), 515- 544; Marion Roth and G. R. Boynton, "Communal Ideology and Political Support," *Journal of Politics,* XXXI (February, 1969), 167- 185; Richard Merelman, "The Development of Political Ideology: A Framework for the Analysis of Political Socialization," *American Political Science Review,* LXIII (September, 1969); 750- 767; Merelman, "Learning and Legitimacy," pp. 548- 561; Jack Dennis, "Support for the Party System by the Mass Public," *American Political Science Review,* LX (September, 1966), pp. 600- 615; Gurr, pp. 1104- 1124; Rodgers and Taylor, *passim*; Murphy and Tanenhaus, pp. 357- 384.

[17]A simple explanation of these assumptions can be found in: Hayward R. Alker, Jr., *Mathematics and Politics* (New York: The Macmillan Company, 1965), pp. 119- 126.

[18]*Ibid., passim.* See also Hubert Blalock, "Controlling for Background Factors: Spuriousness Versus Developmental Sequences," *Sociological Inquiry,* XXXIV (September, 1964), 28- 39.

[19]Dean Jaros, "Children's Orientations Toward the President: Some Additional Theoretical Considerations and Data," *Journal of Politics,* XXIX (May, 1967), 380. Some improvements have been made in the last few years but the literature is still sparse. See for example Dwaine Marvick, "The Political Socialization of the American Negro," *Annals of the American Academy of Political and Social Science,* CCCLXI (September, 1965), 112- 127; Bradbury Seasholes, "Political Socialization of Negroes: Image Development of Self and Polity," in *Negro Self-Concept: Implications for School and Citizenship* ed. by William C. Kvaraceus *et al.* (New York: McGraw-Hill Book Co., 1965), pp. 52- 90; Kenneth P. Langton and M. Kent Jennings, "Political Socialization and the High School Civics Curriculum in the United States," *American Political Science Review,* LXII (September, 1968), 860- 861; Schley R. Lyons, "The Political Socialization of Ghetto Children: Efficacy and Cynicism," *Journal of Politics,* XXXII (May, 1970), 288- 304.

[20]Fred Greenstein, *Children and Politics* (Princeton: Princeton University Press, 1965), p. 102.

[21]Jaros, p. 38.

[22]Edward S. Greenberg, "Black Children and the Political System: A Study of Socialization to Support" (paper delivered at the 65th meeting of the American Political Science Association, New York, N.Y., September, 1969), *passim.*

[23]Previous findings of differences between black and white students on political trust (frequently referred to as political cynicism) have been mixed. Langton and Jennings found no difference between the black and white students in their study. Lyons, however, found that black students in Toledo were

significantly more inclined than white students to manifest political cynicism (low political trust).

[24]See Donald R. Matthews and James W. Prothro, *Negroes and the New Southern Politics* (New York: Harcourt, Brace and World, Inc., 1966), pp. 275–302.

[25]Sixty-five percent (N = 67) of the black students said they had the most confidence in the national government as opposed to 43 percent (N = 84) of the white students (p < .01). Similarly, 83 percent (N = 84) of the black students said they had the least confidence in state or local government whereas only 65 percent (N = 122) of the white students gave this answer (p < .01).

[26]This finding needs to be tested more extensively, but Greenberg's findings are impressive since his data were drawn from racially impacted areas in a large metropolitan area.

Chapter 3

RACE AND COMPLIANCE: DIFFERENTIAL POLITICAL SOCIALIZATION

Richard L. Engstrom

A major focus of research on the political socialization of young children is inquiry into the development of attitudes and behavior patterns important for the maintenance of a political system. One conceptual element of a political system is the regime, the decisional and administrative structures, "together with the rules of the game or codes of behavior that legitimate the actions of political authorities and specify what is expected of citizens or subjects."[1] This research investigates children's orientations to a norm of regime "support," the behavioral expectation of compliance to authority figures.

The understanding of regime supports and their antecedents is clearly of enduring importance, but it seems especially critical in a period of rapid political change. In contrast to even the very recent past, the amount of support—and hence the level of compliant behavior—manifested by some major segments of the American public may be questioned. In particular, the black community is alleged to be increasingly alienated from and decreasingly supportive of the on-going system.

That blacks are becoming less supportive and that this may be importantly related to childhood experiences is increasingly suggested in the literature. Black children may be "undergoing some important new generational experiences" due to unrest in the Negro ghettos.[2] Indeed, it may be that one manifestation of the growth of militancy and the decline of "accommodation" evidenced in the black community[3] would be a decline in the black child's view of the legitimacy of an authority figure,

Reprinted from *Polity,* 3 (Fall, 1970), pp. 100–11, by permission of the author and publisher.

The author wishes to express his appreciation to Professor Dean Jaros for his most instructive guidance and comments during the preparation of this paper.

expressed by a decline in his desire to comply to that authority's commands. Data from the National Opinion Research Center's 1960 national survey, analyzed by Marvick, shows that there appears to be "a level of caution and distrust among Negro Americans toward representatives of the law with whom they have dealings,"[4] and recent research by Greenberg shows that black children are less favorably disposed toward police as they grow older.[5]

Thus, it is quite reasonable to expect substantial differences in propensities to comply to political authority between black and white children, and to expect that this state of affairs may have grave implications. But an understanding of racial differentials in regime support is not only of immediate practical concern; it affords an opportunity for theoretically relevant advances as well. If there is substantial variance in compliant behavior, the task of explaining compliance becomes easier as relationships should stand out more clearly. In a homogeneously supportive population, such as has been the subject of much previously reported research, there is little statistical variance to be accounted for, and the search for antecedents has been difficult.

The explanation of compliance to authority figures in this context therefore has important priority for both practical and theoretical reasons. It is to this task of explanation we now turn. According to Hess and Minturn, "A conception of compliance as the expression of a role relationship between an individual and an institution or an authority figure necessarily places a great deal of importance upon images or attitudes that a child holds toward the authority figure."[6] They present three independent variables likely to affect compliance, "the degree of *attachment and respect* for the institution or figure, the child's *belief about the power* of authority figures to punish disobedience, and the *likelihood of such punishment.*"[7] It is easy to imagine and indeed the literature cited above suggests racial differences on the first of these variables. Specifically, we postulate that the lower level of compliance among black children will be explicable in terms of *lesser attributions of benevolence* to authority figures. Given the importance that has been attached to benevolence attribution as a precursor to political attachment in studies of white children, its absence in black youngsters could be expected to have profound effects. On the other hand, black children (though perhaps to a lesser degree) do comply. This compliance, however, may have different roots. Again, referring to the literature above, one comes quickly to Hess and Minturn's second and third variables. We hold that such compliance as blacks do demonstrate will be associated with a belief in the authorities' ability to administer punishment.

Two authority figures have been shown to be highly visible to children, the president and the policeman.[8] Research stressing the president as both a cognitive and affective introduction to the regime has been prominent for several years,[9] while the policeman's role in this regard has only recently been explored.[10] It appears that the relative deemphasis of policemen may be unfortunate, as Easton and Dennis have found that the policeman plays "an important function in molding the child's understanding of and feelings about political authority,"[11] and thus has "a vital role in laying part of the foundation for the input of support."[12] In addition, Hess and Torney conclude that "To children, the policeman represents the authoritative ruling order."[13] In short, especially if one considers the proximate nature of police operations as opposed to the remote nature of presidential authority, there may be as much justification for studying youthful orientations toward the policeman as there is for investigating reactions to the president. Children's acceptance of the commands of policemen is the immediate topic of this paper.

I. METHOD

Data were collected by administering a paper and pencil questionnaire to 288 public school children, grades four through eight, in Lexington, Kentucky. The multi-purpose survey was conducted within the children's respective classrooms during March, 1969, by political science graduate students. Although, due to the exigencies of school operations, it was not possible to choose classes randomly, purposeful selection acquired a distribution with some variance in social background. The race of each child was recorded by the person administering the instrument.

The compliance dimension was tapped by asking the children, "If you think a policeman is wrong in what he tells you to do, what should you do?" Responses were categorized according to: (1) outright compliance, (2) compliance but a corresponding confrontation with the policeman as to the nature of the command, and (3) resistance or disobedience to the command.[14]

The degree of attachment to the policeman was measured by asking two questions concerning the benevolent qualities of that authority figure: "Do policemen want to help you when you need it?"[15] and "Is a policeman a nice person?" Responses to these items were permitted along a six-point continuum ranging from "never" to "always." An index of the benevolent perception was constructed by first Guttman scaling these two six-category response items. Scale scores ranged from 1 to 11. The distribution of these scores assumed the characteristic of a step function. Therefore, for purposes of analysis, it was deemed appropriate to construct the index by collapsing these scores consistent with the "steps." This produced score groupings of 1 through 4, 5 through 8, and 9 through 11; groupings which may be considered as reflecting low, medium, and high benevolence.

The perception of the policeman's power to punish was measured in the same manner as benevolence. Two questions were asked: "If the policeman wants somebody to do something, who can he make do it?" and "Who can a policeman punish?"[16] There were six response alternatives ranging from "nobody" to "anyone." An index of the power perception was again constructed by first Guttman scaling these two six-category response items. Scores ranged from 1 to 10. The distribution was bi-modal, with the modes appearing at the two extremes. Thus, the index was constructed by grouping the modes and the between region, again providing groupings which may be interpreted as low (1 and 2), medium (3 through 8), and high power (9 and 10).[17]

To determine the child's perception of the probability of punishment, he was asked, "If you do not obey the laws, are you punished by a policeman?" Responses were again arranged along a six-point continuum ranging from "never" to "always." These responses were categorized into low probability (1 and 2), medium probability (3 and 4), and high probability (5 and 6).[18]

II. FINDINGS

The overall distributions on the compliance dimension for the black and white children are presented in Table 1. It is easily ascertained from the percentage distributions that the two groups are *not* differentiated on this variable. Thus, the proposition that the two groups would show differential compliance patterns is not confirmed. This rather surprising

Table 1
Compliance, by Race

	Whites		Blacks	
	%	n	%	n
Acceptance	56.8	(112)	57.3	(51)
Confrontation	39.1	(77)	34.8	(31)
Resistance	4.1	(8)	7.9	(7)
Total	100.0	(197)	100.0	(89)
X^2 goodness of fit = 3.63			p > .05	

result might be interpreted in two ways. First, black and white children may actually look upon this authority figure substantially identically. If this were the case, and the connections between early orientations and later behavior suggested by recent political socialization literature really exist, then there should be few differences between black and white adults in authority orientations. But the literature cited above strongly indicates that this may not be the case. Apparently these identical childhood attributions give way to substantial adolescent and adult differences.

This suggests a second interpretation of the data in Table 1. Though the members of the two races may show similar tendencies toward compliance while young, the elements on which these tendencies are based may be quite divergent. If so, the implications of these identical tendencies could be quite different. Thus, it becomes interesting to note that the races are significantly differentiated on two of the three independent variables, and at a rather comfortable degree of confidence. Tables 2 and 3 show the distribution of index values for benevolence and power, and Table 4 shows the distributions on the probability of punishment dimension.

At first blush one might conclude that the conceptual elements Hess and Minturn posit as determinative of compliance in reality are not operative on that behavior. As Tables 2 and 3 indicate, the black children in the sample see the policeman as both less benevolent and less powerful. This would lead us to suspect that black children would tend to be less compliant as well, unless of course, the perception of the probability of punishment, similarly distributed for each race, was dominant over both the benevolence and power variables. But it remains to examine the nature of the connections between these elements and compliance to the policeman for the two races. When this is done, it becomes evident that the compliance of the blacks is explained in quite different terms from that of the whites.

It is evident from Table 5 that the benevolent perception of the policeman is the strongest factor motivating white children to comply, while there is no interpretable association between this factor and black compliance. On the other hand, there appears a marked relationship between the black child's perception of the policeman's power and his tendency to comply, even though on the whole he sees the policeman as possessing less power than does the white child. It may be that although the black perceives less power, he is more sensitive to that power than is the white child, a possibility supported by the stronger relationship between the perceived probability of punishment and compliance for the black than white child. This power-punishment saliency may be a result

Table 2
Benevolence, by Race

	Whites		Blacks	
	%	n	%	n
Low	3.8	(7)	6.1	(4)
Medium	25.9	(48)	54.5	(36)
High	70.3	(130)	39.4	(26)
Total	100.0	(185)	100.0	(66)
X^2 goodness of fit = 30.765			$p < .001$	

Table 3
Power, by Race

	Whites		Blacks	
	%	n	%	n
Low	29.2	(47)	47.6	(30)
Medium	37.3	(60)	30.2	(19)
High	33.5	(54)	22.2	(14)
Total	100.0	(161)	100.0	(63)
X^2 goodness of fit = 10.573			$p < .005$	

Table 4
Probability of Punishment, by Race

	Whites		Blacks	
	%	n	%	n
Low	40.8	(73)	42.7	(32)
Medium	33.5	(60)	40.0	(30)
High	25.7	(46)	17.3	(13)
Total	100.0	(179)	100.0	(75)
X^2 goodness of fit = 3.05			$p > .05$	

Table 5
Association of Each Independent Variable with Compliance, by Race*

	Whites	Blacks
Benevolence	.30	−.07
Power	.24	.59
Probability of punishment	.04	.24

*The measure of association is Goodman and Kruskal's gamma.

of the "caution and distrust" Marvick found present in the black community.

But it is also apparent that power has some association with compliance for white children as well. However, its meaning may be quite different from that for black children; indeed, one could argue that the white's sensitivity to power is instrumental in the development of benevolent perceptions. This possibility is illuminated when a control is applied for grade in school. (See Tables 6–9 for matrices containing all relationships by race, controlled by school grade.) For elementary school whites, attributions of power, attributions of benevolence, and compliance are all highly interrelated (for power and compliance, $\gamma = .58$; for benevolence and compliance, $\gamma = .31$; for power and benevolence, $\gamma = .62$). These data are consistent with what is called the vulnerability hypothesis." This notion states that a young child escapes feelings of being vulnerable in his relationship with a person occupying a position of power over him by attributing benevolent qualities to that person.[19] This benevolent image of authority figures acquired during childhood is often believed to contribute to a strong attachment to the regime during adulthood; an attachment which is an important source of system support which persists even in the face of perceived governmental level conflict.[20]

Table 6
Matrix of Gamma Coefficients for All Variables,
Elementary School Whites

	Compliance	Benevolence	Power	Probability of Punishment
Compliance				
Benevolence	.31			
Power	.58	.62		
Probability of punishment	.24	.25	.50	

Consistent with the vulnerability notion, the relationship between power and compliance completely disappears for the junior high school whites ($\gamma = -.01$), but an association between benevolence and compliance remains ($\gamma = .14$). There is no relationship between power and benevolence in these older children. This is not surprising if one views a junior high school child's thinking as reflecting a degree of maturation beyond that of the elementary school child's, and does suggest that the benevolent perception acquired during earlier childhood may indeed have some influence in legitimizing authority as the child ages. The role

Table 7
Matrix of Gamma Coefficients for All Variables,
Junior High School Whites

	Compliance	*Benevolence*	*Power*	*Probability of Punishment*
Compliance				
Benevolence	.14			
Power	−.01	.01		
Probability of punishment	.00	.05	.39	

Table 8
Matrix of Gamma Coefficients for All Variables,
Elementary School Blacks

	Compliance	*Benevolence*	*Power*	*Probability of Punishment*
Compliance				
Benevolence	−.30			
Power	.44	−.10		
Probability of punishment	.18	.00	.54	

Table 9
Matrix of Gamma Coefficients for All Variables,
Junior High School Blacks

	Compliance	*Benevolence*	*Power*	*Probability of Punishment*
Compliance				
Benevolence	.00			
Power	.64	.00		
Probability of punishment	.17	.06	.56	

of power attribution, then, is for the whites confined to earlier life and perhaps operative only as an instrument in the development of more permanent attributions of benevolence.

But probably more important than the fact that whites conform to the vulnerability hypothesis is the corresponding finding that blacks do not! Elementary school black youngsters show a high relationship between power and compliance ($\gamma = .44$), but a *negative* relationship between benevolence and compliance ($\gamma = -.30$). The relationship between power and benevolence for these young blacks is slightly negative ($\gamma = -.10$). Clearly, these data support neither the vulnerability hypothesis nor any other scheme which associates perceptions of benevolence and power. On the other hand, the relationships between power and compliance, the perceived probability of punishment and compliance, and power and the perceived probability of punishment all remain. Even for young blacks, the power of police is associated with punishment.

These relationships are not substantially modified for the older black children. For the black junior high school students power and the probability of punishment are still highly associated with compliance, while there is no relationship between benevolence and compliance nor between power and benevolence. But the high relationship between power and the probability of punishment remains to fill out our picture of black compliance resting on the *very opposite* of the benevolent picture whites entertain.

III. CONCLUSIONS

It is clearly evident that the children in this sample have incorporated the compliance norm no matter what their race. Possibly more important than the fact that they comply, however, are the apparent reasons for their compliance. The young child's perception of an authority figure is often considered a determinant of his later orientation to the abstract social system the authority figure represents.[21] It was found that a benevolent basis for compliance was lacking in the black children. The absence of this affective motivation to comply with the authority figure may forewarn a weaker attachment to the regime for the adult black. The power-punishment basis for black compliance to police may indeed be relatively fragile. Our own data suggest that older black children see the policeman as possessing less power and less punishing ability than their younger counterparts.[22] If the age trend continues, even this coercive base might be expected to dissolve.

In summary, the data conclusively show that the black and white children have both incorporated the compliance norm. However, it is highly suggestive that the "why" of compliance is different, a difference that may have important consequences for adult regime support. This proposition is deserving of further tests, not only because it is highly intriguing but because, when placed within the present sociopolitical setting of the United States, it takes on social as well as theoretical significance.

NOTES

[1]David Easton and Robert D. Hess, "The Child's Political World," *Midwest Journal of Political Science,* VI (August, 1962), 233.

[2]David Easton and Jack Dennis, *Children in the Political System: Origins of Political Legitimacy* (New York: McGraw-Hill, Inc., 1969), 242.

[3]See, in this regard, Dwaine Marvick, "The Political Socialization of the American Negro," *Annals* CCCLXI (September, 1965), 112-122.

[4]*Ibid.,* 118. In addition, a recent study of adults in Denver found, ". . . the most important factor influencing people's views of the police is ethnicity. Negroes and Spanish-named persons share among themselves views of the police that are less favorable than those of the rest of the community and which are not materially affected by the success they achieve in life in terms of social and economic position." See David H. Bayley and Harold Mendelsohn, *Minorities and the Police: Confrontation in America* (New York: The Free Press, 1969), 113.

[5]Edward S. Greenberg, "Black Children and the Political System: A Study of Socialization to Support." Paper delivered at the 1969 Annual Meeting of the American Political Science Association, New York City, September 2-6, 1969. See also in this regard Dawson and Prewitt's discussion of the "slum child's" image of the policeman. Richard E. Dawson and Kenneth Prewitt, *Political Socialization* (Boston: Little, Brown and Company, 1969), 79-80.

[6]Robert D. Hess and Leigh Minturn, "Authority, Rules and Aggression: A Cross-National Study of Socialization of Children Into Compliance Systems," mimeo, 5.

[7]*Ibid.* (emphasis added). In addition, Hess and Minturn posit a fourth independent variable not utilized in this study, the perceived reinforcement authority figures provide one another while punishing disobedience.

[8]Easton and Dennis, op. cit., especially chapters 6 and 7; and Robert D. Hess and Judith V. Torney, *The Development of Political Attitudes in Children* (Chicago: Aldine Publishing Company, 1967), 214.

[9]See, for example, Fred I. Greenstein, "The Benevolent Leader: Children's Images of Political Authority," *American Political Science Review,* LIV (December, 1960), 934-943, and "More on Children's Images of the President," *Public Opinion Quarterly,* XXIV (Winter, 1960), 632-644; Dean Jaros, "Children's Orientations Toward the President: Some Additional Theoretical Considerations and Data," *Journal of Politics,* XXX (May, 1967), 368-387; Dean Jaros, Herbert Hirsh, and Frederic J. Fleron, Jr., "The Malevolent Leader: Political Socialization in an American Sub-culture," *American Political Science Review,* LXII (June, 1968), 564-575; and Roberta Sigel, "Image of a President: Some Insights into the Political Views of School Children," *American Political Science Review,* LXII (March, 1968), 216-226.

[10]Easton and Dennis, op. cit., chapters 10 and 11, and Hess and Torney, op. cit., passim.

[11]Easton and Dennis, 221.

[12]Ibid., 240.

[13]Hess and Torney, op. cit., 58.

[14]This question was adopted from the Hess and Torney study, but two additional response options were included. The responses and the categories they were placed into are as follows:

Acceptance
"Do what he tells you because a policeman is never wrong."
"Do what he tells you and forget about it."
"Do what he tells you but tell your father."
Confrontation
"Do what he tells you but ask the policeman why."
"Do what he tells you but tell him he is wrong."
Resistance
"Do not do what he tells you."

[15] This question is taken from Hess and Torney, and Hess and Minturn.

[16] These questions were also adopted from Hess and Torney.

[17] Guttman scaling was employed in constructing the indices not as an attempt to assume that an unidimensional attitude has been tapped, but rather as an attempt to be less arbitrary in assigning scores on these variables and in establishing cutting points for the indices. Unidimensionality should not be assumed with these indices.

[18] A "don't know" option was also included for each independent variable probe. If a respondent answered "don't know" to either of the power or benevolence items, or to the probability of punishment item he was excluded from the computations dealing with that item.

[19] For a statement of the vulnerability hypothesis, see Robert D. Hess and David Easton, "The Child's Changing Image of the President," 643–644. For evidence questioning the applicability of this hypothesis, see Dean Jaros, "Children's Orientations Toward the President."

[20] See Easton and Hess, "The Child's Political World," 242–246.

[21] Hess and Torney, op. cit., 32–37, 110.

[22] The distribution of the power perceptions for the elementary school blacks was 31.0% perceiving low power, 37.9% medium, and 31.0% high. For junior high school blacks the distribution was 61.8% perceiving low power, 23.5% medium, and 14.7% high. X^2 goodness of fit = 15.145 $p < .001$. The distribution on the probability of punishment dimension for elementary school blacks was 28.6% perceiving a low probability, 40.0% medium, and 31.4% high, while that distribution for junior high blacks was 52.8% low, 41.7% medium, and 5.6% high. X^2 goodness of fit = 15.041 $p < .001$.

Chapter 4

THE POLITICAL SOCIALIZATION
OF GHETTO CHILDREN:
EFFICACY AND CYNICISM

Schley R. Lyons

Most American children acquire early in life the belief that individual political action can influence governmental decision making. They demonstrate positive and supportive feelings toward the government and political leaders, develop a sense of efficacy as early as the third grade, believe it is important to vote, and are not as politically cynical as adults.[1] Easton and Hess have described the child's political socialization as follows:

> The child is initiated into a supportive stance by what is probably high exposure to cues and messages about government, even while he is essentially unconcerned with such matters and too young to do much about them even if he wished. He learns to like the government before he really knows what it is. . . . The child has somehow formed a deep sympathy for government even before he knows that he is in some way potentially part of it.[2]

The extreme contrast between adult-child attitudes toward politics has led several researchers to offer explanatory hypotheses. Easton and Hess suggested that adults show a strong tendency to shelter young children from the realities of political life. Adults tend to paint politics for the child in rosier hues and the younger the child the more pronounced is this protective tendency.[3] Greenstein hypothesized that since children cannot be completely insulated from adult attitudes of distrust toward politics they simply misperceive and otherwise screen out the discordant elements in the adult political environment.[4]

Reprinted from *The Journal of Politics,* 32 (May, 1970), pp. 288–304, by permission of the author and publisher.

The above observations have been synthesized from data gathered primarily from white, middle-class children living in urban, industrial communities. In this study a distinctive sub-population of children—those who grow up in a slum—are singled out for attention. In previous socialization studies one seeks with little reward clues about the political socialization of the slum child, particularly the Negro slum child. Greenstein's New Haven sample of 659 children included 20 Negroes. Although the Hess and Torney study was based upon a sample of 17,000 children, only 269 Negroes and Mexicans were included and they were not separated from other respondents for the purpose of comparison. The Easton and Dennis study of efficacy among children was based upon data supplied by 12,052 white public school children. The Survey Research Center's national sample of high school seniors, which provided data for a number of articles, contained 186 Negroes in a total sample of 1,669, and these were disproportionately from the South.[5]

It is obvious, however, that the slum child, particularly the Negro slum child, acquires his political values and beliefs within a milieu of poverty and racial discrimination that differs significantly from that of white, middle-class children.[6] What is the effect of such early life experiences on the slum child's sense of efficacy? Do children who grow up in the deprived milieu of the inner city develop more cynical feelings about government than children who grow up elsewhere?

Efficacy has been defined as the expectation that in democracies citizens will feel able to act affectively in politics.[7] Lane's speculation that a sense of efficacy is established relatively early in life and is not the product of occupational experience so much as of the family and strata where one is reared has been largely supported by recent research.[8] In analyzing the norm of efficacy, Easton and Dennis have suggested the following definition:

> . . . a sense of the direct political potency of the individual; a belief in the responsiveness of the government to the desires of individuals; the idea of the comprehensibility of government; the availability of adequate means of influence; and a general resistance to fatalism about the tractability of government to anyone, ruler or ruled.[9]

The efficacy index employed in this study was based upon agree-disagree responses to the following: (1) What happens in the government will happen no matter what people do. It is like the weather, there is nothing people can do about it. (2) There are some big, powerful men in the government who are running the whole thing and they do not care about us ordinary people. (3) My family doesn't have any say about what the government does (4) I don't think people in the government care much what people like my family think. (5) Citizens don't have a chance to say what they think about running the government.[10]

Political cynicism or distrust relates to a basic and general evaluative posture towards government. The index employed here refers specifically to the government in Washington and taps feelings relating to the honesty, competence, and fairness of government. Cynicism appears to be a manifestation of a deep-seated suspicion of others' motives and actions.[11] Among adults it has been found to be positively correlated with contempt for others, feelings of impotency, and low educational attainment. It is negatively correlated with political participation.[12] The political cynicism index was based upon responses to the following: (1) Do you think that quite a few of the people running the government are a little crooked, not very many are, or do you think hardly any of them are? (2) Do you think that people in the government waste a lot of the money we pay in taxes, waste some of it, or don't waste very much of it? (3) How much of the time do you think you can trust the government in Washington to do what is right—just about always, most of the time, or only some of the time? (4) Do you feel that almost all of the people running the government are smart people who usually know what they are doing, or do you think that quite a few of them don't seem to know what they are doing? (5) Would you say the government is run by a few big interests looking out for themselves or that it is run for the benefit of all the people?[13]

METHODS

Data for the study were obtained from paper-and-pencil questionnaires administered to 2,868 fifth- through twelfth-grade students attending classes in the Toledo City Public School System from October to December 1968. The city's student population was divided into inner-city and non-inner-city groupings. The inner-city schools were defined as those located within Toledo's Model Cities area. This area was Toledo's hard core slum, exhibiting the worst example of physical, social, and economic decay in the city. Population density was more than twice as high as the city average, substandard dwellings made up 30 percent of all units, almost a third of the area's 10,334 families lived on less than $3,000 per year, the unemployment rate was twice as high as that for the city as a whole, a third of all adults had less than eight years of formal education, and rates of juvenile and adult delinquency were almost three times as high as that in the city as a whole.[14]

Two high schools and 11 elementary and junior high schools served the inner-city students. Total student enrollment in the area was 15,174 of which 83 percent were Negroes. In the non-inner-city or control area were six high schools and 52 elementary and junior high schools with a total student enrollment of 42,528 of which 92 percent were white.[15] Most of the children in the control area were from working- or middle-class homes.

The sample was stratified by grade level (5th to 12th) with 14 classrooms randomly selected for each grade and equally divided between the inner-city and control areas. Although sampling by grade level provided no direct evidence of the development of political attitudes, it was a practicable alternative to a more satisfactory longitudinal study. It must be remembered, however, that the assumption underlying sampling across grade levels is that systematic variation from year to year results from "development" rather than from the influence of some uncontrolled variable. The inner-city sample included 1,276 respondents of which 78 percent were Negro and the control area sample included 1,592 respondents of which 91 percent were Caucasian.

The questionnaire was administered to the students during school hours in their classrooms. All questions were read aloud as well as written to insure more adequate measurements of the children's political orientations. Children in the higher grades offered fewer "don't know" responses and at each grade level on both indices the inner-city children opted for the "don't know" response more frequently than did their control area counterparts.[16]

FINDINGS

No significant difference in interest in the general subject of politics was apparent between the respondents in the two subsamples. Fifty-three percent in the inner-city and 55 percent in the control area stated that they thought about what was going on in government and public affairs at least some of the time. Fifty-six and 53 percent, respectively, indicated that they talked about politics and important public events with members of their family at least occasionally and 41 and 46 percent, respectively, talked with their peers about such matters almost as often. Sixty-two percent of the inner-city sample and 59 percent of the control sample had developed a party preference while still in school. Fifty-one percent of the inner-city sample favored the Democratic Party and 11 percent the Republicans while in the control area the percentages were 35 for the Democrats and 24 for the Republicans. Seventy-eight percent in the inner-city and 82 percent in the control area claimed they would vote when they became 21 years of age. Overall, therefore, on the questions that tapped general interest in politics there was a great deal of similarity between the two subsamples.

On the key dependent variables, however, significant differences did exist. The major point to be established in this study is that children who lived in the deprived environment of the inner-city slum had by the fifth grade (roughly 10 to 11 years of age) already become more cynical about politics and lagged behind children who lived elsewhere in developing a sense of political efficacy. The direction of development for the two attitudes after the fifth grade was the same for both subsamples: a higher sense of efficacy and greater feelings of cynicism grew with increased age. However, the rate of development varied within the groups of students. A sense of efficacy tended to peak during junior high school (by age 14) for the control group and thereafter remained relatively stable. Among inner-city respondents a sense of efficacy developed more slowly but continued its upward trend throughout the high school years. Students in both subsamples experienced a similar "de-idealization" of politics and politicians with increased age, and the difference between the inner-city and control area children became progressively smaller at higher grade levels. (See Table 1.)

There are, of course, many factors other than milieu that could explain differences in a sense of efficacy and feelings of cynicism. Explanatory factors investigated in other socialization studies include the family unit, social class, sex, intelligence, school curriculum, peer groups, and the mass media. However, a potentially significant explanatory factor that has received relatively little attention is race.[17] Does the fact that one's skin is black aid in predicting how a child will score on indices measuring a sense of efficacy and feelings of cynicism? After controls were introduced for race, it became evident that the association between milieu, the environment in which the children lived, and the dependent variables was primarily a result of attitude differences between white and black children. (See Tables 2 and 3.)

Theta correlations between efficacy and race and cynicism and race were higher than between milieu and the dependent variables at every grade level with the exception of the fifth and sixth graders on the efficacy index.[18] Negro children regardless of where they lived had a lower sense of efficacy and higher feelings of cynicism than white students. Mean scores for the white and black students on the dependent variables controlled by grade level indicate the magnitude of the difference. Negroes felt less efficacious in high school than whites felt in

Table 1
Sense of Political Efficacy and Cynicism Controlled
by Residence and Grade Level*

	5–6 grades		7–8–9 grades		10–11–12 grades	
	Inner-city	*Control*	*Inner-city*	*Control*	*Inner-city*	*Control*
			Efficacy			
Low	34% (62)	25% (59)	24% (79)	17% (84)	15% (50)	11% (53)
Medium	41 (75)	46 (111)	45 (149)	31 (151)	42 (138)	38 (185)
High	25 (45)	29 (69)	31 (104)	51 (246)	43 (143)	50 (242)
N	(182)	(239)	(332)	(481)	(331)	(480)
	z = 2.066 p<.05		z = 6.196 p<.01		z = 2.154 p<.05	
	CD = .11699		CD = .25434		CD = .08840	
			Cynicism			
Low	36% (81)	52% (144)	31% (114)	43% (237)	26% (99)	31% (158)
Medium	46 (103)	35 (97)	46 (166)	41 (229)	50 (190)	48 (245)
High	18 (44)	13 (35)	23 (85)	16 (190)	24 (91)	21 (108)
N	(228)	(276)	(364)	(556)	(380)	(511)
	z = 4.181 p<.01		z = 4.471 p<.01		z = 2.117 p<.05	
	CD = .21461		CD = .2777		CD = .08205	

*The coefficient of differentiation (theta) is employed in this study to measure association between one nominal and one ordinal scale. Theta measures the degree to which knowledge that an observation falls into a particular nominal class can help in guessing its relative rank on an ordinal scale. The Mann-Whitney U Test is used to determine significance and the 5 percent level was judged to represent significance.

junior high, and Negroes were about as cynical toward politics at the elementary school level as white children were in senior high. (See Table 4.)

Although inner-city white students developed a sense of efficacy more slowly than their control-area counterparts, they did not differ significantly from them by the end of high school. On the cynicism scale there were no significant differences between white students in the two subsamples at any grade level.

A second factor that may help explain the difference between the two subsamples on the two indices was achievement in school.[19] Fourteen percent of the inner-city sample was rated as above average in achievement compared with 31 percent in the control group. Since one of the most important challenges confronting children is coping with the demands of the educational process, the success that a child has in mastering the school environment was considered a probable predictor

Table 2
Sense of Political Efficacy Controlled by Residence,
Grade Level, and Race

	5–6 grades		*7–8–9 grades*		*10–11–12 grades*	
	Inner-city	*Control*	*Inner-city*	*Control*	*Inner-city*	*Control*
			Caucasian			
Low	35% (8)	24% (52)	24% (20)	16% (69)	6% (5)	10% (47)
Medium	43 (10)	47 (103)	41 (35)	30 (130)	38 (31)	38 (173)
High	22 (5)	29 (64)	35 (30)	54 (234)	56 (45)	51 (232)
N	(23)	(219)	(85)	(433)	(81)	(452)
	n.s.		z = 3.178	p<.01 n.s.		
			CD = .21703			
			Negro			
Low	34% (54)	35% (7)	24% (59)	31% (15)	18% (45)	21% (6)
Medium	41 (65)	40 (8)	46 (114)	44 (21)	43 (107)	43 (12)
High	25 (40)	25 (5)	30 (74)	25 (12)	39 (98)	36 (10)
N	(159)	(20)	(247)	(48)	(250)	(28)
	n.s.		n.s.		n.s.	

Table 3
Sense of Political Cynicism Controlled by Residence,
Grade Level, and Race

	5–6 grades		*7–8–9 grades*		*10–11–12 grades*	
	Inner-city	*Control*	*Inner-city*	*Control*	*Inner-city*	*Control*
			Caucasian			
Low	32% (11)	54% (140)	43% (39)	45% (225)	36% (35)	32% (154)
Medium	56 (19)	34 (88)	40 (36)	40 (201)	48 (46)	48 (233)
High	12 (4)	12 (31)	17 (15)	15 (78)	16 (15)	20 (98)
N	(34)	(259)	(90)	(504)	(96)	(485)
	n.s.		n.s.		n.s.	
			Negro			
Low	36% (70)	24% (4)	27% (75)	23% (12)	22% (64)	15% (4)
Medium	43 (84)	53 (9)	47 (130)	54 (28)	51 (144)	46 (12)
High	21 (40)	24 (4)	26 (70)	23 (12)	27 (76)	38 (10)
N	(194)	(17)	(274)	(52)	(284)	(26)
	n.s.		n.s.		n.s.	

Table 4
Mean Scores for Caucasian and Negro Students on
Efficacy and Cynicism Scales Controlled by Grade Level

Grades	Caucasian			Negro		
	%	Not scored	N	%	Not scored	N
			Efficacy			
5-6	8.8	42	(419)	8.3	46	(332)
7-8-9	10.1	24	(678)	8.5	33	(439)
10-11-12	10.3	16	(636)	9.5	23	(363)
			Cynicism			
5-6	4.6	30	(419)	5.5	36	(332)
7-8-9	5.0	12	(678)	5.9	26	(439)
10-11-12	5.6	9	(636)	6.2	15	(363)

of how strong a sense of efficacy he would develop.[20] At every grade level in both subsamples, achievement was, as expected, a predictor of efficacy. It was a particularly good predictor of efficacy among inner-city children during the high school years. (See Table 5.) Overall, achievement was a more useful predictor for the inner-city sample since the

Table 5
Sense of Political Efficacy Controlled by Residence,
Grade Level, and Achievement in School

	5-6 grades				7-8-9 grades				10-11-12 grades			
	Inner-city		Control		Inner-city		Control		Inner-city		Control	
					High Achievement							
Low	26%	(6)	9%	(5)	17%	(9)	10%	(19)	3%	(2)	8%	(13)
Medium	43	(10)	54	(30)	43	(23)	32	(60)	34	(20)	41	(70)
High	30	(7)	38	(21)	40	(21)	57	(106)	63	(37)	51	(87)
N		(23)		(56)		(53)		(185)		(59)		(170)
					Medium Achievement							
Low	32%	(25)	30%	(38)	19%	(28)	18%	(44)	13%	(22)	10%	(16)
Medium	41	(32)	42	(54)	46	(68)	32	(75)	44	(72)	35	(55)
High	28	(22)	28	(36)	35	(52)	50	(119)	42	(69)	55	(86)
N		(79)		(128)		(148)		(238)		(163)		(157)
					Low Achievement							
Low	39%	(31)	29%	(16)	32%	(42)	36%	(21)	24%	(26)	16%	(24)
Medium	41	(33)	49	(27)	44	(58)	28	(16)	42	(46)	39	(60)
High	20	(16)	22	(12)	24	(31)	36	(21)	33	(36)	45	(69)
N		(80)		(55)		(131)		(58)		(108)		(153)

association between achievement and a sense of efficacy was almost twice as high among the inner-city respondents as among those in the control group. (See Table 6.)

The political de-idealization process was so pervasive with increased age in both subsamples that achievement, although significant, was as good a predictor for feelings of cynicism as it was for a sense of efficacy. High achievement and low cynicism were associated during the

Table 6
Association Between Sense of Efficacy and Achievement
in School Controlled by Residence*

Achievement	Low	Medium	High	N
	\multicolumn{3}{c}{Sense of political efficacy — Inner city}		
High	12%	39%	48%	(135)
Medium	19	44	37	(197)
Low	31	43	26	(319)
	z = 6.0138	p<.01	G = .2239	(651)
	\multicolumn{3}{c}{Sense of political efficacy — Control}		
High	9%	39%	52%	(411)
Medium	19	35	46	(523)
Low	23	39	38	(266)
	z = 4.2066	p<.01	G = .1280	(1200)

*G or Gamma is a coefficient of ordinal association. It is essentially a ratio of the amount of agreement between two sets of rankings. G scores showed there was 22 percent agreement in the inner-city between achievement and efficacy while approximately 12 percent agreement in the control area.

junior-high years but lost their association before the end of high school. (See Table 7.) Overall, gamma scores for achievement and cynicism among inner-city and control-area respondents were .0927 (.01 level of significance) and .0559 (.05 level) respectively. These scores indicate the low predictive value of achievement for feelings of cynicism.

Controls were also introduced for sex. Politics is generally considered a "man's game," and evidence indicates that among adults women feel less competent and efficacious in their political activity, are less interested in political matters and elections, and vote less frequently than men.[21] Data in this study, however, indicate that sex differences do not appear prior to the end of high school. There were no significant differences between boys and girls in either subsample in regard to efficacy and cynicism. This finding generally supports previous observations made about sex differences in the development of political attitudes

Table 7
Sense of Political Cynicism Controlled by Residence,
Grade Level, and Achievement

	5-6 grades		7-8-9 grades		10-11-12 grades	
	Inner-city	Control	Inner-city	Control	Inner-city	Control
High Achievement						
Low	37% (11)	68% (43)	42% (22)	49% (99)	31% (19)	27% (49)
Medium	50 (15)	24 (39)	42 (22)	37 (74)	44 (27)	50 (92)
High	13 (4)	8 (21)	16 (9)	14 (28)	26 (16)	23 (43)
N	(30)	(63)	(53)	(201)	(62)	(184)
Medium Achievement						
Low	40% (40)	47% (70)	32% (54)	39% (110)	30% (56)	37% (65)
Medium	39 (39)	38 (57)	49 (84)	44 (125)	48 (90)	42 (73)
High	21 (21)	15 (22)	20 (34)	17 (49)	23 (43)	21 (36)
N	(100)	(149)	(172)	(284)	(189)	(174)
Low Achievement						
Low	31% (30)	48% (31)	27% (38)	39% (28)	18% (23)	29% (44)
Medium	50 (49)	39 (25)	43 (60)	42 (30)	57 (73)	52 (80)
High	19 (19)	13 (8)	30 (42)	18 (13)	25 (32)	19 (29)
N	(98)	(64)	(140)	(71)	(128)	(153)

among children. Hess and Torney stated that girls and boys did not differ in perceiving the government to be all for the best or in their feelings of efficacy.[22] Easton and Dennis could not distinguish between third- to eighth-grade boys and girls on an efficacy index.[23]

Although Greenstein found boys scoring higher than girls on political information items, there were no sex differences on juvenile conceptions of civic duty and political efficacy.[24]

SUMMARY AND CONCLUSIONS

Although limited to one city, the data suggest that being Negro is a much stronger predictor of a low sense of efficacy and feelings of cynicism than milieu. Negro youth were more cynical and felt less efficacious than their white counterparts regardless of where they lived. By the end of elementary school Negro children had been socialized into a level of cynicism that white students did not reach until the high-school years. White children in the control area felt more efficacious in junior-high school than Negroes in senior high. Unlike white, middle-class children, Negroes developed negative attitudes toward government long before adolescence.

Achievement in school was a predictor of a sense of efficacy, but it was a stronger predictor among Negro and white slum children. Achievement in school is equated with more than just intellectual ability; it is probably a manifestation of the personality as a whole. Various studies have found that "bright" children are superior to others in physique, health, and social adjustment. They tend to be self-confident, self-assured, and are free from unsubstantiated fears and apprehensions.[25] It is quite plausible, therefore, that achievement in school measures a range of psychological predispositions that carry over into the child's attitudes about politics. The greater association between achievement and a sense of efficacy among inner-city children appears to arise from the fact that being Negro and a low achiever significantly depresses a sense of political efficacy. In contrast, high achievement and the range of psychological predispositions that are probably measured by achievement apparently aid the Negro child in developing a sense of political effectiveness.

On the other hand, achievement was a relatively poor predictor of political cynicism. Feelings of cynicism were sufficiently generalized among children by senior high school that the association between achievement and cynicism completely disappeared. Although there remained in senior high school a significant difference between white and black students on the cynicism index, the difference had narrowed.

Sex has been found to be an important discriminating variable among adults for both political attitudes and behavior. However, the findings of political-socialization studies of children suggest that male-female differences are narrowing. This study supports such a proposition since there were no significant differences between boys and girls in either subsample on the dimensions explored.

What are the implications of these findings? First, the widely accepted model of political socialization among children assumes rapid socialization during the elementary school years with relatively little change thereafter. The samples that provided data for the above hypothesized pattern contained an urban, white bias and as a result may be descriptive of only the white child from a working- or middle-class home. Such a model was not descriptive of the Negro child's political socialization on the dimensions explored here—efficacy and cynicism; nor was it descriptive of the white slum child's acquisition of a sense of efficacy.

The high-school years were a time of rapid change in the political attitudes of black and disadvantaged white children. Evidence that this may be the case in settings other than Toledo was provided by Langton and Jennings in their effort to measure the effects of the high-school civics curriculum on twelfth graders. They observed that when white and Negro students were considered separately it became clear that the curriculum exerted more influence on the latter. They offered the explanation that the curriculum had a lower level of informational redundancy for Negro students than for white students. Negro students were, therefore, more likely to encounter new or conflicting perspectives and content while the white student encounters a further layering of familiar materials.[26] Whether this is the case or not, evidence presented here indicates that the high-school years are a more critical period in the political socialization of Negro and white slum children than they are for other children.

Aside from adding to our knowledge of childhood political socialization, a second implication of these findings is that the prospects for the Negro fulfilling his aspirations through widespread use of the ballot are not encouraging. For adults a sense of political efficacy and low feelings of cynicism are positively related to political involvement. The weaker the sense of efficacy and the stronger the feelings of cynicism the less likely one is to participate in the political process.

In recent years legal barriers hindering the full participation of the Negro in the political process have been largely stripped away. The federal government is attempting to stimulate a kind of "grassroots" democracy among Negroes and the urban poor through the poverty and model cities programs. Various black spokesmen striving to arouse the Negro poor out of their apathy and self-hate have captured the headlines and news bulletins. Nevertheless, black youth continue to develop early in life fundamental political orientations that suggest that "nothing very basic is happening." When one projects into the future the kind of political behavior correlated with the low-efficacy and high-cynicism orientations of Negro youth, one is led to speculate that the next generation of Negro adults will still be operating far below its potential in the political arena.

NOTES

[1]Most of the published work in the field of political socialization is summarized in the following: Herbert H. Hyman, *Political Socialization* (Glencoe, Ill.: The Free Press, 1959); Jack Dennis, "Major Problems of Political Socialization Research," *Midwest Journal of Political Science,* 12 (February 1968), 85–114;

John J. Patrick, *Political Socialization of American Youth: Implications for Secondary School Social Studies* (Washington: National Council for the Social Studies, 1967); Richard E. Dawson and Kenneth Prewitt, *Political Socialization* (Boston: Little, Brown, 1969).

[2]David Easton and Robert Hess, "The Child's Image of Government," *Annals of the American Academy of Political and Social Science,* 361 (September 1965), 56.

[3]David Easton and Robert Hess, "The Child's Political World," *Midwest Journal of Political Science,* 6 (August 1962), 214. One piece of direct empirical evidence to support this proposition is that parents did not pass on to their children suspicions of a conspiracy at work in the assassination of President Kennedy. Karen Orren and Paul Peterson, "Presidential Assassination: A Case Study in the Dynamics of Political Socialization," *Journal of Politics,* 29 (May 1967), 404.

[4]Fred I. Greenstein, "The Benevolent Leader: Children's Images of Political Authority," *The American Political Science Review,* 54 (December 1960), 941. One reported exception to this general pattern was a group of children from a poor, rural Appalachian County who were significantly more cynical than children from other parts of the country. See Dean Jaros, Herbert Hirsch, Frederic Fleron, "The Malevolent Leader: Political Socialization in an American Sub-Culture," *The American Political Science Review,* 62 (June 1968), 564–575.

[5]Since there is a correlation between a slum milieu and the lower socioeconomic strata, many of the observations made about children from lower SES families are probably applicable to slum children. Greenstein observed that lower-status children do not share the explicit unwillingness to participate in politics found among adults of the same background. They do show, however, a greater deference toward political leadership and indicate that their judgments are not worth acting upon. Easton and Dennis reported that at every grade level the child higher on the social ladder is likely to be a step or two higher in his relative sense of political efficacy. Hess and Torney found that lower-status children more frequently accepted authority figures as correct and relied upon their trustworthiness and benign intent. Fred I. Greenstein, *Children and Politics* (New Haven: Yale University Press, 1965), 94–106; David Easton and Jack Dennis, "The Child's Acquisition of Regime Norms: Political Efficacy," *The American Political Science Review,* 61 (March 1967), 35; Robert Hess and Judith Torney, *The Development of Political Attitudes in Children* (Chicago: Aldine Publishing Company, 1967), 154.

[6]The effect of milieu on learning and behavior has been demonstrated in many different contexts. See: Richard Boyle, "The Effect of the High School on Students' Aspirations," *American Journal of Sociology,* 71 (May 1966), 628–639; Edgar Litt, "Political Cynicism and Political Futility," *Journal of Politics,* 25 (May 1963), 312–323; Bonnie Bullough, "Alienation in the Ghetto," *American Journal of Sociology,* 72 (March 1967), 469–478 [reprinted here as Chapter 6]; Bryan T. Dowes, "Municipal Social Rank and the Characteristics of Local Political Leaders," *Midwest Journal of Political Science,* 12 (November 1968), 514–537; Robert Green, Louis Hofmann and Robert Morgan, "Some Effects of Deprivation on Intelligence, Achievement, and Cognitive Growth," *The Journal of Negro Education,* 36 (Winter 1967), 5–14.

[7]Easton and Dennis, "Child's Acquisition of Regime Norms," 26.

[8]Robert E. Lane, *Political Life* (Glencoe, Ill: The Free Press, 1959), 151.

[9]Easton and Dennis, "Child's Acquisition of Regime Norms," 29.

[10]This index has been used in a number of previously reported studies. However, neither slum children nor Negroes were singled out for separate analysis and none reported data for children beyond the eighth grade. See Hess and Torney, *Political Attitudes in Children;* Easton and Dennis, "Child's Acquisition of Regime Norms"; Elliott S. White, "Intelligence and Sense of Political Efficacy in Children," *Journal of Politics,* 30 (August 1968), 710-731.

[11]M. Kent Jennings and Richard E. Niemi, "The Transmission of Political Values From Parent to Child," *The American Political Science Review,* 62 (March 1968), 177.

[12]Robert E. Agger, Marshall Goldstein and Stanley Pearl, "Political Cynicism: Measurement and Meaning," *Journal of Politics,* 23 (August 1961), 487-494; Edgar Litt, "Political Cynicism," 312-323.

[13]The cynicism index has also been used in previously reported research. See Jennings and Niemi, "Transmission of Political Values"; Jaros, Hirsch, and Fleron, "Malevolent Leader."

[14]Application to the Department of Housing and Urban Development for a grant to Plan a Comprehensive City Demonstration Program for Toledo, Ohio, City Manager's Office, City of Toledo, April 28, 1967, 5-7.

[15]Two vocational schools were excluded from the sample since their student bodies were drawn from all parts of the city.

[16]In scoring the indices, the procedure followed was to add up the scores for each item; these could run from one to four for the efficacy index and one to three for cynicism (eliminating the "don't know" option). Scores ranged from 5 to 20 for efficacy and 5 to 15 for cynicism. For a child who answered four of five questions other than "don't know" on each scale, his four-item score was multiplied by 5/4. Children who failed to answer at least four questions for each index were not scored. The following percentages by grade level were not scored and therefore dropped from the analysis.

| | Efficacy | | | | Cynicism | | | |
| | Inner-city | | Control | | Inner-city | | Control | |
Grades	%	N	%	N	%	N	%	N
5-6	48	169	40	161	35	123	31	124
7-8-9	32	159	23	146	26	126	11	71
10-11-12	24	103	15	85	12	54	10	54

[17]For a general discussion of political socialization among Negroes, see Bradbury Seasholes, "Political Socialization of Negroes: Image Development of Self and Polity," in *Negro Self-Concept: Implications for School and Citizenship* by William C. Kvaraceus *et al.* (New York: McGraw-Hill, 1965), 52-90; Dwaine Marvick, "The Political Socialization of the American Negro," *The Annals of the American Academy of Political and Social Science,* 361 (September 1965), 112-127.

[18]Theta correlations for race and the two dependent variables were as follows:

	Cynicism	Efficacy
5-6 Grades	.23357	.10753
7-8-9 Grades	.22186	.28329
10-11-12 Grades	.15750	.16328

The finding on cyncism conflicts with that reported for a national sample of 12th-grade students. Langton and Jennings stated that while Negroes are less politically efficacious than whites, they are not at the same time more cynical. Kenneth P. Langton and M. Kent Jennings, "Political Socialization and the High School Civics Curriculum in the United States," *The American Political Science Review,* 62 (September 1968), 860–861 [reprinted here as Chapter 5].

[19]The cumulative records of each pupil in grades 5 through 8 were used to obtain academic achievement level. For grades 9 through 12 the teacher gave the achievement level of each student relative to the entire school population. Although there is probably some error in judgment on the part of the teachers, it is believed this procedure will produce data as valid as I.Q. or other test scores, especially among the inner-city sample.

[20]Easton and Dennis reported that the higher the intellectual ability (I.Q.) the higher the sense of efficacy. "Child's Acquisition of Regime Norms," 35; White claimed that in addition to grade level, individual intelligence as measured by national standardized intelligence tests was the single best indicator of efficacy. "Intelligence and Sense of Political Efficacy," 731.

[21]Angus Campbell *et al., The American Voter* (New York: John Wiley, 1964), 255–261.

[22]Hess and Torney, *Political Attitudes in Children,* 188.

[23]Easton and Dennis, "Acquisition of Regime Norms," 36.

[24]Greenstein, *Children,* 115–116.

[25]White, "Political Efficacy in Children," 723–724.

[26]Langton and Jennings, "Political Socialization," 866.

Chapter 5

POLITICAL SOCIALIZATION AND THE HIGH SCHOOL CIVICS CURRICULUM IN THE UNITED STATES

Kenneth P. Langton
M. Kent Jennings

III. FINDINGS FOR THE NEGRO SUBSAMPLE

Although the Negro portion of the sample is not as large as one might desire for extensive analysis (raw N = 186, weighted N = 208), it is sufficiently large to permit gross comparisons with White students of similar social characteristics and also permits some analysis within the Negro subpopulation. The subsample size and the fact that the dropout rate is appreciably higher among Negroes than Whites underscores the admonition that this subsample should not be extrapolated to the Negro age cohort in general. It should also be noted that the subsample contains twelve respondents classified as non-Whites other than Negro.

Demographically, the Negro students are located disproportionately in the South (55 percent versus 25 percent for Whites) and come from more disadvantaged backgrounds than do the Whites. The latter is true despite the fact that the backgrounds of Negro students who have persevered through high school are undoubtedly less deprived than are those of their cohort who dropped out. Social status differences between Negroes and Whites are more pronounced in the South than in the North.

Negro and White students have taken civics courses in approximately the same proportions (Negroes 63 percent, Whites 68 percent). When the association between the civics curriculum and the dependent

Reprinted from *The American Political Science Review,* 62 (September, 1968), pp. 859–65, by permission of the authors and publisher. Footnotes and tables have been renumbered; some have been deleted. Sections I and II have been omitted.

variables discussed above was reexamined within both racial groups, some intriguing differences appeared. These caused us to reassess the place of the civics curriculum in the political socialization of American youth.

Political Knowledge

White students score more highly on the knowledge scale than do Negroes; and when parents' education is controlled the differences persist at all levels. Civics courses have little effect on the absolute political knowledge level of Whites (beta = .08). The number of courses taken by Negroes, on the other hand, is significantly associated with their political knowledge score (beta = .30). The civics curriculum is an important source of political knowledge for Negroes and, as we shall see later, appears in some cases to substitute for political information gathering in the media.

Although the complex multivariate analysis holds parental education constant, it does not allow us to observe easily the singular role of this crucial socialization factor upon the relationship between curriculum and political orientations. Therefore, contingency tables were constructed with parental education controlled for all relationships between the number of government courses taken on the one hand, and each political orientation on the other. All instances in which education makes a distinctive imprint are reported.[1] For the case at hand—political knowledge—controls for parental education did not alter the effects of the curriculum among either Whites or Negroes.

In another attempt to measure political knowledge as well as ideological sophistication, students were asked which political party they thought was more conservative or liberal. Each party has its "liberal" and "conservative" elements, but studies of roll call voting in Congress as well as the commentary of the politically aware places the Republican party somewhat to the right of the Democrats. Forty-five percent of students said that the Republicans were more conservative than the Democrats. Thirty-eight percent confessed to not knowing the answer.

In answering this question the student was faced with a problem not of his own making. It can be presumed that some respondents made a random choice (i.e., guessed) to extricate themselves. One gauge of the frequency of guessing is how often the Democrats were assigned a conservative position (17 percent). If we make the reasonable assumption that this form of random guess is symmetric around the midpoint of the response dimension, we can say that an additional 17 percent of the students guessed "correctly" by putting the Republicans in the conservative column. Accordingly, we may deduct 17 percent from the 45 percent who said Republicans were more conservative, leaving 28 percent who are able to connect the conservative label to the Republican party.[2]

We are less interested in the absolute number of students who are able to connect symbol with party than with the role the civics curriculum plays in this process. Again we see that course work has little impact on White students while the percent of Negroes who "know" the parties' ideological position increases as they take more civics courses (Table 1).

Table 1
The Relation Between the Civics Curriculum and Knowing the Ideological Position
of the Republican and Democrat Parties Among Negro and White Students

Number of civics courses	Adjusted percentages of correct responses			
	Negro		White	
	%	N	%	N
0	0	(72)	29	(543)
1+	19	(122)	31	(1184)

These findings using both measures of political knowledge offer an excellent example of redundancy in operation. The clear inference as to why the Negro students' responses are "improved" by taking the courses is that new information is being added where relatively less existed before. White students enrolled in the courses appear to receive nothing beyond that to which their non-enrolled cohorts are being exposed. This, coupled with the great lead which Whites in general already have over the Negro students, makes for greater redundancy among Whites than Negroes.

One should not deduce from these results that the White students have a firm grasp on political knowledge; as Table 1 and other data indicate, they clearly do not. Rather, White students have reached a saturation or quota level which is impervious to change by the civics curriculum. From their relatively lower start the Negro students' knowledge level can be increased by exposure to the civics curriculum.

Political Efficacy and Political Cynicism

Almost twice as many Negro students as White scored low on the political efficacy scale. When the effect of parental education is partialed out the racial differences remain at each educational level, although they are somewhat diminished. Interestingly enough, the difference in the percentage of those who scored low is less between Negro and White students whose parents have had only an elementary school education (13 percent) than between Negro and White students whose parents have had a college education (24 percent).

The number of civics courses taken by White students has little perceptible effect on their sense of political efficacy (beta = .05). Among Negroes, though, course exposure is moderately related to a sense of efficacy (beta = .18). As can be seen in Table 2, this is particularly true for Negroes from less educated families. The strength of the relationship decreases significantly among higher status students. Course-taking among the lower-status Negroes acts to bring their scores into line with their higher status cohorts. There is but a faint trace of this pattern among White students.

Table 2

The Relation Between the Number of Civics Courses Taken and Political Efficacy Among Negro Students, by Parental Education*

	Political efficacy				
Number of civics courses	*Low* %	*Medium* %	*High* %	*N*	*Gamma*
		Elementary			
0	64	20	16	(18)	
1+	30	27	43	(39)	.56
		High School			
0	56	20	24	(41)	
1+	34	27	39	(62)	.36
		College			
0	32	32	36	(15)	
1+	37	19	44	(24)	.02

*Parental education was set by the highest level achieved by either parent. "Elementary" means neither parent exceeded an eighth grade education; "high school" that at least one parent had one or more years of high school training; and "college" that at least one parent had one or more years of collegiate experience.

Although Negro students at all levels of parental education feel less efficacious than their White counterparts, it must be concluded that without the civics curriculum the gap would be even greater. As in the case of political knowledge, we have another illustration of less re-dundancy at work among the Negro subsample. For a variety of reasons the American political culture produces a lower sense of efficacy among

Negro youths compared with Whites. But by heavily emphasizing the legitimacy, desirability, and feasibility of citizen participation and control, the civics course adds a new element in the socialization of low and middle status Negro students. Since those from the less educated families are more likely to be surrounded by agents with generally low efficacy levels, the curriculum has considerably more effect on them than on their peers from higher-status environments. Leaving aside the possible later disappointments in testing the reality of their new-found efficacy, the Negro students from less privileged backgrounds are for the moment visibly moved by course exposure.

While Negroes as a whole are less politically efficacious than Whites, they are not at the same time more politically cynical. The proportion of twelfth graders falling into the three most cynical categories of a six point political cynicism scale includes 21 percent of the White and 23 percent of the Negro students. This relatively low level of political cynicism among Negroes may seem ironic, but it is consistent with their view of the "good citizen" role (discussed later). The high school civics curriculum has only a slight effect upon the cynicism level of Whites (beta = .11) and none among Negroes (beta = .01). However, this difference suggests that the cynicism of the latter may be somewhat less moveable than that for Whites.

Civic Tolerance

One of the abiding goals of civic education is the encouragement and development of civic toleration. Negroes as a whole score lower on the civic tolerance scale than do Whites. When parental education is controlled the racial differences remain at each education level, although they are moderately attenuated. Again, as with political efficacy, the differences in the percentage of those scoring low is less between Negro and White students whose parents have had only an elementary school education (18 percent) than between Negro and White students whose parents have had a college education (28 percent). What we may be witnessing is the result of Negro compensation for the White bias in American society—a bias to which higher status Negroes may prove most sensitive.

The number of civics courses taken has little effect on White students' civic tolerance scores (beta = .06), with somewhat greater impact being observed on those from homes of lower parental education. There is, however, a moderate association between exposure and Negro students' sense of civic tolerance (beta = .22). The more courses they take, the higher their level of tolerance. Negroes are more intolerant even when educational controls are introduced, but the civics curriculum appears to overcome in part the environmental factors which may contribute to their relatively lower tolerance. The items on which the civic tolerance measure is based all have to do with the acceptance of diversity. Aggregate student and parent data suggest that these items tap a dimension of political sophistication less likely to be operative in the Negro subculture. To the extent that the civics courses preach more tolerance, the message is less likely to be redundant among the Negroes than the Whites. Unlike political knowledge and efficacy, though, course-taking exerts its main effect on Negro twelfth graders from better-educated families, thereby suggesting that a threshold of receptivity may be lacking among those from lower-status families.

Politicization — Interest, Discussion, and Media Usage

Students were asked about their interest in public affairs and how often they discussed politics with their friends outside class. There is little difference between racial groups among those who expressed high interest in politics or said they discussed politics weekly or more often with their friends. Nor did controls for parental education uncover aggregate racial distinctions. Moreover, the civics curriculum appears at first glance to have little impact upon these two indicators of politicization among Negroes (beta = .15 and −.07 respectively) or Whites (beta = .06 and .04). Yet an examination of Table 3 indicates that cur-

Table 3
Gamma Correlation Between Number of Civics Courses Taken and Political Interest and Discussion with Peers Among Negro Students, by Parental Education

Parental education	Political interest	Political discussion
Elementary	+ .31	+ .20
High school	− .18	− .31
College	− .21	− .36

riculum effect is differentially determined by the educational level of the Negro students' parents (in contrast to a lack of variation among Whites). The differential effect may account for the low beta coefficient in the multivariate analysis.

As Negroes from less educated families take more civics courses their political interest and frequency of political discussion with peers increases. Since less educated parents ordinarily evince lower states of politicization, one could explain this in terms of nonredundant information spurring an upsurge in student politicization. Students from higher status families, however, actually appear to undergo depoliticization as they move through the civics curriculum.

In their excellent social and psychological inquiry into the personality of the American Negro, Abram Kardiner and Lionel Ovesey observed that it is the higher status Negro who is most likely to identify and have contact with Whites and their culture.[3] But due to their race, the disappointments are more frequent and their aspirations more likely to founder on the rock of unattainable ideals.

Because of his parents' experiences, the higher status Negro student may have received a more "realistic" appraisal of the institutional and social restrictions placed upon Negro participation in the United States. Upon enrolling in the civics course he finds at least two good-citizen roles being emphasized. The first stresses a politicized-participation dimension. The second emphasizes a more passive role: loyalty and obedience to authority and nation. If he has absorbed from his parents the probability of restrictions, the participation-politicization emphasis in the curriculum may have little impact upon the higher status Negro student. Redundancy is low because the information conflicts with previous learning. The "reality factor" causes him to select out of the curriculum only those role characteristics which appear to be more congruent with a preconceived notion of his political life chances. As we shall see later, higher status Negro students' perception of the good citizen role is compatible with the above interpretation.

Students were also asked how often they read articles in newspapers or magazines or watched programs on television that dealt with public affairs, news, or politics. In the aggregate, students from each racial grouping employ newspapers and magazines at about the same rates; but Negro students use television more often than do Whites, and at all levels of parental education. The civics curriculum has a different impact upon political media usage among Whites and Negroes. Table 4 shows that for White students there is a consistent—but very weak—association between taking civics courses and use of the media as an access point to political information. Among Negroes there is a consistently negative but somewhat stronger association between the civics curriculum and political media usage.

Observing the same relationship within contingency tables under less severe control conditions, the civics curriculum continues to have a negative—although fluctuating—impact upon political media usage among Negroes at all levels of parental education (Table 5).

Table 4

Partial Beta Coefficients Between Number of Civics Courses Taken and Political Media Usage Among Negro and White Students

Media	Negro	White
Newspapers	−.17	+.07
Television	−.21	+.04
Magazines	−.10	+.10

Table 5

Gamma Correlations Between Number of Civics Courses Taken and Political Media Usage Among Negro Students, by Parental Education

| Media | Parental education | | |
	Primary	Secondary	College
Newspapers	−.07	−.36	−.28
Television	−.39	−.42	−.17
Magazines	−.27	−.07	−.42

Negative correlations among Negroes might be explained on at least two dimensions: substitution and depoliticization. A civics course may increase a student's political interest while at the same time acting as a substitute for political information gathering in the media. This is what appears to be happening among Negroes from less educated families. Negative associations between course work and media usage suggest that the former may be substituting for political information gathering in the media. But as we saw before, there is a significant increase in political interest among lower status Negroes as they take more civics courses. The lack of depoliticization in this group was further confirmed by the positive correlation between the civics curriculum and discussing politics with one's school friends (Table 3).

The case of the higher status Negro seems to be of a different order. Negative correlations between the civics curriculum and media usage may indicate substitution, but what is even more apparent is the general depolitication of higher status Negroes as they move through the curriculum. The more courses they take the less likely are they to seek political information in newspapers, magazines, and television. In addition there is also a decrease in their political interest and propensity to discuss politics with their friends.

Citizenship Behavior

Interjecting race adds a special complexity to the relationship between the civics curriculum and the student's belief about the role of a good citizen in this country. Students were asked:

> People have different ideas about what being a good citizen means. We're interested in what you think. Tell me how you would describe a good citizen in this country – that is, what things about a person are most important in showing that he is a good citizen.

Taking only their first responses, 70 percent of the Whites and 63 percent of the Negroes fell along two general dimensions: loyalty and political participation. Within these two response dimensions there are distinct racial differences. Sixty-one percent of the Negro responses focus on loyalty rather than participation. Only 41 percent of the White students, on the other hand, see the "good citizen" role as being one of loyalty rather than political participation. When we probe the relationship between taking civics courses and citizenship orientation some interesting differences are revealed. More civics courses mean more loyalty and less participation orientation for Negroes. In Table 6 there is a 24 percent difference in loyalty orientation between those Negroes who have taken no civic courses and those who have taken one or more. Civics course work has a slightly opposite effect among White students.

In other words, while the civics curriculum has little impact upon the White Student's view of the good citizen role, it appears to inculcate

Table 6
The Relationship Between Civics Curriculum and Good Citizenship
Attitudes Among Negro and White Students

Number of civics courses	Loyalty %	Participation %	N*
	Negroes stressing		
0	51	49	(41)
1+	75	25	(85)
	Whites stressing		
0	46	54	(395)
1+	39	61	(803)

*These Ns run lower than corresponding Ns in other tables because those respondents not mentioning either loyalty or participation in their first response are not included in the base.

in Negroes the role expectation that a good citizen is above all a loyal citizen rather than an active one. Yet looking at this same relationship among Negroes under the more severe multivariate control conditions the size of the beta coefficient $(-.10)$ is not large.[4] While it is predictably negative (i.e., loyalty orientation increases with course work), the magnitude of the coefficients reduces our confidence in the earlier contingency table.

The difference in findings may be the result of moving from a relatively simple bivariate analysis with no controls for other possible intervening variables to a more sophisticated mode of multivariate analysis under more rigorously controlled conditions. This undoubtedly accounts for part of the difference, but we also found, as before, that the civics curriculum has a differential effect upon Negroes depending on the educational level of their parents.

Negro students whose parents have some secondary school or college education increase their loyalty orientation by 36 percent and 28 percent, respectively, as they take more civics courses (Table 7). Negroes from less educated families, however, increase their participation orientation much like White students. Due to the small N for Negro students who have taken no courses and whose parents have an elementary school education or less this relationship should be treated quite cautiously. Although differences between Negroes from different levels of parental education have been mentioned before, the most one would want to say here is that the civics curriculum seems to increase the loyalty orientations of higher status Negroes while having a slightly opposite effect among lower status Negro students.

Table 7
The Relationship Between Civics Curriculum and Citizenship Attitudes Among Negro Students, by Parental Education

Number of civics courses	Loyalty %	Participation %	N
		Elementary	
0	83	17	(6)
1+	63	37	(28)
		High School	
0	54	46	(24)
1+	90	10	(41)
		College	
0	32	68	(11)
1+	60	40	(17)

A number of interpretations can be placed on these findings. Both loyalty and participation are emphasized in the civics curriculum, and for White and lower status Negro students the dual emphasis has about equal effect. But as we noted earlier, the higher status Negro may have received from his more active parents a "realistic" appraisal of the institutional and social restrictions placed upon Negro participation in American politics. Consequently, the participation emphasis in the curriculum has little impact. The reality factor may cause the higher status Negro to select out of the curriculum only those role characteristics which appear to be most congruent with a preconceived notion of his political life chances.

Another rationale for the findings might be found in the relative fulfillment of White and Negro needs to belong, to be accepted in this society. If we assume that the Negro is cut off from many of the associational memberships and status advantages that most Whites take for granted, then his unfulfilled need to belong and to be accepted is probably greater than that of his white counterparts. This may be particularly true of the higher status Negro and his parents. Because of their relatively higher education in the Negro community, they have had more contacts with Whites—contacts which, because of their race, have led to more frequent rebuffs. The one association not explicitly denied Negroes is that of being a loyal American. It is entirely possible that the psychic relief a higher status Negro receives in "establishing" his American good-citizenship is greater than that of his White counterpart or his lower status racial peer. As a consequence, the loyalty emphasis in the curriculum may have the most impact on the higher status Negro.[5]

Regional Effects

The Negro students are located disproportionately in the southern part of the United States. Because of possible cultural differences we thought it advisable to control for region as well as parental education. Therefore the Negro subsample was divided into South and non-South with controls for high and low parental education employed in each region.[6]

When controlled for region as well as parental education, the effects of the civics curriculum upon political knowledge, interest, discussion, television-newspaper-magazine usage, and loyalty-participation orientations were consistent with the results for the Negro subsample as a whole in all except two cases. Among the seven variables discussed above there are 28 cases (two for each region because of the education control or four for each variable) in which a possible deviation from the

Negro subsample as a whole could occur. Due to the small marginals and the fact that there were 26 consistent findings, we attach little conceptual significance to these two exceptions.

In both regions the civics curriculum continued to be negatively associated with political media usage at all educational levels except for newspaper reading among higher status students outside the South. The relationships are slightly stronger in the South than in the non-South. The differential consequences of parental education were remarkably consistent across both regions. As before, civics courses had a negative effect upon the political discussion (and political interest in the South) of higher status Negroes while having a positive impact upon lower status Negroes. Finally, in both regions the civics curriculum continued to have its greatest negative effect on the participatory orientations of Negro students from the more educated families.

There appeared to be different regional effects on only three of the dependent variables. The first of these was political cynicism. In the South course work increases cynicism slightly among high and low status Negroes while in the North political cynicism decreased as the student was exposed to the civics curriculum. However, in both regions the outcome of taking a civics course is to make the student from the higher educated family relatively more cynical than his lower status peer. As with cynicism, exposure to civics means a slight decrease in civic tolerance among high and low status southern Negroes. This is also true of lower status Negroes outside the South. For all three cases the magnitude of the relationships are quite small, the highest being a Gamma of −.14. It is only among higher status non-southern Negroes that a stronger, positive relationship develops − +.39.

The political efficacy of lower status students in the South was increased much more by the civics curriculum (.64) than was the efficacy of their higher status peers (.32). This is consistent with the picture for the entire subsample. However, while there was a positive relationship between exposure and increased efficacy among higher status students in the non-South there was a negative relationship among lower status students. We are at a loss to explain this negative sign other than point to the small frequencies which may account for this departure. . . .

NOTES

[1]Parental education was used as a summary control variable because we felt that it best captures the tone of the whole family environment as well as other sources of socialization.

[2]We have borrowed this method of adjusting "correct" answers from Donald E. Stokes, "Ideological Competition of British Parties," paper presented at 1964 Annual Meeting of the American Political Science Association, Chicago, Illinois.

[3]Abram Kardiner and Lionel Ovesey, *The Mark of Oppression* (Cleveland: The World Publishing Co. [a Meridian book], 1962).

[4]The beta coefficient for White students is + .04.

[5]In 1942 Gunnar Myrdal completed a comprehensive codification of the Negro culture and circumstances in America. He maintained that Negroes in this country were "'exaggerated Americans," who believed in the American Creed more strongly than Whites. Gunnar Myrdal, *An American Dilemma* (New York: Harper & Brothers, 1944).

[6]The Negro subsample was not large to begin with, and a regional control in addition to the control for parental education reduced cell frequencies even further. Because the differential effects of parental education were found primarily between students whose parents had only an elementary school education versus those with high school or college education, we combined students from the latter two categories into one category. This retained the substance of the original education break in the South, but it still left only a small number of students outside the South whose parents had an elementary school education or less. In order to enlarge this latter group the parental education cutting point in the non-South was moved to a point between those parents who were at least high school graduates and those who had only some high school or less. If there are important regional differences in curriculum effect they should be apparent under these control conditions.

The respective raw and weighted N's for the four groupings are as follows: southern low educated – 33, 44; southern high educated – 48, 64; non-southern low educated – 45, 42; non-southern high educated – 53, 50.

PART TWO

Attitudes of Black Adults

For more than a century blacks have been seeking equal treatment. In recent decades equal treatment has often been synonomous with integration, the paramount objective of much civil rights activity since the early 1950s. Even today, when a great deal of publicity is accorded black militants' demands for racial separation, this position is embraced by only a splinter of the black population. As recently as 1971 only 3 percent of a black sample in Detroit chose total school separation while 68 percent opted for integration with the remainder favoring an unspecified intermediate solution.[1] Even those blacks not desiring integration tend to strongly endorse equality of opportunity which would permit although not require integration.

In Part Two we include articles focusing on some aspects of black attitudes toward integration and equal treatment that have implications for system support. The first reports on the impact of milieu on black attitudes, comparing blacks living in integrated neighborhoods with economically similar blacks in segregated areas. The second reports on changes in black attitudes toward whites over time. The last two selections are studies of the political support found among riot area residents.

The article by Bonnie Bullough reports on the relationship between alienation and whether one lives in a largely white or all-black neighborhood. Anomia, powerlessness, and isolation, three of the five variants of alienation distinguished by Seeman[2] are used as dependent variables by Bullough. Blacks who have left all-black communities differ from their peers in evincing less powerlessness and less anomia, as well as severing ties with the ghetto subculture while becoming more oriented toward middle class America. The scars of encounters with hostile whites produce a sense of powerlessness in many segregated blacks that reduces the likelihood of their attempting to move into an integrated area. Blacks, who in the face of white opposition become quickly discouraged, may conclude, at times unjustly, that the government has again failed to ensure equal opportunities for all races.

The implications of integration for the incidence of alienation among blacks is summed up by Bullough:

Segregation and all that is associated with it emerges as such a critical problem for Negroes that successful experiences with integration seem to raise the general level of expectation for control [i.e., efficacy].

Finifter has suggested that "alienation . . . may be conceived as one end of a continuum whose opposite extreme is defined by the concepts of support or integration."[3] From this perspective the implications of Bullough's research are that through integration potentially dangerous alienation may be averted and diffuse political support may be developed. Finifter has speculated that low political powerlessness and low perceived political normlessness may be concomitants of political integration; people who score at the other (high) end of these scales may engage in political violence or else withdraw altogether from political participation.[4] Either action, if widespread, may constitute a dangerously low level of support.

Bullough's conclusions that segregation causes anomia are tempered by Wilson's study of anomie (attitudes toward social structures as opposed to personal relations) in three largely black working class areas of one city. He found that among blacks "anomie is highest when racial mixture approaches 50 percent white and 50 percent Negro."[5] In Wilson's study anomie was lowest in Ghetto (96 percent black) and highest in West Side (63 percent black). Contextual variables, particularly community stability, are important in accounting for the variations observed by Wilson. Disparities between the findings of Bullough and Wilson may spring from differences in 1) the social class of the subjects (Bullough interviewed middle class blacks; Wilson used lower class); 2) the racial composition of the research sites (Bullough compared blacks in an all-black ghetto with those in an almost all-white suburb; Wilson worked in urban areas 63 to 96 percent black); 3) individual motivations (those who move into largely unintegrated areas may have quite different personalities from those who enter a neighborhood undergoing racial transformation); and 4) the measures used for alienation.

Wilson, however, is not the only one to observe negative consequences of integration. From a 1970 study of St. Louis junior college students, Holtzman finds that those who attended integrated high schools and/or had frequent biracial social interaction at the junior college were less trusting of other people. Nor was there any convincing evidence that biracial social interaction in an educational milieu produced a stronger sense of political efficacy among blacks.[6]

On the other hand, benefits linked with integrated experiences include moderating unfavorable stereotypes, a greater willingness to participate in biracial environments, and the acquisition of better-paying jobs.[7] There is evidence that the earlier one comes into contact with members of another race the more likely that attitudinal changes leading to a more favorable evaluation of the other race will occur.[8] When initial experiences with members of another race do not come until adulthood, changes in attitudes are less likely to be observed.

Jeffery Paige, in the second article in Part Two, presents evidence that suggests that young blacks in northern ghettoes are increasingly unwilling to participate in integrated social situations because of growing antipathy toward whites. Paige explains why at various points in time different components of the black population have displayed the strongest anti-white attitudes. He concludes that because of changes in the sociopolitical situation and resultant changes in blacks' perceptions of their situation vis-a-vis whites, poor, young blacks have come to see more to gain from trying to wrest control of their environment from whites rather than from relying upon the aid of white liberal allies to produce improvements. In support of this speculation, respondents who had participated in the Newark riots were demonstrably more hostile toward whites than were nonparticipants. Evidence that young blacks in Newark are rejecting white society and its values is in keeping with the recent emphasis on racial pride, culture, and history.

The Holtzman study, with respondents not from riot areas, presents findings somewhat at variance with Paige's. Holtzman's junior college students were overwhelmingly favorable to integrated employment (97 percent), political representation (95 percent), public accommodations (94 percent), and housing (66 percent).[9] The great majority of a nationwide sample of blacks polled by Gallup in 1969 also gave pro-integration responses when asked about schools (78 percent) and housing (74 percent).[10] Also at variance with Paige's observations are slight indications noted by Holtzman that middle class blacks may be more separatist than working class blacks, with the greatest difference (ten percentage points) being in the realm of housing.[11]

Paige's finding that blacks who want to live in all-black neighborhoods are less anomic than those who look favorably upon integrated living should not be viewed as necessarily contradicting Bullough. Perhaps the crucial difference between the studies is that Bullough's subjects were middle class while Paige dealt with lower class blacks. The different times at which the interviews were conducted (Bullough in 1964–65; Paige in 1968) may also be an intervening variable.

The relationship between integration and black attitudes is, to say the least, complex. Available survey data contain clues suggesting that over the last few years, as the range of equal opportunities has been expanded, dissatisfaction with the system among blacks has been increasing. From the available evidence some illustrative findings are:

1. Between 1966 and 1968 the alienation scores for samples of blacks increased from 34 to 54 in comparison with an increase from 24 to 30 for the national samples.[12]

2. Between 1966 and 1968 the proportion of blacks doubting that they had as good a chance to succeed as others in society rose from 33 to 56 percent. In 1968 only 17 percent of the white sample held this negative outlook.[13]

3. Between 1970 and 1971 blacks became more critical in their evaluations of whites. A majority of blacks agreed with nine or ten negative statements about whites, with a high of 81 percent thinking that most whites consider blacks inferior. In contrast the same Harris poll found that whites were less likely to entertain negative stereotypes of blacks in 1971 than in 1963. For example, in 1971 only 22 percent of the whites acknowledged believing blacks to be inferior.[14]

4. The proportion of blacks thinking whites were hostile or indifferent toward them rose from 54 to 69 percent between 1966 and 1969.[15]

The prevalence of negative images of whites held by blacks may indicate that the "moving against" trend noted by Paige is growing, particularly among lower class blacks, even though there may be no great desire for racial separation. What we are witnessing seems to be the growing commitment among blacks to "make sure the Negro has all that any other American has."[16]

The Bullough and Paige articles may be viewed as tapping attitudes of the least and most alienated blacks. Blacks who have succeeded in achieving economic and social equality are, as Bullough finds, less anomic and have a greater sense of efficacy. They have successfully followed a strategy of moving toward white America and, we can speculate, probably have support levels comparable to those of their white neighbors. On the other hand, blacks with less extensive biracial experiences, for example those studied by Holtzman and Wilson, may well be more alienated, less trusting, and less efficacious, while political support may be least among blacks who are moving against the white majority.

The last two articles, by Sears and by Aberbach and Walker, deal with the attitudes of those who have experienced urban riots. There is disagreement about the full implications of urban riots[17] and these two articles seek to provide answers to some critical questions: 1. Are the riots signs of widespread revolt by blacks or are they merely the acts of a small criminal element bent on "fun and profit"?[18] 2. Do the riots indicate black estrangement from the political system and its institutions or do they indicate disaffection only from current public leaders and policies? 3. What factors produce a disposition to riot? 4. Are blacks most likely to attempt to change the system in the future by violence or through more peaceful types of demand articulation?

Many white Americans, including a sizable number of public officials,[19] have dismissed the riots as meaningless, haphazard expressions of criminal behavior participated in, and supported by, only a small fraction of the black citizenry. In the selection by David Sears and in another article by Sears and T. M. Tomlinson[20] (not reprinted here) such contentions are found incorrect. Analysis of interviews with 586 blacks from the Watts area after the riot of 1965 indicate that some 15 percent of the blacks surveyed participated in the disorders, and that support for the riot was rather substantial.[21] Thirty-four percent of the blacks said they supported the riot and 56 percent said they had opposed it.[22] Sympathy for the riot was also indicated by the selection of militant terms such as "revolt," "revolution," and "insurrection" by 38 percent of the blacks to describe the Watts disorder.

Fifty-eight percent of the blacks interviewed considered the riot to be a purposeful protest that would have predominantly beneficial effects on their lives; only 26 percent anticipated primarily unfavorable consequences.[23] Most blacks believed that the riot was useful in calling white attention to black problems. Similarly, Gary Marx found that an average of 50 percent of the blacks surveyed in five northern and southern cities believed that riots "do some good because they make whites pay attention to the problems of Negroes."[24]

Blacks attributed the riot to specific grievances such as racial discrimination, unemployment, and deprivation. The *Report of the National Advisory Commission on Civil Disorders* (referred to hereafter as the Kerner Report) arrived at the same conclusion: "White racism is essentially responsible for the explosive mixture which has been accumulating in our cities since the end of World War II."[25]

The selection by Joel D. Aberbach and Jack L. Walker, "Political Trust and Racial Ideology," provides insight into the development of a disposition to participate in riots. Aberbach and Walker's study was conducted in Detroit, Michigan, shortly after a riot in the summer of 1967. The authors compare data based on interviews with 394 whites and 461 blacks to examine the concept, antecedents, and consequences of various levels of political trust. The critical function of political trust for the polity is demonstrated in a number of findings. For example,

Aberbach and Walker report that blacks who manifest low political trust are more affected by experiences of discrimination than are blacks who are high in trust. "Persons who are low in trust seem to interpret each experience of discrimination as further proof that the political system is evil and must be dealt with by any means, while those who are trusting have a less severe reaction to these experiences." High trust in the system, which is a form of political support, is a resource that the government can draw on in time of crisis to provide the time and stability needed to make adjustments necessary to alleviate political grievances. For citizens with low trust, however, there is no reservoir of good will (diffuse support) that can be tapped when political outputs do not meet expectations. Thus Aberbach and Walker find that low trust on the part of blacks is correlated with a willingness to engage in riots. The findings of the Kerner Report support this conclusion: "The typical rioter was . . . proud of his race, extremely hostile to both whites and middle-class Negroes and, although informed about politics, highly distrustful of the political system."[26]

Recalling that a substantial number of black citizens were inclined to be sympathetic to the riots and to consider them beneficial, the two readings reflect on a broader question: Does black support for the riots denote disaffection from the political system and its institutions or only dissatisfaction with current incumbents and policies? A study conducted on the riots of April 1968 in Chicago reported a "growing feeling among blacks that 'the existing system must be toppled by violent means.' "[27] Is this representative of black feelings in riot-torn cities? The evidence is not completely clear but studies do not indicate widespread estrangement from the political system on the part of the great majority of blacks. Sears finds that blacks in Watts were more inclined than whites to manifest low trust for elected officials, and were more dissatisfied with their representation in the system, but he concludes that this discontent reflects enmity toward white political leaders and their policies rather than a rejection of the American political system. "It would appear that the rejection of white dominated local government is not a rejection of the political system, but a complaint about inadequate attention and inadequate service." The Kerner Report arrived at a similar conclusion: "What the rioters appeared to be seeking was fuller participation in the social order and the material benefits enjoyed by the majority of American citizens. Rather than rejecting the American system, they were anxious to obtain a place for themselves in it."[28]

The one exception in Sears' data is young blacks (15–29) who tend to be considerably more dissatisfied with white leadership, more racially partisan, and more politicized. "The data do not indicate that . . . (young blacks) yet are estranged from the system, but that appears to remain an open possibility."

Aberbach and Walker also have data that bear on black commitment to the system. Typically studies have found that black faith in the national government is high but Aberbach and Walker's analysis may indicate a serious erosion in black trust. When the authors compare blacks and whites they find the blacks to be less trusting of the national government. These lower levels of trust are best explained by expectations about treatment from government officials, feelings of deprivation, and beliefs about the acceptability of one's group in society. An emerging racial ideology in the black community that provides insight into black support is also identified by Aberbach and Walker.

> The elements of this belief system include a favorable interpretation of black power, the choice of militant black leaders as representative of one's own point of view on race relations and a revolutionary interpretation of the meaning or significance of the 1967 disturbance.

This ideology, which cuts across class lines in the black community, does not embrace racial separation, but instead calls for speedy and substantial efforts to improve the condition of all black people.

In contrast, a considerable proportion of the white population interviewed by Aberbach and Walker demand racial separation and an end to programs designed to aid blacks. Indeed, the black respondents seem to be much more sanguine about the future of race relations than do whites. Rising black demands and frustrations accompanied by "an expressed willingness to resort to almost any means necessary to achieve their goals," in conjunction with increasing bitterness on the part of many whites (especially lower class whites) led Aberbach and Walker to conclude that: "emerging from our analysis are the outlines of an ominous confrontation between the races."

The question of black support for the system is illuminated also by investigation of the means that blacks consider feasible for gaining improved conditions. Sears and Tomlinson asked their respondents "What must Negroes do to get when they want?" Only 3 percent felt that resort to violence would be necessary.[29] The great majority of blacks seemed committed to working for change through the traditional political processes. Blacks remained strong Democrats and manifested high support for local black politicians and national civil rights leaders, but harbored some reservations about black nationalists. Encouragingly, Sears concludes that the pattern "seems to be more one of racial partisanship and self-interest than estrangement from the American political system." However, although the blacks had about the same number of political contacts, voting rates, and political participation, they (especially the young and better educated) felt much less able to influence public policy than did whites. As Sears concludes: "This is, then, a troublesome combination among the young and better-educated blacks; relatively high levels of political activism, but little confidence that the system as it currently exists will be responsive to them."

There are both positive and negative implications for support for the political system in the research conducted on the attitudes of riot-area blacks. On the positive side there seems to be no sizable number of blacks bent on destruction of the political system. Of course, it takes only a small percentage of the black population to start and maintain a riot. Still, even though Aberbach and Walker's more recently drawn data are more somber than Sears', the evidence seems to indicate that most blacks are not disaffected from the system and its institutions so much as they have lost faith in current political leaders and policies. When one considers the deprivation and discrimination that blacks have endured and continue to be subjected to in our society, the lack of widespread estrangement seems an amazing testimony to the strength of citizen support for the American system. Some of this support, of course, is simply a form of apathy. General findings that the poor and uneducated tend to be apathetic suggest that regardless of how harsh the ghetto environment, many blacks would not be politically active. Further, many blacks, particularly older ones and those in the South, may still, to use Pettigrew's words, "be moving toward" whites or else be culturally unequipped to challenge white America.[30] Finally, on the positive side are indications that most action-oriented blacks are willing to try to produce change through political activism, despite low faith in the political system.

On the debit side are higher levels of political distrust on the part of blacks, impatience for change, low political efficacy, and substantial support for past riots. Aggravating these attitudes are the slow response of political leaders to black needs and the limited sympathy on the part of substantial numbers of whites for black demands. As Aberbach and Walker point out, these conditions could lead to a serious confrontation between the races.

NOTES

[1]Joel D. Aberbach and Jack L. Walker, "Citizen Desires, Policy Outcomes, and Community Control," paper presented at the 1971 Annual Meeting of the American Political Science Association, Chicago, Illinois, September 7-11, p. 6.

[2]Melvin Seeman, "On the Meaning of Alienation," *American Sociological Review*, 24 (December, 1959): 783-91. Scholars have used a variety of concepts in explicating and measuring alienation. This brief note is not the place to discuss the extensive literature on alienation. The reader who is interested may find good, brief literature reviews in Joel B. Aberbach, "Alienation and Political Behavior," *American Political Science Review*, 63 (March, 1969): 86-99, and Ada W. Finifter, "Dimensions of Political Alienation," *American Political Science Review*, 64 (June, 1970): 389-410.

[3]Finifter, "Dimensions," 389.

[4]Finifter, "Dimensions," 407.

[5]Robert A. Wilson, "Anomie in the Ghetto: A Study of Neighborhood Type, Race, and Anomie," *American Journal of Sociology*, 77 (July, 1971): 66-88.

[6]S. Jo Holtzman, *Relationships of Social Characteristics, Attitudes, and Political Behavior of Inner-City Community College Students* (Washington: Office of Education, 1971), pp. 74-90.

[7]Thomas F. Pettigrew, "Racially Separate or Together," *Journal of Social Issues*, 25 (January, 1969): 43-69; Robert L. Crain, "School Integration and Occupational Achievement of Negroes," *American Journal of Sociology*, 75 (January, 1970): 593-606.

[8]Holtzman, *Relationships;* "Small Cities Hail Full Integration," *The New York Times* (October 18, 1970), p. 1.

[9]Holtzman, *Relationships,* p. 106.

[10]"Report from Black America," *Newsweek* (June 30, 1969), p. 20.

[11]Holtzman, *Relationships,* pp. 106-7.

[12]Data collected by Louis Harris and reported in Hazel Erskine, "The Polls: Negro Philosophies of Life," *Public Opinion Quarterly*, 33 (Spring, 1969): 152.

[13]Erskine, "The Polls," p. 151.

[14]Louis Harris, "Black Animosities Found Increasing," *Washington Post* (October 6, 1971), p. A-8.

[15]Nationwide polls reported in "Report from Black America," p. 22.

[16]A 29-year-old black electrician quoted in "Report from Black America," p. 21.

[17]The magnitude of these disorders is pointed out by Professor Bryan T. Downes who reports that from 1964 to 1968 there were 225 hostile outbursts in American cities with 49,607 persons arrested, 7,942 wounded, and 191 killed. See "Social and Political Characteristics of Riot Cities: A Comparative Study," *Social Science Quarterly*, 49 (December, 1968): 509.

[18]See Edward C. Banfield, *The Unheavenly City* (Boston: Little, Brown, 1970), pp. 185-209.

[19]Harlan Hahn and Joe R. Feagin, "Rank-and-File Versus Congressional Perceptions of Ghetto Riots," *Social Science Quarterly*, 52 (September, 1970): 363-65.

[20]David Sears and T. M. Tomlinson, "Riot Ideology in Los Angeles: A Study of Negro Attitudes," *Social Science Quarterly*, 49 (December, 1968).

[21]Sears and Tomlinson, "Riot Ideology," 487.

[22]Sears and Tomlinson, "Riot Ideology," 488. In a 1968 sample of 236 Newark black males living in the area torn by the 1967 riots, 44 percent mentioned participating in the lawlessness. Jeffrey M. Paige, "Changing Patterns of Anti-White Attitudes Among Blacks," *Journal of Social Issues,* 26 (1970): 68–86.

[23]Sears and Tomlinson, "Riot Ideology," 490.

[24]Gary T. Marx, *Protest and Prejudice* (New York: Harper & Row, 1969), p. 32.

[25]*Report of the National Advisory Commission on Civil Disorders* (Kerner Report) (New York: Bantam, 1968), p. 10.

[26]Kerner Report, p. 7.

[27]"Survey of Chicago Riots Reveals 'Black Racism,' " *Baton Rouge Morning Advocate* (August 8, 1968), p. 12-D. Cited in Jewel L. Prestage, "Black Politics and the Kerner Report: Concern and Direction," *Social Science Quarterly,* 49 (December, 1968): 456.

[28]Kerner Report, p. 7.

[29]Sears and Tomlinson, "Riot Ideology," 501. A Gallup poll of a national sample of blacks in 1969 reported that 63 percent thought they could win their rights without violence while 21 percent felt violence would be necessary. See "Report From Black America," p. 23. Harris polls of blacks in 1963 and 1966 found 22 percent and 21 percent respectively thought violence would be necessary. See William Brink and Louis Harris, *Black and White* (New York: Simon and Schuster, 1967), p. 260. Aberbach and Walker ("Citizen Desires, Policy Outcomes, and Community Control") report that the proportion of blacks favoring school integration and supporting demonstrations that risk violence declined from 66 percent in 1967 to 29 percent in 1971. During the same period the proportion opposing demonstrations which risk violence rose from 30 to 59 percent (p. 6).

[30]Thomas F. Pettigrew, *A Profile of the Negro American* (Princeton, N.J.: Van Nostrand, 1964).

Chapter 6

ALIENATION IN THE GHETTO[1]

Bonnie Bullough

Thirty years ago Chicago sociologists described the pattern of the urban Negro ghetto. The center of the "black belt" was occupied by the new arrivals to the city who were often unskilled and unemployed. The more successful and better-educated residents tended to move farther out toward the periphery of the area; occasionally they even moved a short distance beyond the concentrated Negro area, so that there were neighborhoods which were temporarily integrated as the ghetto expanded.[2] In spite of the current revolutionary drive for integration, this over-all pattern has not changed much in the large cities of the North and West. Even in the sixteen states that have laws making discrimination in housing illegal there has been no massive movement toward residential desegregation.[3]

Recently, however, it has been reported that in Boston, Seattle, and Philadelphia there are isolated Negro families who have moved completely away from the old ghettos and have settled in previously all white areas.[4] In Los Angeles, where a similar movement has taken place, a small but growing number of Negro families have moved into the previously all white areas of the San Fernando Valley. Although actually a part of the sprawling city of Los Angeles, "the Valley" is separated from the older, central portion of the city by the Santa Monica mountain range. It is one of the fastest growing areas in the country, having developed in the last twenty years from a few scattered communities to one large solidly settled area with almost a million inhabitants. Even before the postwar building boom it contained one predominantly Negro community called Pacoima, which reported a Negro population of 9,000 in 1960,[5] but the remaining large expanse of the Valley was

Reprinted from "Alienation in the Ghetto," *American Journal of Sociology,* 72 (March, 1968), pp. 469–78, by permission of the author and the University of Chicago Press. Copyright 1967 by the University of Chicago.

until recently almost "lily white." It is too soon to say whether the movement of these scattered Negro families in Los Angeles or else-where portends future urban integration, but such a possibility cannot be discounted. In any case these first families, which I have called "barrier breakers," seemed like an interesting group of people to study.

Preliminary investigation of the families in Los Angeles who had made this move indicated that they tended to be well educated and occupationally successful, which is consistent with the findings reported in the other cities mentioned. Since portions of the Los Angeles ghetto also contain areas in which there are many well educated and successful Negroes, it was reasoned that socioeconomic status was not the only factor that determined who would be able to break through the barriers of housing discrimination. The problem for research, then, was to deter-mine some of the social-psychological characteristics that distinguish the barrier breakers from other middle-class Negroes.

The main theoretical framework used to investigate the social psy-chological barriers to integration was an alienation one. Alienation would seem to be particularly important since it has been mentioned as an aspect of ghetto life by many writers, both popular and scholarly.[6] The alienation of many Negro residents of Los Angeles was dramatical-ly demonstrated in smoke and flames across the skies of Watts during the riots. The rioters, however, were drawn primarily from the poorly educated, unemployed youths,[7] and the focus of this research, which was actually completed before the riots, was on the consequences of alienation for the well-educated, employed middle-class ghetto dwellers.

Previous studies have suggested that those who are less alienated are more likely to seek integration. Researchers in a southern Negro college found that students who felt that they themselves could control their own fate were more willing to participate in a civil rights demon-stration.[8] In a study done in Nashville the Srole anomia scale was used to predict which families would seek an integrated school for their children.[9] Based on the conceptualization developed by Melvin Seeman, alienation in this research was viewed as not just a single attitude but as a group of attitudinal variables, which under certain conditions can be related, but which for conceptual clarity should not be confused with each other.[10] Three aspects of the alienation complex were investigated: (1) powerlessness; (2) anomia, which in Seeman's scheme is called normlessness; and (3) an orientation toward or away from the ghetto, which in his scheme would be called a type of value isolation. In conceptualizing the direction of orientation as a type of alienation it should be noted that the alienation can be from the values and in-stitutions of the Negro subculture or from the dominant society. It was hypothesized not only that powerlessness and anomia would be associated with ghetto life but that they played a key role in holding people within the old residential patterns. It was also hypothesized that the subjects would turn their attention away from the strictly segregated institutions of the ghetto as they moved out into integrated neighborhoods.

Sixty-one Negro families, scattered throughout the predominantly white section of the Valley, were located and interviewed during the winter and spring of 1964–65. All available Negro adult members of the household were included in the sample (three non-Negro spouses were excluded).[11] This yielded a sample of 104 persons, 54 men and 50 women. The names and addresses of these subjects were obtained through the efforts of members of the Valley Fair Housing Council, a local civil rights group. Members of the council used a wide variety of contacts to locate the subjects, including other organizations, work contacts, schools, and so on. The subjects themselves were able to furnish the names of some other Valley Negro families known to them. A control group of 106 persons, 48 men and 58 women from sixty-five families, was obtained by randomly sampling two middle-class neighborhoods with Negro populations of over 90 percent. One of these areas was in the Pacoima section of the Valley, and the other was in central Los Angeles, several miles to the north of the now famous Watts area. Actually, the physical characteristics of all the sampled areas, integrated and ghetto, were somewhat similar. Most of the dwellings were single family with just an occasional apartment building; the neighborhoods were attractive and the yards well kept. Sixty-three persons from Pacoima and forty-three from the central Los Angeles area were interviewed; two white spouses were excluded from the sample. There seemed to be little difference between the two ghetto areas; the educational, occupational, and income levels were similar, as well as the findings on the alienation scales, so the two areas were combined for the final analysis.

The powerlessness scale that was used measures the extent to which the subject feels that he himself can control the outcomes of events that concern him.[12] The conceptualization of powerlessness is based on the social-learning theory of Julian B. Rotter, which, stated in a simplified way, holds that behavior is a function of values and expectations.[13] It has been argued that people tend to develop generalized expectancies, including those for control or lack of it. Since integration seems to be a commonly held value among Negroes, at least on the surface, it would seem that the expectation for successful integration would play an important role in determining who would make the effort to move into the integrated or predominantly white neighborhood. The powerlessness scale uses a forced-choice format so that subjects chose between pairs of items such as the following: (1) I have usually found that what is going to happen will happen, no matter what I do. (2) Trusting to fate has never turned out as well for me as making a definite decision.

The Srole anomia scale was selected as a second alienation measurement because it seems to be a more global type of measurement of the subject's lack of integration into the ongoing society. The Srole scale also captured the feelings of hopelessness and despair expressed by some of the subjects. It is a five-item Likert-type scale made up of statements such as the following:[14] In spite of what some people say, the lot of the average man is getting worse. A ten-item factual test was constructed to assess the amount of information subjects had about housing integration and the legal rights of minority people in the housing market. It included items such as: Restrictive housing covenants are still legal in California (false) and real-estate offices were defined as places of public accommodation so they are not supposed to discriminate (true).

A fourth scale, which measures the orientation toward or away from the ghetto, was built from information obtained in the interview schedule. It actually measures reported behavior rather than an attitude, but the behavior suggests an underlying orientation toward the Negro subculture of the ghetto or away from it. Subjects indicated what organizations they belonged to, their church affiliations, their chief leisure-time activities, the newspapers and magazines they read regularly, the schools they sent their children to, the racial identities of their close friends, and the degree of integration in their work situations. Each of these items was rated as to whether it was exclusively Negro or was reflective of an integrated situation.[15] It was expected that there would be some drifting away from a strictly segregated life as a part of the process of moving out of the ghetto. Obviously, some of the items in this scale, such as the school, the church, and even the friendship choices, are affected by place of residence, so the fact that the ghetto dwellers and the outsiders would differ was to be expected. It nevertheless proved to be a useful device for looking at what happens to people when they move out.

A special methodological problem in a study such as this one is the possible biasing effect of the race of the interviewer. Approximately half of the interviews were done by white and half by Negro interviewers. The data were therefore analyzed controlling for this factor. Slight differences (not statistically significant) were found in the answers about the racial characteristics of friends; more people indicated that they had non-Negro friends when the interviewer was white. There did not seem to be other differences in responses that could be related to the race of the interviewer.

FINDINGS

As had been anticipated, the educational and income levels of the barrier breakers were high. Their median income was approximately $11,000 a year, which is well over the average Valley income.[16] The hope was that the ghetto samples would be of the same socioeconomic level as the people in the integrated sample, but due to the rather wide variety of income levels found in segregated neighborhoods the median income for the ghetto samples was lower, being approximately $9,700. There were, however, only six persons in the ghetto and two persons in the Valley-wide sample who reported family incomes of less than $5,000, so that poverty was not a factor in either area. Part of the difficulty in matching socioeconomic levels was due to the decision to avoid the mixed neighborhoods on the edge of the ghetto where the incomes might well have been more uniformly high but where some of the impact of segregated life would have been lost.

There were some factors that were similar in and out of the ghetto. The majority of people in both samples said they saw some value in living in an integrated or predominantly white neighborhood; 87 percent of the Valley-wide group and 80 percent of the ghetto dwellers indorsed such a statement, although the Valley residents could think of more concrete reasons why they felt that way. Both groups seemed to be made up of occupationally mobile people. The Bogue scale was used to assign numerical ratings to occupations, and about half of the people in each sample had moved up forty or more points beyond the level of their parents' occupations.[17] It was, for example, not at all unusual to find people with technical or professional jobs whose fathers had been laborers or their mothers domestic workers. This finding supports observations made by such writers as the late Franklin Frazier that there is a new and rapidly growing Negro middle class.[18] Possibly also related to the recent development of this middle class was the scarcity of older people in both groups. The median age in both samples was thirty-nine, but there was just one person over sixty in the Valley group, and in the ghetto sample there were just four.

When the powerlessness scores of the two groups were compared, significant differences were found; the people in the ghetto sample have a mean powerlessness score of 3.01, while the outsiders' mean score is

Table 1
**Mean Powerlessness and Anomia Scores in the Valley-wide and Ghetto Areas
When Education, Income, and Sex Are Controlled**

Control	Powerlessness		Anomia	
	Valley-wide (N = 101)	Ghetto (N = 105)	Valley-wide (N = 103)	Ghetto (N = 105)
Education:				
College graduate	2.14 (N =43)	2.88 (N = 32)	9.67 (N = 43)	11.72 (N = 32)
Some college or technical education	2.73 (N = 42)	3.15 (N = 39)	10.90 (N = 42)	12.54 (N = 39)
High school or less	2.75 (N = 16)	2.97 (N = 34)	12.17 (N = 18)	14.38 (N = 43)
Income:				
$15,000 and over	2.05 (N = 34)	3.05 (N = 22)	9.91 (N = 34)	12.60 (N = 22)
$7,800–$15,000	2.59 (N =49)	2.80 (N = 56)	10.26 (N = 50)	11.77 (N = 56)
Below $7,800	3.00 (N = 18)	3.27 (N = 26)	12.79 (N = 19)	15.19 (N = 26)
Sex:				
Male	2.55 (N = 53)	2.77 (N = 48)	10.77 (N = 54)	12.65 (N = 48)
Female	2.42 (N = 48)	3.21 (N = 57)	10.42 (N = 49)	13.08 (N = 57)

2.48 ($t = 2.07$; $P < .05$). The people who have moved out thus indicate that they feel that they have more control over their own lives. Table 1 shows these scores with education, income, and sex controlled. As can be noted in the table, the greatest differences in powerlessness between the in- and out-of-the-ghetto samples show up in the high income and educational levels. This suggests that when the objective criteria for overcoming the barriers of housing discrimination are most favorable, the expectation for control of one's life helps predict who will actually make the move.

The anomia scores follow a similar pattern. In the ghetto the mean score on the anomia scale is 12.9; in the integrated community the mean score is 10.6; these differences are also significant ($t = 4.24$; $P < .001$). The controls for income and education indicate that, although the anomia scores vary more in relation to these factors, the area of residence still makes a difference at each level. There is a correlation between anomia and powerlessness; inside the ghetto it was $r = .43$ and outside it was $r = .37$. This suggests that there is indeed a relationship between these two kinds of alienation in this situation, although the two scales are not measuring the same thing.[19]

Most of the people now living in the Valley spent their childhoods in the ghetto or on its edge (only twelve people reported having grown up in predominantly white neighborhoods). Some explanation should be given as to why the two groups of people scored differently on the alienation scales. This paper cannot, of course, supply all of the answers to that question, but if we look at some of the other factors associated with anomia and powerlessness some clues are offered. Anomia seems to correlate negatively with almost any of life's advantages,[20] so it would seem that the people with lower scores on the Srole scale, including those who moved out of the ghetto, somehow escaped some of the worst disadvantages. Table 2 shows the small but consistently negative corre-

Table 2
Correlations (Pearson's *r*) of Powerlessness and Anomia*[a]* with Selected Factors

	Powerlessness		Anomia	
	Valley-wide	*Ghetto*	*Valley-wide*	*Ghetto*
Father's occupational level	−.04	−.004	−.04	−.20*
Employed subject's occupational level	−.31**	−.05	−.22**	−.22**
Present income	−.18*	−.03	−.23**	−.28**
Educational attainment	−.17*	−.07	−.28**	−.31**
Amount of integrated schooling	−.22**	−.10	−.13	−.19*
Neighborhood of childhood (segregated to integrated)	−.30**	−.24**	−.12	−.27**

*[a]*The numbers varied in these correlations from 79 to 105.
*Significant ($P < .05$).
**Significant ($P < .01$).

lations with several of these factors. Since powerlessness is a less global sort of attitude it does not correlate highly with as many variables; in this study the development of a high expectation for control seems most related to past and present experiences with integration, not only in housing but also in other aspects of life. Segregation and all that is associated with it emerges as such a crucial problem for Negroes that successful experiences with integration seem to raise the general level of expectation for control. Notice that the childhood experiences most related to lower powerlessness scores are those of integrated school experience and living in a racially mixed neighborhood while growing up.

It was expected from the beginning of the study that the Valley-wide residents would have lost some of their ties with the strictly segregated institutions within the ghetto. In fact, giving up some of the old customs and ties seems to be the price paid by any minority group that is assimilated. It was therefore not surprising that the Valley group had a mean score of 13.0 on the "ghetto-orientation" scale, while the mean of the ghetto sample was 9.7 ($t = 7.99$; $P < .001$). This wide difference on the ghetto-orientation scale indicates that the various aspects of integration tend to be related to each other; moving out of the ghetto is one part of a total life pattern. That this change in pattern is a long-term process is suggested by the fact that the last residence of 61 percent of the Valley group was described as predominantly white or mixed, while only 23 percent of the ghetto sample reported that the place they lived in last had even token integration.

It was of interest to find out that within each sample the drift away from a ghetto orientation was related to a greater expectation for control and to lower anomia scores. Table 3 shows the differences in powerlessness and anomia when the two samples are split at the median on orientation. As an alienation measurement the orientation scale is two

Table 3

Mean Powerlessness and Anomia Scores in the Valley-wide and Ghetto Areas
When the Samples Are Divided at the Median[a] on Orientation

Orientation	Valley-wide	Ghetto
Powerlessness		
Integrated orientation	2.38	2.63
	($N = 49$)	($N = 57$)
Ghetto orientation	2.75	3.45*
	($N = 52$)	($N = 48$)
Anomia		
Integrated orientation	10.00	11.86
	($N = 49$)	($N = 57$)
Ghetto orientation	11.19*	14.10**
	($N = 54$)	($N = 48$)

[a]The median scores on the orientation scale were 13 in the valley-wide area and 9 in the ghetto.
*Differences between the mean scores of those with integrated or ghetto orientations were significant ($P < .05$).
**Significant ($P < .01$).

sided. It indicates the degree to which the customs and associations of the subculture are selected over those of the mainstream of the society; movement away from one pole implies a movement toward the other. This type of value isolation is alienation of a different dimension than that assessed by the Srole scale in which movement away from the mainstream could mean a withdrawal into apathy. The concept of value isolation has been used to describe the alienation felt by intellectuals, although presumably members of any subculture that holds values that deviate from the commonly held societal values would be alienated in this sense.[21] Of course it is also possible to be alienated from the subculture. Since the ghetto orientation was related to both powerlessness and anomia, regardless of place of residence, it would seem that the securely "locked-in" position within the Negro ghetto was not a particularly desirable state. The "marginal" or moving-out position may not be as undesirable as it is sometimes considered. Of course it can be argued that, since Negroes are already familiar with American culture, and yet not completely accepted by it, their position in the ghetto is already a marginal one.

One of the items used to make up the orientation scale was the racial makeup of the subject's church congregation. In addition to the racial characteristics of the individual congregation, the denominational identification also turned out to have predictive value. As can be noted in Table 4, not only were members of Baptist and Holiness churches more powerless than others, they were seldom found outside the ghetto.

Table 4
Mean Powerlessness Scores and Religious Identification*

Religion	Valley-wide (N = 101)	Ghetto (N = 105)
Baptist	3.29 (N = 7)	3.62 (N = 29)
Methodist	2.17 (N = 23)	2.95 (N = 19)
Holiness	3.00 (N = 3)	3.63 (N = 8)
Other Protestant	2.10 (N = 28)	2.27 (N = 22)
Catholic	1.96 (N = 24)	2.28 (N = 17)
None	3.45 (N = 16)	2.70 (N = 10)

*Differences in religious affiliation in the two areas: $\chi^2 = 19.4$ $(P < .01)$.

Methodists, whose churches also have been segregated historically, did not score so high on the powerlessness scale, and they were well represented in the Valley-wide area. Members of other Protestant churches, Catholics, and non-church members were the best represented in the Valley. The church is the focus of much of the social life within the ghetto, so that it may sometimes act as a positive tie to hold people within the segregated areas.[22] These differences by denomination were not adequately anticipated in the planning of the study, so that data were not obtained about past religious identification. It is therefore not known whether certain church affiliations are associated with staying in the ghetto or whether people change their religious identifications when they move out.

Having found that Negroes who live outside the ghetto feel less powerless and less of the hopeless detachment measured by the anomia scale still leaves an unanswered question; are the feelings of alienation a selective factor that keeps some people from moving out, or does the experience of having successfully moved lessen the feelings of alienation? Probably both happen, but the evidence for alienation as a negative selective factor is strongest. Some of the correlations associated with childhood conditions suggest that feelings of alienation are fairly stable attitudes, developing sometimes over a lifetime. When the powerlessness scores of the Valley residents who have lived outside of the ghetto for more than five years were compared with the newcomers, the older residents did have lower scores, but even the newcomers were lower in alienation than the average for the ghetto.

As suggested by other research on alienation, one of the mechanisms by which higher expectation for control fosters integration is probably through its relationship with more effective social learning.[23] People who feel less powerless would thus be expected to have learned more about their rights in the housing market and how they might be able to secure a house or an apartment in an integrated area. Table 5 shows the differences in scores on the housing-facts test with the subjects divided at the median on their powerlessness scores; the low powerlessness group does tend to have learned more of these facts.

Both powerlessness and anomia seem to act as psychological deterrents to people making the kind of sustained effort that is necessary to be successful in overcoming the barriers to integration. Subjects in the

Table 5
Mean Scores on the Housing-Facts Test When Divided at the Median
in Each Area on the Powerlessness Scale[a]

Powerlessness	Valley-wide	Ghetto
Above median or at the median	7.10	6.27*
	(N = 47)	(N = 61)
Below median	7.37	7.02
	(N = 54)	(N = 44)

[a]Both samples were split at 2.
*The differences in the ghetto sample were significant (P < .05).

ghetto were asked if they had ever looked for housing in an integrated or predominantly white neighborhood. Fifty-six of the people in that sample said they had done so at some time in their lives. However, when the ghetto sample was divided by this factor, the anomia scores were the same for the two groups (12.9), and the powerlessness scores were actually higher for the group that said they had looked (3.20 mean score as compared with 2.80). Just looking at these scores it would seem that alienation was not a selective factor. However, when these people were asked to elaborate on their experiences in looking, they characteristically told of a single experience in which they looked and were rebuffed. When the Valley residents told of their experiences they sometimes described years of searching until they were finally successful. Occasionally these accounts included reports of open refusals, but more often they were faced with a long series of evasions and trickery including realty salesmen who were "out" or ran to hide from them in the other room, managers who had no authority to rent the apartments, owners who could not be located, forms that could not be processed, returned deposits, and so on. The persistence shown by some of these people in the face of one disappointment after another is worthy of note. It would seem, then, that alienation as a selective factor may function more in fixing the amount of determination and effectiveness that the subjects bring to the task, rather than merely selecting who will make a single attempt. The people who were successful in moving out, despite the present barriers of discrimination, were unwilling to accept one act of prejudice as their final answer, and here an ultimate belief in a manageable world undoubtedly helped them.

SUMMARY AND CONCLUSIONS

When a group of integrated middle-class Negro subjects was compared with another group of middle-class subjects who remained within the traditional Negro ghettos, significant differences in alienation were found. The integrated subjects had greater expectations for control of events that concerned them and less of a feeling of anomia. They also tended to orient themselves toward the mainstream of society rather than toward the segregated institutions of the Negro subculture. Alienation within the ghetto takes on a circular characteristic; not only is it a product of segregated living, it also acts to keep people locked in the traditional residential patterns.

The fact that alienation is such a circular process does not mean that nothing can be done to deal with the problems of segregation. It does mean that antidiscriminatory legislation alone cannot bring about instant integration. Instead such legislation would be more effective if accompanied by other efforts to overcome the psychological barriers to integration. The fact that anomia correlated with almost any kind of deprivation suggests the need for effective programs to combat poverty, unemployment, and lack of educational opportunity in the ghetto; these programs are needed not only for their own intrinsic worth but also to combat the feelings of hopelessness and despair that are a part of the ghetto attitude. The fact that choosing the integrated way of life in one sphere is related to choosing it in others suggests that any sort of program aimed at decreasing segregation is worth trying. A fair-employment-practices act can even help bring about more housing integration by giving the workers the experience of working together. Integrated school or church experiences give children the opportunity to set up patterns of mixed associations. However, the solution to the problems of segregation are not easy; the old patterns, supported by the psychological barriers of alienation, do not change rapidly.

NOTES

[1]The author is indebted to Melvin Seeman for advice and help in all stages of the research and in preparation of this manuscript. Computing assistance was obtained from the Health Sciences Computing facility of the University of California, Los Angeles, sponsored by National Institutes of Health grant FR-3. The author is supported by a U.S. Public Health special-nurse fellowship.

[2]E. Franklin Frazier, "The Negro Family in Chicago," in Ernest Burgess and Donald Bogue (eds.), *Contributions to Urban Sociology* (Chicago: University of Chicago Press, 1964), pp. 404–18. A similar pattern was described by St. Clair Drake and H. R. Cayton in *Black Metropolis* (New York: Harcourt, Brace & Co., 1945), pp. 174–213.

[3]"How the Fair Housing Laws Are Working," *Trends in Housing,* IX (November–December, 1965), 3–4, 7–10.

[4]Helen MacGill Hughes and Lewis G. Watts, "Portrait of the Self Integrator," *Journal of Social Issues,* XX (April, 1964), 103–15; L. D. Northwood and Ernest A. T. Barth, *Urban Desegration: Negro Pioneers and Their White Neighbors* (Seattle: University of Washington Press, 1965); and Commission on Human Relations, *Some Factors Affecting Housing Desegregation* (Philadelphia, 1962).

[5]Marchia Meeker and Joan Harris, *Background for Planning* (Los Angeles: Research Department, Welfare Planning Council, Report # 17, 1964), pp. 55–60. A Negro population of 334,916 was reported in 1960 in the city of Los Angeles; see Los Angeles County Commission on Human Relations, *Population*

and Housing in Los Angeles County: A Study in the Growth of Residential Segregation (Los Angeles, 1963), p. 1.

[6]See, e.g., James Baldwin, *The Fire Next Time* (New York: Dial Press, 1963); Charles Silberman, *Crisis in Black and White* (New York: Random House, 1964), pp. 189–223; James Coleman, "Implications of the Findings on Alienation," *American Journal of Sociology,* LXX (July, 1964), 76–78; and Russel Middleton, "Alienation, Race and Education," *American Sociological Review,* XXVIII (December, 1963), 793–97.

[7]John A. McCone (chairman), *Violence in the City—An End or a Beginning? A Report by the Governor's Commission on the Los Angeles Riots* (Los Angeles: State of California, 1965).

[8]Pearl Mayo Gore and Julian B. Rotter, "A Personality Correlate of Social Action," *Journal of Personality,* XXXI (March, 1963), 58–64.

[9]Eugene Weinstein and Paul Gusel, "Family Decision Making over Desegregation," *Sociometry,* XXV (March, 1963), 58–64.

[10]Melvin Seeman, "On the Meaning of Alienation," *American Sociological Review,* XXIV (December, 1959), 783–91.

[11]Both spouses were included in the sample because there was some question ahead of time as to which one would be the more significant in deciding about moving and in carrying through the decision. As it turned out, there was agreement in most families, although in some one partner was a stronger force in the decision, but it could be either the husband or the wife.

[12]The powerlessness scale was developed by Shephard Liverant, Julian B. Rotter, and others. For a discussion of its use and development see Melvin Seeman, "Alienation and Social Learning in a Reformatory," *American Journal of Sociology,* LXIV (November, 1963), 270–84.

[13]Julian B. Rotter, *Social Learning and Clinical Psychology* (Englewood Cliffs, N.J.: Prentice-Hall, Inc., 1954).

[14]Leo Srole, "Social Integration and Certain Corollaries: An Exploratory Study," *American Sociological Review,* XXI (December, 1956), 709–16.

[15]The items in this scale of ghetto (versus outside) orientation were scored in the following way: 0 if the activity was ghetto and only that, 1 if no direction could be determined, and 2 or 3 if the activity was clearly integrated or pointed to an outside interest. Eight items were included in the scale, and a range of scores from 0 to 19 was possible, with the low scores pointing toward the ghetto and the high scores indicating an outside interest.

[16]Meeker and Harris, *op. cit.,* p. 53.

[17]Donald Bogue, *Skid Row in American Cities* (Chicago: University of Chicago Press, 1963), Appendix.

[18]E. Franklin Frazier, *Black Bourgeoisie* (Glencoe, Ill.: Free Press, 1957).

[19]The relationship of powerlessness and anomia is discussed by Arthur Neal and Melvin Seeman, "Organization and Powerlessness: A Test of the Mediation Hypothesis," *American Sociological Review,* XXIX (April, 1964), p. 222 n.; see also Arthur G. Neal and Salomon Rettig, "Dimensions of Alienation among Manual and Non-Manual Workers," *American Sociological Review,* XXVIII (August, 1963), 189–202.

[20]Dorothy L. Meier and Wendell Bell, "Anomia and Differential Access to the Achievement of Life Goals," *American Sociological Review,* XXIV (April, 1959), 189–202.

[21]Seeman, "On the Meaning of Alienation."

[22]E. Franklin Frazier, *The Negro Church in America* (New York: Schocken Books, 1964); Joseph R. Washington, Jr., *Black Religion* (Boston: Beacon Press, 1964).

[23]Seeman, "Alienation and Social Learning in a Reformatory"; see also Melvin Seeman and J. W. Evans, "Alienation and Learning in a Hospital Setting," *American Sociological Review,* XXVII (December, 1962), 772–82.

Chapter 7

CHANGING PATTERNS OF ANTI-WHITE ATTITUDES AMONG BLACKS

Jeffery M. Paige

In the period from the end of World War II to the middle sixties social psychological research on anti-white attitudes among blacks has attempted to find a general psychological mechanism to account for black hostility to whites. Although at present it would seem that most blacks have eminently rational reasons for resenting their treatment by the white majority, it was possible for some time to believe that anti-white attitudes were held by an unrepresentative minority of blacks. Attitude surveys conducted at widely different times in the post-war period found that few blacks were willing to express anti-white attitudes to interviewers, even when the interviewers themselves were black. In addition, the same studies found that the best educated, best informed, and most militant blacks were the least anti-white. These findings were interpreted in a theoretical tradition based on the authoritarian personality studies (Adorno et al., 1950). Since most blacks were at least overtly pro-white it seemed reasonable to inquire what special personality characteristics led to anti-white feelings among the rest. Authoritarianism, self-hatred, lack of education, and Southern socialization were all suggested as possible sources of anti-white sentiment. While the findings from such studies are discussed as if they were general characteristics of minority group personality, it is clear that the generality of such assertions is limited by the particular historical and social situation in which the original studies were conducted.

Reprinted from *The Journal of Social Issues,* 26 (1970), pp. 69–86, by permission of the author and publisher.

This essay was one of three awarded honorable mention in the 1968 Gordon Allport Intergroup Relations essay contest. The research upon which this discussion is based was supported by a grant from the National Advisory Commission on Civil Disorders supervised by Nathan Caplan. Details of the sampling procedure and various indices used may be found in the report of the National Advisory Commission (1968) and in Paige (1968).

The social context of black attitudes has clearly changed since the late forties and fifties when much of the research on minority group attitudes was originally carried out. During this period the most active and militant black spokesmen stressed cooperation with white allies, increased contact with whites and the integration of previously all white institutions. Since the Watts riot in the summer of 1965, militant black leaders have increasingly emphasized racial pride and distrust of white institutions and intentions. Thus it would be reasonable to ask whether the correlates of anti-white attitudes among blacks have changed along with the nature of inter-group conflict. It is the general hypothesis of this study that the correlates of anti-white attitudes *have* changed and that they have changed in response to the exigencies of political conflict. The results of studies carried out in a period of integration cannot therefore be extrapolated to a period of direct and often violent conflict.

While the generality of findings from the 1945–1965 period may be limited, there is remarkable agreement on the patterns of correlations among attitude measures reported by a number of different researchers. Grossack (1957), Steckler (1957), Noel (1964), and Marx (1967) agree on the following statements about black attitudes:

> (1) Authoritarianism as measured by items derived from the California F scale (Adorno et al., 1950) is positively associated with anti-white feeling and negatively associated with in-group solidarity or racial pride.
> (2) Anti-white attitudes are positively associated with black self-hatred measured either by acceptance of the white stereotype of blacks or by agreement with more general deprecatory statements about blacks.
> (3) Militance as measured by concern with black rights or by protest activity is positively associated with in-group pride and negatively associated with anti-white feeling.

PERSONALITY EXPLANATIONS OF ANTI-WHITE ATTITUDES

These empirical relationships have typically been explained in terms of underlying personality dynamics. The fundamental assumption of such arguments is that attitudes reflect personality characteristics which, in turn, are a product of early socialization experiences. Even if one accepts this general causal scheme there are a number of difficulties in accounting for the observed relationships. The relationship between black self-hatred and anti-white feeling is usually explained by postulating a psychological mechanism associating low self-acceptance with distrust of other people (see the discussions of Pettigrew, 1964, pp.

35–36, and Marx, 1967, p. 196). This explanation has also been suggested in a number of studies of anti-Semitism among Jews (Himmelhoch, 1950; Adelson, 1953; Radke-Yarrow & Lande, 1953; Sarnoff, 1951). In all these studies rejection of the in-group (Jews in this case) was positively associated with rejection of various out-groups. The low self-acceptance argument does not, however, provide a parallel explanation for rejection of out-groups among members of majority groups. In this case, extreme positive attitudes toward the in-group, such as super-patriotism, are associated with rejection of minority out-groups. It is not clear why the psychological mechanism linking self-acceptance and acceptance of other should cause in-group pride to be associated with high prejudice in majority group members and low prejudice in minority group members.

The association between high levels of authoritarianism and anti-black feeling is usually explained by noting the authoritarian's concern with power and dominance and the relatively powerless position of most minorities. Black authoritarians would be more likely to accept the negative stereotypes of bigoted members of white society since they will tend to adjust their views to conform with those of people in positions of authority, and most such positions will be occupied by whites. This explanation is inconsistent with the fact that authoritarianism is correlated with anti-white attitudes among blacks. If authoritarian blacks perceive whites as a dominant group, why do they not show the appropriate respect for those in power? In order to explain the black authoritarians' anti-white attitudes it is necessary to invoke the general distrust of other people which is said to be characteristic of white authoritarians.

Research on the demographic correlates of anti-white attitudes among blacks, like that on the psychological correlates, shows a surprising amount of agreement over the period from 1945 to 1965. Two major studies of black attitudes conducted 15 years apart report surprisingly similar results. A research group under the general direction of Robin Williams at Cornell conducted surveys in four cities (Elmira, New York; Steubenville, Ohio; Bakersfield, California; and Savannah, Georgia) in 1948 and 1949 (summarized in a series of publications: Noel, 1964; Johnson, 1957; Williams, 1964). The Cornell group found that anti-white attitudes were more frequent among the old, among women, among the married, among the poorly educated, and among Southern-born migrants living in the North. Marx (1967), in a survey of black attitudes in metropolitan areas conducted in 1964, reports that anti-white attitudes are more common among women, among those not oriented toward "intellectual values," and among Southern migrants living in Northern cities. Marx, however, found that anti-white attitudes were more common among the young rather than the old, the reverse of the Cornell group's finding. While a number of *ad hoc* explanations of these relationships are provided by Williams (1964) and Marx (1967), the most convincing overall interpretation is provided by Johnson (1957) in his discussion of the Cornell survey results for Elmira, New York. He distinguished between an old black creed based on avoidance, apathy, self-hatred, and hostility toward whites and a new black creed stressing militance, integration, and lack of prejudice toward whites. Studies conducted in a period of social change would show a mixture of both strategies with the more conservative, tradition-oriented groups within the black community supporting the old creed of withdrawal and distrust. Thus the older blacks, women, the married, and the Southern-born should be less likely to adopt the new strategy of militance, integration, and pro-white attitudes and would still subscribe to the old pattern of avoidance and distrust of whites.

Johnson's line of reasoning can easily be extended to account for the attitudinal as well as the demographic correlates of anti-white attitudes. Since the new black creed of militance requires collective action to achieve integration, it would be difficult for a militant black to support anti-white attitudes. Similarly, if pro-black attitudes are understood as a measure of commitment to blacks as a group, and if those individuals most committed to group concerns are the most militant, then the more pro-black individuals should also be the most pro-white in the social context of a movement toward integration. Finally, authoritarianism, by definition, represents support for traditional values and submission to authority. Thus authoritarian attitudes would be inconsistent with movements aimed at change, especially change in the structure of white-black authority relationships. Similarly, belief in the positive qualities of blacks would be inconsistent with the contrary view of many whites in positions of authority. Anyone subscribing to authoritarian ideology then would appear as anti-white only relative to the more militant, pro-black individuals who are concerned with integration. This argument does not depend on assumptions about the nature of underlying personality structure or about practices of child rearing. It is, of course, dependent on the nature of the political struggle between blacks and whites.

STRATEGIC FUNCTIONS OF ANTI-WHITE ATTITUDES

The dominant issues at the time Johnson's research was conducted – the late forties – involved a shift from a strategy of distrust and withdrawal to one of trust and integration. In the late sixties it would seem that a third strategy involving direct confrontation with the white authority structure had become increasingly important. A similar set of three strategies has been described by both Pettigrew (1964) and Simpson and Yinger (1962) in discussions of the general pattern of minority response to discrimination by majority groups. Pettigrew describes three responses of minorities to majorities: moving away, moving toward, and moving against. "Moving away" in Pettigrew's terminology means either passive withdrawal or active separatism, and resembles closely Johnson's old black creed of withdrawal. "Moving toward" includes efforts to achieve integration or to adopt white manners and attitudes, and corresponds closely to Johnson's new black creed. "Moving against" takes the form of direct confrontation with whites and may lead to the overt aggression of a riot. This strategy would seem to describe the pattern of racial confrontation of the late sixties. The importance of this typology of strategies for the present analysis is that each strategy includes a corresponding ideology with regard to whites. Moving away would be associated with distrust and fear of whites; moving toward, with trust and affiliation; moving against, with open hostility. In each case attitudes toward whites are part of a broader political ideology which suggests practical strategy for dealing with the white majority. As the usefulness of a political strategy increases, the attitudes associated with it will become more widespread. This does not necessarily imply that every black calculates his own best interest and decides to adopt the appropriate views about whites, although this may be the case for some political leaders. It only suggests that once a new political strategy has proved successful for any substantial number of blacks, there will be a strong tendency for those who have adopted the successful strategy to resolve the dissonance between their behavior and their attitudes by changing the attitudes.

The usefulness of a particular strategy depends on a number of political factors, such as the political resources of the minority, the willingness of the majority group to use force, or the availability of allies within the majority group. In a situation of rigid caste segregation such as that which existed in the United States before World War II, direct attempts at integration or expressions of hostility toward whites would be useless if not dangerous to blacks as a group. Violations of the caste line or demands for increased access to jobs or public facilities were met by severe sanctions including the Southern lynching and the Northern urban pogrom or "race riot." In a segregated system in which infractions of caste barriers are met with force, the safest strategy is one of disengagement and withdrawal. This passive adjustment would be expected among most blacks during the early part of this century in both the North and the South.

In a slightly more open system in which some white institutions are open to small numbers of well-educated middle-class blacks, attitudes of withdrawal and distrust would no longer be useful for advancing black interests. Anti-white attitudes would be inconvenient since the admission of talented blacks to predominantly white institutions depends on the sympathy of white liberals. Thus moving toward is the most practical strategy, at least for the politically active middle class, and it is the one which the most ambitious and militant blacks would be expected to adopt. Militant action to increase integration became a useful strategy with the opening of previously all white institutions to limited numbers of blacks in the period beginning with the end of World War II. In the late sixties it became possible for small numbers of blacks to move into white institutions and to use public facilities. In fact these rights were frequently guaranteed by law. The success of the predominantly middle class movement for integration probably exerted considerable influence on attitudes in the black community in the period when most of the studies reviewed above were conducted.

In the late sixties, however, blacks in urban ghettos in the North became increasingly important as political actors and the strategies which had dominated the movement at the time of middle-class leadership were no longer adequate. Jobs for well-educated blacks are of little utility if ghetto schools are incapable of providing a reasonable education. Access to public facilities is relatively meaningless if the facilities themselves are starved for funds. Guarantees of civil liberties for blacks are of little importance if the police force supposedly defending these liberties behaves like an occupying army. Since schools, public facilities, and police were all controlled by white-dominated city governments, political action increasingly took the form of demands for black control alternating with violence against white property and struggles to defend blacks against the activities of predominantly white police forces. Thus the nature of political conflict changed to direct confrontation between urban blacks and white political power. The mobilization of large numbers of blacks in urban ghettoes provided the opportunity for the development of a more militant, nationalistic, anti-white leadership.

In summary then, in a period of strict caste segregation, most blacks adopted a strategy of moving away; in a period of limited integration for middle class blacks, political ideology was dominated by the drive for increased integration; and in a period of urban ghetto mobilization, moving against became an increasingly important strategy among black leaders. This analysis of changing strategies permits predictions to be made about the attitudinal and demographic correlates of anti-white attitudes in the late sixties. If we assume that moving against is a new and increasingly important strategy in ghetto areas, then the sub-groups most receptive to change would be the most likely to adopt the new strategy and its corresponding anti-white attitudes. Johnson argued that young, single, Northern-born males should be the least traditional groups and consequently should have been more receptive in 1948 to the developing strategy of militant action for integration. In the context of the late sixties, the groups most receptive to change would adopt the new strategy of moving against. While conservatism in 1948 meant distrust of whites, it now implies relatively less hostility toward whites than does the more radical position. Thus the old, the female, the married, and the Southern born should now be *less* anti-white than the young, the male, the unmarried, and the Northern born.

Similar predictions can be made concerning the attitudinal correlates of anti-white attitudes. If pro-black attitudes are considered as indicating a commitment to group political action, and if this action increasingly tends toward moving against, then anti-white attitudes would be associated with pro- rather than anti-black attitudes and with high rather than low levels of militance. As long as whites remain in a position of dominance, authoritarian attitudes will be associated with the whites' negative assessment of blacks. Hence authoritarianism should continue to be associated with anti-white attitudes. The changing relationship of anti-white and pro-black attitudes would suggest, however, that high authoritarianism would be *negatively* associated with anti-white feeling. Since favorable attitudes toward blacks are associated with negative attitudes toward whites, it should follow that authoritarians, who are less favorable toward blacks, would be less anti-white. The shift from moving toward to moving against then leads to a shift in the social and psychological correlates of out-group rejection to a pattern similar to that observed in majority groups. Group pride and solidarity are positively associated with militant attitudes toward out-groups.

If these deductions about the relationship of anti-white attitudes to strategies of inter-group conflict are correct, and if furthermore it may be assumed that the strategy is changing from moving toward to moving against, then the following predictions can be made:

(1) Young black males who are most receptive to new strategies should have higher absolute levels of anti-white attitudes in the late sixties than during the period of activity in support of integration.

(2) Tradition-oriented elements in the black community should now be less anti-white; the old, the female, and the Southern born should be less prejudiced than the young, the male, and the Northern born.
(3) Authoritarianism should continue to be negatively associated with racial pride, but should now also be negatively associated with anti-white feeling.
(4) Racial pride should be positively associated with anti-white feeling.
(5) Militance should be positively associated with in-group pride and anti-white feeling.

SURVEY DESIGN AND ANALYSIS

In order to test these predictions a number of questions on attitudes toward blacks and whites were included in a survey concerned with patterns of participation in the July, 1967 riot in Newark, New Jersey. Interviews were conducted with a probability sample of 236 black males between the ages of 15 and 35 who lived in the Newark riot area. The interviews were conducted by black interviewers in January and February of 1968. In order to insure comparability with earlier research, a number of questions used by the Cornell research group in 1949 were repeated in the Newark Questionnaire. Despite the obvious differences which may exist between the two samples, it is possible to make some general statements about temporal differences in the results reported in 1949 and in 1968. Two indices of anti-white feeling from the Cornell research were used in Newark. The first of these presented the respondent with the statement, "Sometimes I hate white people," and asked for an agree/disagree response. The second was a modified three-item social distance scale which presented three progressively more intimate situations and asked the respondent if he would find each distasteful if the person or persons involved were white. The three situations were eating at the same table with a white person, going to a party where most of the people there were white, and marrying a white person. In the analysis that follows respondents who found two or more of the situations distasteful have been classified as high on social distance feelings.

Increased Anti-white Attitudes of Young Males

The first prediction above calls for a higher level of anti-white attitudes in 1968 than in 1949 among young males. Since the 1949 sample consisted of males and females 16 years of age and older and included a Southern city (Savannah), it is not directly comparable with the Newark data. It will be recalled, however, that in the Cornell study the youngest blacks were the least prejudiced, females were more prejudiced than males, and Southerners were more prejudiced than Northerners. Thus, the level of anti-white attitudes for young Northern-born males in the 1949 sample must be lower than the value reported for the sample as a whole.

As the data in Table 1 indicate, only 28 percent of the respondents in the Cornell sample as a whole agreed that "Sometimes I hate white people." Williams said of this low level of agreement, "This may appear to be one of the more remarkable findings of this study, the more so because the item said 'sometimes' and the responses were given without exception to Negro interviewers [1964, p. 281]." In the Newark sample the level of anti-white feeling is more than twice as high. In fact there has been a shift from a small minority saying in 1949 that they sometimes hate white people to a numerical majority in 1968.

Table 1
Hatred of Whites and Social Distance
(percentages)

	Newark Sample 1968	Cornell Sample 1949
	Sometimes I hate white people[a]	
Agree	61	28
Disagree	39	72
Total N	(234)	(655)[b]
	Social distance[c]	
3 (high)	18	17
2	17	18
1	32	24
0 (low)	33	41
Total N	(235)	(805)

[a]$\chi^2 = 64.90, p < .001$.
[b]Does not include Steubenville, Ohio.
[c]$\chi^2 = 7.19, p < .10$.

Social distance feelings on the other hand do not seem to show a similar dramatic increase. As the data in Table 1 indicate, there has been only a small increase in the proportion of anti-white responses. Such a difference given the crude nature of the comparison is clearly insufficient to reject the null hypothesis. Thus there seems to be a sizeable increase in direct expression of hostility toward whites without a similar increase in social distance feelings. This difference may in part reflect the differing nature of the two attitude indices. Social distance reflects outright hostility, but it is also a measure of fear and distrust. Williams reports no significant relationship between these two measures of prejudice in his total four-city sample. The substantial difference on the hatred of whites measure, however, lends some support to the initial prediction.

Conservative Blacks Are Less Anti-white

The second set of predictions concerned change in the demographic characteristics of anti-white individuals. Specifically, the more conservative elements in the black community – the old, the female, and the Southern born – should now be less rather than more anti-white than the young, the male, and the Northern born. Age is a particularly important variable since it can be understood as an index of generational change. If a study is conducted at a single point in time, it is impossible to distinguish between generational change and maturation effects. There is no reason to assume that people grow more ethnocentric as they grow older, but even if this were the case, the effect should be repeated in studies conducted at other times. Thus if the young are more anti-white than the old in 1968, this reversal can be understood as an index of the direction of attitude change within the black community. The reader may recall that Williams (1964) and Marx (1967) report opposite findings on the relationship between age and anti-white attitudes. In the 1949 Cornell study, the young were less anti-white; in the 1964 Marx survey, the young were more anti-white. If these differences are real, it suggests that some change in black attitudes had begun to take place as early as 1964. The data presented in Table 2 replicate Marx's finding. The young are distinctly more anti-white than the old on both hatred of whites and social distance measures.

Unfortunately the Newark sample consisted entirely of males, so it is not possible directly to test change in the relationship between sex and anti-white attitudes. Data are available, however, from a survey conducted by Meyer and Caplan in Detroit just after the July riot (Meyer, 1967). Their sample consisted of 437 black Detroit residents 15 years of age or older. As was the case in Newark, the sample was drawn from the riot area and all interviewers were black. No direct questions on anti-white attitudes were included in their questionnaire, but there was one indirect question. Respondents were asked to indicate whether the following statement was true or false: "Civil rights groups with both white and Negro members would be better off without the whites." Of 181 males, 27 percent considered the statement to be true; of 192

Table 2
Hatred of Whites and Social Distance by Age in Newark
(percentages)

	Age	
	15–25	*26–35*
	Sometimes I hate white people[a]	
Agree	67	55
Disagree	33	45
Total N	(138)	(92)
	Social distance[b]	
High	39	22
Low	61	88
Total N	(137)	(92)

[a]$\chi^2 = 4.76, p < .05.$
[b]$\chi^2 = 8.26, p < .005.$

females, 21 percent gave that response. Thus there was a small (non-significant) tendency for men to be more anti-white in their responses than women, the reverse of earlier findings.

The final measure of tradition orientation is the region in which the respondent grew up. Both Marx and the Cornell group found that those who were born in the South were considerably more anti-white than those born in the North. As the data in Table 3 indicate, just the opposite is the case for the Newark sample. On both measures, those who reported that they grew up in the North were more hostile to whites than those who said they had grown up in Southern or border states.

Table 3
Hatred of Whites and Social Distance by Region of Socialization
(percentages)

	Region	
	North	*South*
	Sometimes I hate white people[a]	
Agree	69	51
Disagree	31	49
Total N	(141)	(89)
	Social distance[b]	
High	38	29
Low	62	71
Total N	(143)	(87)

[a]$\chi^2 = 7.68, p < .01.$
[b]$\chi^2 = 2.30, p < .25.$

Thus the changing pattern of demographic correlates of anti-white attitudes tends to support the predictions based on the changing context of black-white relations. Those sub-groups in the black community which might be expected to be slowest to accept a new mechanism for dealing with whites are the least anti-white. The prediction was strongly confirmed for age and region of socialization and less strongly supported for sex.

Authoritarianism, Racial Pride, and Anti-white Feelings

The predicted changes in the social psychological correlates of anti-white attitudes were similarly tested by including survey questions dealing with authoritarianism and attitudes toward blacks. Respondents were asked to respond either "agree" or "disagree" to four items from the California F scale and to five items from McClosky's study of anomie (McClosky & Schan, 1965). The following items were utilized for authoritarianism: (1) Human nature being what it is, there will always be war and conflict; (2) A few strong leaders could make this country better than all the laws and talk; (3) What young people need most of all is strict discipline by their parents; and (4) Sex criminals deserve more than prison; they should be publicly whipped or worse. For anomie the items were: (1) Everything changes so quickly these days that I often have trouble deciding which are the right rules to follow; (2) With everything in such a state of disorder, it's hard for a person to know where he stands from day to day; (3) The trouble with the world today is that most people really don't believe in anything; (4) People were better off in the old days when everyone knew just how he was expected to act; and (5) What is lacking in the world today is the old kind of friendship that lasted for a lifetime.

Authoritarianism has been found to be associated empirically with a social psychological measure of anomie developed by Srole (1956a, 1956b). Srole (1956b) and Roberts and Rokeach (1956) have both demonstrated that anomie as measured by Srole's scale is independently associated with ethnocentrism. McClosky's measure is similar and is also empirically associated with ethnocentrism. The anomie items were included as a check on the expected relationship between authoritarianism and attitudes toward the in-group and out-group. If anomie behaves the same way as does authoritarianism in black samples, it should be negatively associated with racial pride and positively associated with anti-white feeling. For these predictions to hold there should also be a high correlation between the two measures, an effect which has been demonstrated by Srole and by Roberts and Rokeach. The item responses on the authoritarianism and anomie scales were summed and the mean score used as an overall index, high scores indicating high authoritarianism and/or anomie.

Black self-hatred was measured by an item taken from Noel's (1964) study of anti-Negro feeling ("Negroes are always shouting about their rights but have nothing to offer") and by two additional indices constructed for this study. The first of these asked the respondent to indicate whether he would prefer to live in a neighborhood that was all Negro, mostly Negro, 50/50 Negro and white, or mostly white. Responses to this item were organized on a four point scale with a high score indicating choice of an all Negro neighborhood. Near the beginning of the interview respondents were asked what racial term they preferred to use in describing themselves; the choices were "black," "Negro," "colored," and "no preference." The term "black" was considered the most positive of the racially descriptive terms (as in "black is beautiful") and a preference for this term was considered an index of positive identification with the in-group.

The interrelationships among these indices and the two measures of anti-white attitude are presented in Table 4. Social distance was measured by the number of situations the respondent found distasteful, with a possible range from 0 to 3. For the hatred of whites item, a high score

Table 4
Intercorrelations Among Personality and Attitude Indices

Variables	X_2	X_3	X_4	X_5	X_6	X_7
X_1 Authoritarianism	.41	−.32	−.23	.26	−.09	−.08
X_2 Anomie	−	−.30	−.20	.43	.14	−.05
X_3 Prefer Black Neighborhood	−	−	.45	−.19	.44	.22
X_4 "Black" Identity	−	−	−	−.11	.31	.18
X_5 Self-Hatred	−	−	−	−	−.03	−.02
X_6 Social Distance	−	−	−	−	−	.22
X_7 Hatred of Whites	−	−	−	−	−	−

indicated an agree (anti-white) response. It is clear from Table 4 that the measures of authoritarianism and anomie used in the Newark survey are highly associated (r = .41), as was the case in the Srole and in the Roberts and Rokeach work with white samples. Similarly the relationship between authoritarianism and rejection of the in-group (anti-black feeling) was replicated in the Newark data: the higher the authoritarianism score, the lower the preference for an all Negro neighborhood (r = −.32) and the less likely the respondent is to prefer being called black (r = −.23). Finally, the higher the authoritarianism score, the greater the tendency to express anti-Negro feeling as measured by Noel's item (r = .26).

A similar pattern can be observed for the anomie index. Those high on anomie are less likely to want to live in an all Negro neighborhood (r = −.30) and are less likely to want to be called black (r = −.20). There is a strong tendency (r = .43) for those high on anomie to disparage other Negroes. Thus the relationship between authoritarianism and anti-Negro prejudice among blacks found in earlier research has been replicated in this study, and the results for the anomie measure are parallel, as would have been expected from research on white samples.

The predictions made for the remaining relationships of interest, however, differ from those expected on the basis of past research. Although the previous work on minority group attitudes indicated that self-hatred is associated with hatred of out-groups, the opposite is, in fact, true of the data in Table 4. Those who are most strongly identified with being black are the most likely to be anti-white. This pattern is, of course, what one would expect to find for a majority group, but it is unusual for a minority. Preference for a Negro neighborhood is strongly related (r = .44) to social distance feelings and to expressed hatred of whites (r = .22). Self-description as black is also associated with both social distance (r = .31) and hatred of whites (r = .18). There is no significant relationship between hatred of Negroes and anti-white feeling (r = −.03 for social distance, −.02 for hatred of whites).

The data in Table 4 also indicate that while authoritarianism and anomie are not positively associated with hatred of whites or social distance feelings as was the case in past research, the association is non-significant rather than positive. Despite the negative relationship between authoritarianism and in-group pride and the positive relationship between pride and hostility to whites, the predicted relationship between authoritarianism and anti-white attitudes does not appear in these data.

The other correlations however, tend to support the relationships between in-group solidarity and out-group rejection which would have been expected if moving against were the dominant reaction to white discrimination. The general psychological mechanism associating acceptance of self and acceptance of others does not seem to be the correct explanation of the previously observed anti-black, anti-white relationship. Instead this relationship was apparently a result of a particular historical circumstance − the existence of a civil rights movement aimed at increased integration.

Militance, Black Pride, and Anti-white Feelings

The final group of predictions concerned the relationship of militancy and anti-white and anti-black attitudes. When civil rights activity or support for civil rights actions was used as an index of militance, pro-black and pro-white attitudes predicted militance. In the current social context, moving against is the most widespread strategy; consequently anti-white attitudes should be associated with current forms of militance. Pro-black attitudes, since they can be seen as indicating concern for blacks as a group, should be associated with collective action whatever its particular social form.

The index of militancy used in this study was self-reported riot participation, an extreme form of moving against but one in which large numbers of urban blacks have become involved. In the Newark survey, participation in the July 1967 riot was determined by asking two questions at different points in the interview. The first of these simply asked if the respondent had been active in the riot and listed the following alternatives: "very active," "somewhat active," "slightly active." The respondent had actively to deny riot participation since this alternative was not provided. The second question, later in the interview, consisted of a list of specific riot-related activities. The respondent was asked to indicate whether he had engaged in any of the listed activities, and was classified as a rioter if he either admitted some degree of activity *or* said that he had engaged in one of the specific forms of riot activity, or both. The specific activities which led to classification as a rioter were yelling at police and soldiers, picking up goods and taking them home, breaking windows, entering stores, making fire bombs, throwing fire bombs. Almost all the respondents who admitted some specific form of riot activity indicated they were involved in looting (picking up goods, breaking windows, entering stores), while relatively few were involved in arson.

The data for testing the predicted relationship between this index of militancy and attitudes toward blacks and whites are presented in Tables 5 and 6. Table 5 indicates that self-reported riot participants are considerably more hostile to whites on both measures of anti-white attitudes. Table 6 demonstrates the less obvious relationship between in-group pride and riot participation: the greater the preference for a Negro neighborhood and the greater the preference for being called black, the greater the riot participation. Consequently, the predicted relationship between militance and both anti-white and pro-black feeling is strongly supported by the survey data. The changing pattern of militant behavior has produced a corresponding change in attitudes toward whites. The association between in-group pride and militance – which is based on the idea that those more committed to Negroes as a group would be more likely to participate in collective action in support of group demands — remains 'unchanged whether the militance involved civil rights activity or riot participation.

Table 5
Self-Reported Riot Participation and Anti-white Attitudes
(percentages)

Participation pattern	Hate white people[a]		Social distance[b]	
	Agree	Disagree	High	Low
Rioter	55	32	56	39
Non-rioter	45	68	44	61
Total N	(142)	(72)	(81)	(155)

[a] $\chi^2 = 12.33, p < .001$.
[b] $\chi^2 = 7.16, p < .01$.

Table 6
Neighborhood Preference, Black Identity, and Riot Participation

Participation pattern	Neighborhood preference[a]				Self-description[b]	
	All N	Most N	50/50	Most W	Black	Other
Rioter	65	40	38	33	57	38
Non-rioter	35	60	62	67	43	62
N	(51)	(60)	(97)	(3)	(97)	(137)

[a] $\chi^2 = 10.75, p < .025$.
[b] $\chi^2 = 8.59, p < .005$.

CONCLUSIONS

Both the demographic and psychological determinants of anti-white attitudes have changed markedly as the social context of group conflict has changed. In a period of transition between an older black creed of distrust and avoidance and a newer creed of militance and integration, the more conservative elements in the black community were more likely to be distrustful and unfavorable toward whites. At present the transition is between the older idea of integration and moving toward, and the newer ideology of hostility and moving against. The same conservative elements are now less anti-white, again finding themselves behind in the pace of social change. The relationship between in-group and out-group pride, frequently described as a general psychological mechanism, is actually tied to the nature of the conflict situation. Those high on racial pride are more likely to adopt attitudes which are useful for satisfying group goals at a particular historical period. In the fifties this meant being pro-integration and pro-white; in the late sixties it has come to mean strong anti-white feelings and violence directed against white property and institutions. Because of the relatively constant power differential between the races, authoritarian attitudes are associated with anti-black attitudes regardless of the nature of the ongoing social conflict. The association between authoritarianism and anti-white feeling, on the other hand, seems to be closely tied to this conflict.

These findings have three direct implications. First, psychological mechanisms such as scapegoating or low self-esteem frequently used to explain attitudes concerning ethnicity are unlikely to be useful in understanding anti-white attitudes among blacks. In fact any explanation, including authoritarianism, which postulates relatively enduring personality mechanisms would be unable to account for three different correlational patterns found during a twenty-five year period. If it can be demonstrated that ethnic attitudes change rapidly in response to political change, it would be contradictory to explain these same attitudes by postulating particular child-rearing practices or elaborate psychoanalytic processes when the explanation must be revised every five or ten years.

Second, attempts to describe feelings about whites in the black community as a whole will yield ambiguous results. A national sample of black Americans at present would include large numbers of older blacks living in the rural South who still believe in moving away and hence distrust and fear whites, a substantial middle-class group both North and South who still support integration as a goal and hence are relatively pro-white, and an increasingly large group of urban blacks who are hostile to whites. Viewing blacks in the United States as a homogeneous group has probably always been an over-simplification, but seems particularly unfruitful with regard to attitudes about whites at present.

Finally, since 1968 when the survey reported here was conducted, the Black Panther party has achieved national prominence. Whatever its actual base of support, it is clear that the party strategy of coalition with poor or radical whites suggests that the findings reported here may rapidly become obsolete even among young, urban blacks in the North on whom the findings are based. The specific findings would change, but the principle that attitudes follow the pattern of political conflict would be confirmed.

REFERENCES

ADELSON, J. B. A study of minority group authoritarianism. *Journal of Abnormal and Social Psychology,* 1953, 48, 477-485.

ADORNO, T. W., FRENKEL-BRUNSWICK, E., LEVINSON, D. J., & SANFORD, R. N. *The authoritarian personality.* New York: Harper, 1950.

GROSSACK, M. N. Group belongingness and authoritarianism in Southern Negroes: A research note. *Phylon,* 1957, 46, 125-131.

HIMMELHOCH, J. Tolerance and personality needs: A study of the liberalization of ethnic attitudes among minority group college students. *American Sociological Review,* 1950, 15, 79-88.

JOHNSON, R. Negro reactions to minority group status. In M. L. Barron (Ed.), *American minorities.* New York: Knopf, 1957.

MARX, G. *Protest and prejudice: A study of belief in the community.* New York: Harper and Row, 1967.

MCCLOSKY, H., & SCHAN, J. H. Psychological dimensions of anomie. *American Sociological Review,* 1965, 30, 14-39.

MEYER, P. *Detroit Free Press,* August 29, 1967, p. 11.

NATIONAL ADVISORY COMMISSION ON CIVIL DISORDERS: Report, New York: Bantam, 1968.

NOEL, D. L. Group identification among Negroes: An empirical analysis. *Journal of Social Issues,* 1964, 20(2), 71-84.

PAIGE, J. M. Collective violence and the culture of subordination: A study of the July 1967 riots in Newark, New Jersey, and Detroit, Michigan. Unpublished doctoral dissertation, University of Michigan, 1968.

PETTIGREW, T. F. *A profile of the Negro American.* Princeton: Van Nostrand, 1964.

RADKE-YARROW, M., & LANDE, B. Personality correlates of differential reactions to minority group belonging. *Journal of Social Psychology,* 1953, 38, 253-272.

ROBERTS, A. H., & ROKEACH, M. Anomie and authoritarianism: A replication. *American Journal of Sociology,* 1956, 61, 355-358.

SARNOFF, I. Identification with the aggressor: Some personality correlates of anti-Semitism among Jews. *Journal of Personality,* 1951, 20, 199-218.

SIMPSON, G. E., & YINGER, J. M. *Racial and cultural minorities* (3rd ed.) New York: Harper and Row, 1962.

SROLE, L. J. Anomie, authoritarianism, and prejudice. *American Journal of Sociology,* 1956, 62, 63-67. (a)

SROLE, L. J. Social integration and certain corollaries: An exploratory study. *American Sociological Review,* 1956, 21, 709-716. (b)

STECKLER, G. A. Authoritarian ideology in Negro college students. *Journal of Abnormal and Social Psychology,* 1957, 54, 396-399.

WILLIAMS, R. M. *Stranger next door.* Englewood Cliffs: Prentice-Hall, 1964.

Chapter 8

BLACK ATTITUDES TOWARD THE POLITICAL SYSTEM IN THE AFTERMATH OF THE WATTS INSURRECTION

David O. Sears

Until recently Negroes have been a "silent minority" in the American political system. Their direct political impact has been relatively slight, except for their rather special influence on Southern politics, which has not generally involved much overt political action on their part. This low level of political activity has, of course, coexisted with chronic discrimination and mistreatment by most American institutions and by many individual whites.

This paper is addressed to the contemporary black man's political response to this situation.[1] Unequal and hostile treatment might be expected to produce antagonistic attitudes toward the American political system. It would be understandable if Negroes felt the system was not working in their behalf, and sought radical changes in it. Indeed widespread revolutionary sentiment would not be surprising. On the other hand, many observers have felt that Negroes were, in Myrdal's phrase, "exaggerated Americans who believe in the American creed more passionately than whites."[2]

... The Watts riots may have marked a real watershed in black political orientations. It, and the riots that have followed, have approximated as closely as anything else in this century mass revolutionary uprisings against constituted authority. The major question we wish to pose in this paper is whether or not the dissatisfaction that Negroes have

Reprinted from "Black Attitudes toward the Political System in the Aftermath of the Watts Insurrection," *Midwest Journal of Political Science*, 13.4 (November, 1969), pp. 515–44, by permission of the Wayne State University Press. Copyright 1969 by the Wayne State University Press. Footnotes and tables have been renumbered; some have been deleted.

typically felt with government has, in the aftermath of insurrection, been converted into estrangement from the American political system. Second, what has been the riot's effect upon the degree of political mobilization in the black community? Is there evidence of increased racial partisanship and political effectiveness? We wish to determine whether estrangement or politically effective partisanship is now more common.

Of course much has happened since the Watts riot in the black and white communities alike. The black community has apparently moved increasingly toward the militants, though the degree is a matter of controversy. If we cannot be entirely clear about where matters stand at the present time, at least we can gain clarity about where it began, in the community just then recovering from the most massive Negro rebellion the country had ever known. The picture that emerges from the Watts of late 1965 is one, we think, that renders explicable much of what has happened subsequently throughout the nation. The nature of racial partisanship that becomes clear then makes the subsequent "racism" more comprehensive.

THE DATA

The data on which this paper is based were obtained from interviews conducted with two samples of respondents in Los Angeles County in late 1965 and early 1966. The most important was a representative sample ($n = 586$) of Negroes living in the large area (46.5 square miles) of South-Central Los Angeles sealed off by a curfew imposed during the rioting. The curfew zone contains about three-fourths of the more than 450,000 Negroes living in Los Angeles County, and is over 80 percent Negro. Hence it represents the major concentration of Negroes in the Los Angeles area. Black interviewers living in the curfew zone did the interviewing. Though the interviews were long (averaging about two hours), interest was high and the refusal rate low. Checks were run on the possible biases introduced by the interviwers' own views and these do not give unusual reason for concern.

The sampling was done by randomly choosing names from the 1960 census lists, then over-sampling poverty level census tracts by a cluster sampling procedure to compensate for the underrepresentation of low income respondents due to residential transience. While sampling biases are common in surveys of black ghettoes, we believe this sample is as close to being representative of the area as is normally achieved.

The other sample included 583 white respondents from six communities in Los Angeles, half of which were racially integrated and half non-integrated, with high, medium, and low socio-economic levels. This sample is thus not wholly representative of the County, overrepresenting high SES and racially integrated areas. Some, but not all, of the items on the Negro interview schedule were also used with white respondents. Our main emphasis in this paper is upon Negro opinion, so the white sample is not referred to except when explicitly indicated.[3]

BLACK DISAFFECTION

Trust of Government

First let us make an overall assessment of the Negro community's attachment to conventional political mechanisms. Blacks clearly felt considerable ambivalence about the adequacy of their representation and whether or not they could trust their political representatives. Fifty percent felt that "elected officials can generally be trusted," while 45 percent felt they could not be. In contrast, 79 percent of the whites trusted elected officials, and only 17 percent did not. Forty-two percent of the blacks responded positively to "how do you feel about the way you are represented? and 42 percent responded negatively. Whites saw the Negro's situation much more favorably: when asked "Do you think the Negro is fairly represented politically?" 55 percent said "yes," and 22 percent said "no." These measures, then, indicate substantial black disaffection.

National Partisan Politics

The "Negro vote" has in recent years become of keen interest to the national political parties and their candidates. Most Negroes today have a basic loyalty to the Democratic party, though their votes often "swing" rather easily from one side to the other, as illustrated by the fact that only about 60 percent of Negro voters supported the Democratical presidential candidate in 1956, while almost all voted for Lyndon B. Johnson in 1964 and Hubert Humphrey in 1968.

Quite aside from the importance of these votes to the two parties, vigorous electoral partisanship reflects acceptance of and participation in the traditional mechanisms of the American political system. A rabid partisan also tends to be a loyal democratic American.[4] Did the use of violence in rioting lead Negroes to reject the act of commitment to one of the conventional partisan alternatives, reflecting a more general loss of faith in the American system?

Los Angeles Negroes did not withdraw from the arena of national partisan politics after the riot. Almost all regarded themselves as Democrats, and held far more favorable attitudes toward the Democratic party and its leaders than toward the Republicans. When asked the standard Survey Research Center item on party identification, 84 percent of the Negroes sampled indicated they were Democrats, 6 percent Republicans, and 5 percent Independents. Their presidential votes in 1964 had been equally strongly pro-Democratic; 71 percent had voted for Johnson, 2 percent for Goldwater, and many of the remainder failed to vote only because they were not eligible to do so. In both cases their level of partisanship compared favorably with that of whites, 84 percent of whom claimed identification with one party or the other, and 73 percent of whom voted for president in 1964.

This preference for the Democrats was not simply a preference for the "lesser of two evils." As shown in Table 1, attitudes toward the Democratic party and toward its two most visible leaders, President Johnson and then-Governor Brown, were highly favorable. The Republican party and conservative Senator George Murphy both were regarded highly unfavorably. Thus, Democratic party identification meant positive regard for the Democrats and active rejection of the Republicans. Most Los Angeles blacks seem to have maintained their pro-Democratic partisan commitments, even in the wake of the riot, and had not rejected their traditional white liberal allies. . . .

Federal and local government. . . . Each respondent was asked which government does the best "for your problems." Four percent said the City government was best, 6 percent said the State government, and 58 percent cited the Federal government. Most of the rest (25 percent) said they were all about the same.

Evaluations of the several legislative bodies show the same pattern, as Table 2 indicates. First, blacks are generally less satisfied with their work than whites: the Congress "represented well" 47 percent of the blacks and 65 percent of the whites; the state legislature 30 percent and 49 percent respectively; and the County Board of Supervisors, 28 percent and 36 percent.

Second, the federal Congress is praised considerably more by blacks than are the local bodies. . . .

This greater support for federal officials and agencies, and the serious dissatisfaction with local government, is one of the most striking findings of this study. As might be expected, it is more obvious as a general disposition, and with respect to the most visible individuals at each level of government (such as the President, Governor, Mayor, and

Black Attitudes after Watts   119

Table 1
Evaluations of Leaders and Groups in National Partisan Politics

	Evaluations			
Leaders and groups	Favorable (1)	Unfavorable (2)	Net affect (1-2)	No opinion
Democrat				
Lyndon B. Johnson, President	95%	3%	+92%	1%
Democratic Party	89	4	+85	7
Edmund G. ("Pat") Brown, Governor	81	12	+69	6
AFL-CIO	58	16	+42	26
Mean	81%	9%	+72%	
Republican				
George Murphy, U.S. Senator	15	33	-18	52
Republican Party	30	56	-26	15
Mean	22%	44%	-22%	

Note: The items used were of a standard evaluation type: "How good a job is President Johnson doing? Is he doing well, doing fairly well (both favorable), doing nothing, or doing harm (both unfavorable)?" The proportions "doing well" were 63%, 64%, 34%, and 35% respectively, for the pro-Democratic set. The "no opinion" column includes those who "never heard of him," "don't know how he does," and those who failed to answer.

Table 2
Evaluations of Legislative Bodies

	Evaluations			
	Favorable (1)	Unfavorable (2)	Net affect (1-2)	No opinion
U.S. Congress	82%	10%	+72%	8%
California state legislature	70	13	+57	17
L.A. County Board of Supervisors	70	16	+54	14
Los Angeles City Council	73	15	+58	12
Mean	74%	14%	+60%	

Note: The item reads, "Do you feel that the U.S. Congress speaks for you or represents you well, a little (both favorable), or doesn't represent you (unfavorable)?" The evaluation item cited in previous tables was very highly correlated with this item when both referred to the same attitude object. Thus "net affect" scores can be meaningfully compared across tables.

Police Chief) than with respect to minor political officials at each level. . . .

Black Leadership

Much of the black community's political disaffection seems to be due to the preponderance of white faces in political office. Black leaders were preferred; 62 percent felt that "Negro elected officials" could be trusted, as opposed to the 50 percent who felt elected officials in general could be. This preference for black leadership also emerged in responses to the question "who do you think really represents the Negro?" Fifty-eight percent cited some Negro or Negro group (the most common, Martin Luther King, was cited by 24 percent), while 24 percent said "no one" or did not know. Only 9 percent cited white people or white leaders and 3 percent some political office. Perhaps, then, the generalized disaffection cited earlier refers primarily to white leadership. It may reflect dissatisfaction with current incumbents (who are mostly white) more than estrangement from the system. . . .

Civil rights and racial nationalism.   The other major sources of black leadership stem from more national individuals and groups; most originally centered around civil rights organizations. Two contradictory assertions were especially common in the aftermath of the riot about support for this leadership. Some said that the black community had become too militant for the moderates in the civil rights movement, and thus had rejected their leadership in favor of violence and anarchy. On the other hand, the Mayor and the Police Chief, and many other white people, alleged that the violence was inspired by the preaching of civil rights spokesmen and demonstrators.

The data suggest that both views were incorrect; that, in fact, racial partisanship, rather than militant radicalization or particular attraction to civil rights leadership, was the dominant pattern. In the first place, there is no evidence of broad public rejection of the civil rights movement as a whole, or even of any specific groups of leaders. All civil rights groups and leaders were evaluated positively, whether "assimilationist" or "protest" in orientation. These data are shown in Table 3.

Second, the main exceptions to this were the radical Muslims, the most visible black nationalists of the day. The sample as a whole consistently evaluated the Muslims negatively. The proportion of those who are positive is fairly stable across questions, ranging from 22 percent to 29 percent. The percent negative varies considerably across questions, as shown in Table 3, but it is consistently higher than the percent

Table 3
Evaluation of Black Leaders and Organizations

	Evaluations			
	Favorable (1)	Unfavorable (2)	Net affect (1-2)	No opinion
Assimilationists				
NAACP	91%	2%	+89%	7%
Urban League	83	4	+79	13
Ralph Bunche	70	5	+65	26
United Civil Rights Council	60	6	+54	34
Thurgood Marshall	50	3	+47	47
Reverend H. H. Brookins	42	9	+33	49
Mean	66%	5%	+61%	
Protest				
Martin Luther King	92%	4%	+88%	4%
SCLC	83	2	+81	15
CORE	77	4	+73	18
SNCC	60	8	+52	32
Mean	78%	4%	+74%	
Nationalism				
John Shabazz	22%	23%	− 1%	55%
Elijah Muhammed	22	46	−24	32
Black Muslims	29	54	−25	17
Mean	24%	41%	−17%	

Note: For the Urban League, SCLC, and SNCC, the standard representation item was used (see Note to Table 2). In all other cases, the standard evaluation question was used (see Note to Table 1).

positive. The stability of positive ratings and the variability of negative ratings across items suggests that Muslim support was fairly well informed and constant, whereas Opposition was more common but less informed.

Aside from the Muslims, however, preferences among these several leaders and organizations seem to have been based more upon their relative visibility than their militancy. As Table 3 reveals, the proportion receiving negative evaluations is very small in every instance. Insofar as they were known at all, they were positively evaluated. The same point may be made by comparing the relative militancy of the most popular (e.g., Martin Luther King and the NAACP) and the least popular (Thurgood Marshall and the Reverend Brookins, the central individual in the local unified moderate civil rights effort). They scarcely represented polar opposites on a militancy dimension.

If anything, the most popular national groups and leaders were those that represented a position of open collective protest rather than more passive or individualistic strategies. Racial partisanship, rather than individual assimilation or racial nationalism, was the most popular stance.[5] . . .

Political Effectiveness

Given the racial partisanship of the black community, what about the other necessary ingredient for political effectiveness, the level of political mobilization? Do blacks have political contacts, do they vote regularly, do they participate politically in other ways, and do they have confidence in their own ability to influence political decisions?

Negroes in Los Angeles were almost as likely as whites to know someone politically influential. Eighteen percent of the Negroes did, as did 22 percent of the whites. Similarly, blacks were about as politically active as whites. In 1964, 73 percent of our black sample voted for a presidential candidate, while 78 percent of the white sample did so. In 1964, 53 percent of the blacks reported they had voted on Proposition 14, a referendum repealing fair housing legislation, whereas 63 percent of the whites reported having voted. When asked, "Did you do anything besides voting in the 1964 election?" 24 percent of the blacks, and 22 percent of the whites, said they had. These several measures indicate that racial differences in participation were small, though whites were generally somewhat more active.

However, blacks had a great deal less confidence in their own political effectiveness, as measured by two items from the Survey Research Center's scale of "political efficacy." Sixty percent of the blacks and 27 percent of the whites agreed that "public officials don't care what people like me think." And 78 percent of the blacks and only 47 percent of the whites agreed that "voting is the only way people like me can have any say about how the government runs things." Thus, despite approximate equality in political contacts, in voting rates, and in other forms of political participation, blacks felt much less able to influence public policy.

RACIAL PARTISANSHIP VS. ESTRANGEMENT

The central question of this paper is whether or not the black community in a riot-torn city has become estranged from government and from conventional societal institutions. Indeed, blacks trusted elected officials considerably less than did whites, and felt quite unhappy about the way they were represented politically. However, the most likely in-terpretation is that this discontent reflects dissatisfaction with current political incumbents and their policies, rather than a more general loss of attachment to the American political system. There are several reasons for reaching this conclusion.

First, Negroes have in recent years consistently expressed firm support for American democracy. In a revolutionary era, historical prec-edent may not seem to count for much, but at least it does not indicate widespread black estrangement. A variety of indicators make the point. Wartime loyalty has appeared to be at a reasonably high level. Brink and Harris report that only 9 percent of the Negroes in 1966 felt the country was not worth fighting for, despite the lack of hospitality shown blacks by other Americans, and the growing opposition to the Vietnam war.[6] Negroes also have been at least as staunch defenders of democratic ideology as whites. There are few racial differences on issues of civil liberties such as freedom of speech; Negroes have generally been some-what *less* anti-Semitic than whites; they consistently favor living in racially mixed areas more than do whites or do not care about the racial composition of their neighborhood; and are generally more egalitarian and more willing to mix racially on the job.[7]

Attachment to the American system is also suggested by the gener-al rejection of violence and separatism as solutions to racial conflicts. A major survey of urban areas conducted in 1968 showed Negroes were only slightly more willing to engage in rioting than whites, and non-rioting Negroes typically have rejected the actions of the rioters despite expressing sympathy for the rioters and their motives. Similarly, separatist ideology has attracted very little broad-based support in the black community.[8]

Negroes also have consistently regarded the present conditions of their personal lives as improvements over previous years, and have expected continued improvement. When asked directly about the Ameri-can system, substantial minorities do report dissatisfaction; for example, Beardwood found 43 percent of a 1967 Negro sample said they could not get what they want under the U.S. system, and Cantril reports a large minority of Southern Negroes felt they would be treated no worse if the Nazis or Japanese conquered the United States.[9] Historically, then, Negroes have expressed discontent with their lot but have appar-ently supported the American democratic system as completely as have whites.

Second, the Los Angeles black community's discontent is focused upon local government and upon white incumbents in it. It is great-est with respect to local government's most visible symbols, such as the

Mayor, the school system, the Police Chief and the police force, but it is discernible with respect to almost all local agencies, and even the local newspapers. However, local black politicians are most important exceptions to this. The highly favorable attitudes toward local black politicians indicate dissatisfaction not with local government per se but with *white* local government.

And the black community seems not to have rejected its liberal allies. There is little evidence of withdrawal from national partisan politics after the riot; blacks remain strong Democrats, and apparently feel that the Democratic party is an attractive partisan champion of their cause. Similarly, they are much more favorable to the federal government than to local government.[10] So it would appear that the rejection of white-dominated local government is not a rejection of the political system, but a complaint about inadequate attention and inadequate service.[11]

The pattern thus seems to be more one of *racial partisanship* and self-interest than of *estrangement* from the American political system. This resembles some elements of the notion of black power, especially (1) mistrust of whites and dissatisfaction with politics that are dominated by whites, (2) racial partisanship, and (3) active political participation.

From this one might think that "black power" ideology would attain some considerable popularity in the black community, particularly those versions of it that stress black political control over arms of government that most immediately affect the black community. It is a little surprising, then, that nationalist leaders have not generally enjoyed wide popularity among blacks. However, these same leaders have tended to advocate separatism as well as increased black political power, and separatism has been much less popular. The greater approval given local black politicians may be due to their support of enhanced political power for the black community, without the implication of separatism.[12]

THE NEW GENERATION

What can be expected about black political attitudes in the future? One indicator is the degree of disaffection in the new generation. The old, Southern-born, rural semi-literates are swiftly being replaced by better-educated urban Northerners. How do the political attitudes of the young and the better-educated differ from those of older and less-educated persons?[13]

First, lack of trust in elected officials is substantially greater among the younger and better-educated. Table 4 gives the data. The same holds

Table 4
Percent Saying Elected Officials Can Be Trusted by Age, Education, and Race

| | | *Respondent's race* | |
	White	*Black*	*Racial difference*
Age			
15–29	76%	42%	+34%
30–44	79	49	+30
45+	81	60	+21
Education			
College	85%	46%	+39%
High School graduate	76	47	+29
Some high school	71	47	+24
Grade school	63	64	− 1
Total	79%	50%	+29%

for feelings of adequacy of representation. Of the college educated, 54 percent felt badly represented, whereas only 39 percent did so among the grade-school educated; among those under thirty, 47 percent felt badly represented, as did 37 percent of those 45 years of age and above. On a generalized scale of disaffection, including these two items and two others on trust and adequacy of representation, the young proved to be significantly more disaffected than the old ($F = 7.80$, $2/477$ df, $p < .001$), and greater education was also associated with greater disaffection, though not significantly so ($F = 1.10$, $3/477$ df, n.s.).[14]

This greater disaffection of the young and better-educated blacks is an important, and disturbing, departure from the pattern that has been typical in America. Previous studies of whites have found almost without exception, that education is strongly and positively related to democratic beliefs and attachment to the political system, and in most cases, so is youth as well.[15] Table 4 also gives the data for our white sample, and confirms this general expectation. Greater education substantially decreased disaffection from the political system, and age made relatively little difference. The greater black disaffection was most vivid among precisely those groups rising in political importance in the black community: the young and the well-educated.

Looking at more specific instances of discontent, there is a clear tendency for the young to be especially disenchanted with white leadership, whether national and liberal, or local and not so liberal. The young were less positive on a scale of attitudes toward white liberals (listed in Table 1; $F = 7.40$, $2/494$ df, $p < .001$); they were more inclined to criticize the several legislative bodies ruling them (listed in Table 2;

$F = 5.33$, $2/516$ *df*, $p < .005$); and they were less favorable toward the several white officeholders asked about (the President, Governor, Mayor, and local white legislators) ($F = 12.74$, $2/521$ *df*, $p < .001$). Education affected none of these significantly, though in each case the college-educated were least favorable.

Dissatisfaction with local government is particularly common in the black community, as indicated above. Perhaps for this reason, there is nothing especially unique about the discontent of the young and better educated. The young were more negative ($F = 3.33$, $2/519$ *df*, $p < .05$) on a scale of attitudes toward the local political structure; they were more inclined to believe in widespread police brutality ($F = 4.65$, $2/511$ *df*, $p < .01$); and more likely to criticize the fairness of local white media's coverage of the black community, to criticize the performance of local service agencies, and to perceive racial discrimination in their operation (though not significantly so). There was also a nonsignificant tendency for the better-educated to be more dissatisfied in each case.

Discontent with the local situation was sometimes more closely related to education (e.g., regarding the Los Angeles *Times,* which is read primarily by better-educated persons) and sometimes to age (e.g., with respect to the police, who are in more contact with the young than the old). But the striking thing is that on virtually every one of the dimensions tested for, the young and better-educated are more dissatisfied than are the older and less-educated.

The greater disaffection and dissatisfaction with the political system in general, and with white leadership in particular, among the young and well-educated implies some greater realism in their views. More generally, they express more skepticism about people in general than do older blacks, or whites of any age, as shown in Table 5. They seem to have a more vivid impression of the selfishness or the self-interestedness of people's behavior. This too may contribute to increasing racial partisanship and political participation; if one cannot trust others' altruistic impulses, one needs to have power over their behavior. Black power advocates emphasize this very point.

Political Mobilization

However, it is not so clear that the new generation is moving toward effective political participation, by the several criteria advanced earlier. First, the young are less likely to be strong Democrats. Of those under 30, 61 percent were strong Democrats, while of those over 44, 76 percent were. And the young tended to be less positive toward noted white liberals ($F = 7.40$, $2/494$ *df*, $p < .001$; education had no effect:

Table 5
Percent of Blacks Trusting People by Age and Education

	Age		
Education	*15–19*	*30–44*	*45+*
College	47%	70%	86%
High school graduate	57	65	69
Some high school	48	63	71
Grade school	29	74	73
Total	51%	66%	72%

Note: Over 80% of the whites in each category said they trusted people.

$F < 1.0$). However, this does not mean they were more attracted to the Republican party. On a scale of attitudes toward the G.O.P., neither age ($F = 1.40$, 2/492 *df*, n.s.) nor education ($F < 1$) had a significant effect. Thus the young are simply more indifferent partisans rather than being potential converts for the Republican party.[16]

Second, what about black leadership? The degree of positive feeling toward black leaders and black organizations actually *increased* with greater education, quite unlike the situation with white leadership. However, with respect to age the familiar pattern holds: the young tend to be the less enthusiastic about most traditional leaders. Specifically, the old and the well-educated were more enthusiastic than the young and the poorly-educated about assimilationist leaders (such as Martin Luther King, the NAACP, etc.), civil rights organizations (ranging from the Urban League and the NAACP to CORE and SNCC), and local black politicians.[17] Before too much is made of this, it should be noted that even among the young and the poorly educated negative evaluations were very rare. Thus these effects are due more to differential familiarity with the leaders than to differential antagonism toward them. Considering everything, therefore, no great disaffection from black leadership appears among the young and college-educated, quite unlike the situation with white leadership.

And in fact the reverse held with the nationalist Black Muslims, toward whom the young were actually more favorable. It is apparent that while sympathy with racial nationalism is not universal in the black community, it is greatest among the young.

Third, the young and better-educated seem to be more politicized than the older generation. By every standard, greater education is related to greater political mobilization. For example, the better-educated vote more frequently, and have more political knowledge. They were higher on a general scale of familiarity with white politicians ($F = 7.60$,

3/461 df, $p<.001$), and on a scale of familiarity with poverty agencies ($F = 5.18$, 3/499 df, $p<.005$). Only 31 percent of the college-educated, as against 57 percent of the grade school educated, did not know of Councilman Bradley; the percentages for then-Assemblyman Dymally were 34 percent and 73 percent respectively; for CORE, 3 percent and 25 percent.

The young appear to be as politicized as the old, contrary to the pattern that normally holds for white Americans.[18] They voted at approximately the same rate as older blacks in 1964, and they were not universally less informed than their elders. They were less informed about white politicians ($F = 10.37$, 2/461 df, $p<.001$), but the young and old alike were better informed than the middle age group (30–44) about poverty agencies ($F = 4.32$, 2/499 df, $p<.025$); and with respect to black leaders, age differences varied widely depending upon the individual in question. For example, 16 percent of the old, and 10 percent of the young, were unfamiliar with the Muslims, while 38 percent of the old and 49 percent of the young were unfamiliar with Councilman Bradley.

Two disturbing signs accompany this high level of politicization in the coming generation. One is a discouraging sense of political ineffectiveness. The sense of political efficacy does not increase with education among blacks. Of the several combinations of age and education afforded by our standard cut-off points, the greatest efficacy is among the middle-aged (30–44) college-educated whites, as might be expected. Eighty-two percent disagreed that "I don't think public officials care about people like me." However, the lowest were the young black (15–29) high school graduates, of whom only 30 percent disagreed. This is, then, a troublesome combination among the young and better-educated blacks; relatively high levels of political activism, but little confidence that the system as it currently exists will be responsive to them.

The other is that local black political leadership appears to be out of touch with much of the black community. Among blacks it is primarily the old and well-educated who are in contact with political influentials, as shown in Table 6. To a degree the same holds for whites, but with far less serious consequences, because those in contact are more numerous. Whites are more than twice as likely to have been to college, and young whites are not as numerous, not as politically significant, and not as removed from political influentials as young blacks.[19]

The dangers in this situation have been clear for some time to the moderate political leadership of the black community. Their lack of contact with the young and the lower class sometimes leaves them more conservative than the black community as a whole. Clearly the potential

Table 6
Percent Knowing Someone Politically Influential by Age and Education

	White	Black	Racial difference
		Respondent's race	
Age			
15–29	21%	13%	+8%
30–44	24	18	+6
45+	20	24	−4
Education			
College	32	29	+3
High school graduates	13	14	−1
Some high school	8	15	−7
Grade school	10	18	−8
Total	21%	18%	+3%

for racial solidarity exists, as witnessed by young blacks' readiness to endorse black leadership. However, the preconditions for truly effective leadership may be difficult to achieve; for example, leaders must maintain contact throughout the black community, and factionalizing must not reach bitterly competitive heights. In this sense the future depends to a large degree on the capabilities of leadership elements within the black community; the opportunities are there. . . .

NOTES

[1]This research was conducted under a contract between the Office of Economic Opportunity and the Institute of Government and Public Affairs at UCLA as part of the *Los Angeles Riot Study,* Nathan E. Cohen, Coordinator. Thanks are due to the many people who worked on this study, particularly to Paula Johnson, John B. McConahay, Diana TenHouten, T. M. Tomlinson, and Richard E. Whitney.

[2]D. Marvick, "The Political Socialization of the American Negro," *The Annals of the American Academy of Political and Social Science,* 1965, 361, p. 122.

[3]For more complete accounts of the method, see T. M. Tomlinson and Diana TenHouten, "Method: Negro Reaction Survey," and R. T. Morris and V. Jeffries, "The White Reaction Study," in Nathan E. Cohen (Ed.), *Los Angeles Riot Study: A Socio-Psychological Study* (New York: Praeger, 1969).

[4]See R. D. Hess and Judith V. Torney, *The Development of Political Attitudes in Children* (Chicago: Aldine, 1967); H. McClosky, "Consensus and

Ideology in American Politics," *American Political Science Review,* 1964, 58, pp. 361-382.

⁵This general pattern, of consistent and strong support for moderate black leadership, and only minority support for militancy, has been obtained repeatedly in other surveys. See A. Campbell and H. Schuman, "Racial Attitudes in Fifteen American Cities," in *Supplemental Studies for the National Advisory Commission on Civil Disorders* (Washington, D.C.: Government Printing Office); W. Brink and L. Harris, *Black and White* (New York: Simon and Schuster, 1966); G. T. Marx, *Protest and Prejudice* (New York: Harper Torchbook, 1969). However, the power of militant organizations and leaders may not be indexed at all well by their general popularity throughout the black community. For example, since the rioting, all black leaders have moved toward more militant positions because of pressures from within the black community. For analyses of subgroups which were considerably more favorable to the militants than was the black community as a whole, see D. O. Sears and J. B. McConahay, "The Politics of Discontent: Blocked Mechanisms of Grievance Redress and the Psychology of the New Urban Black Man," and T. M. Tomlinson, "Ideological Foundations for Negro Action: A Comparative Analysis of Militant and Non-militant views of the Los Angeles Riot," *Los Angeles Riot Study, op. cit.*

This overwhelming support for local black politicians was again demonstrated in the 1969 mayoralty race in Los Angeles, in which the moderate liberal black councilman, Thomas Bradley, received almost unanimous support from an unprecedentedly high turnout in black precincts. See Riley, *et al.,* "Race, Unrest, and the Old Angeleno: The Bradley Defeat in Los Angeles" (Unpublished manuscript, Harvard University, 1969).

⁶Brink and Harris, *op. cit.*

⁷S. A. Stouffer, *Communism, Conformity, and Civil Liberties* (New York: Doubleday, 1955); Hazel Erskine, "The Polls: Religious Prejudice, Part 2: Antisemitism," *Public Opinion Quarterly,* 1965, 29, pp. 649-664; "The Polls: Negro Housing," *Public Opinion Quarterly,* 1968, 32, pp. 134-153. This preference for racial integration among Negroes is obviously based on more than just adherence to democratic ideology. However, the point is that insofar as democratic ideology can be operationally defined, Negroes have consistently been on the supportive side more often than the opposition side.

⁸See footnote 5.

⁹R. Beardwood, "The New Negro Mood," *Fortune,* 1968, 78, 146 ff; Brink and Harris, *op. cit.;* D. R. Matthews and J. W. Prothro, *Negroes and the New Southern Politics* (New York: Harcourt, Brace and World, Inc., 1966); H. Cantril, *Gauging Public Opinion* (Princeton, N.J.: Princeton University Press, 1944), p. 116.

¹⁰This preference for the Federal government has been shared in recent years by most Americans, see D. O. Sears, "Political Behavior," in G. Lindzey and E. Aronson (Eds.), *Handbook of Social Psychology* (Revised Edition), Vol. 5 (Reading, Mass.: Addison Wesley, 1969). It may in addition be a short-term consequence of the more sympathetic attention given to Negro problems by all branches of the Federal system, whether executive, legislative, or judicial, than by local and State systems in the few years preceding the study.

One does sense, though, that much of the Negro's ultimate faith in the benevolence and attentiveness of the white community rests upon the reputation of the Federal government. No doubt Negro attachment to the American political system is sturdy. One does wonder nevertheless, about the consequences of a possible change in Federal policy to a more punitive, less generous stance. It would certainly remove one currently important prop from that basic commitment to the American system, but how much actual change would occur is unclear.

[11]The theme of concern about inadequate attention is a salient one in the black respondents' answers to open-ended questions throughout the interview schedule. To use just one objective index of white attention to the black community, the amount of coverage of blacks in local newspapers has consistently lagged far behind the proportion of the population that is black. See Paula B. Johnson, D. O. Sears, and J. B. McConahay, "Black Invisibility and the Los Angeles Riot," paper presented at the 1969 meetings of the Western Psychological Association, Vancouver, British Columbia.

[12]This is also unusual in that support for a charismatic leader often outstrips the support for his ideology. For examples, see the cases of Father Coughlin, Senator Joseph McCarthy, the John Birch Society, and numerous other domestic political movements [S. M. Lipset, "Three Decades of the Radical Right: Coughlinites, McCarthyites, and Birchers − 1962," in D. Bell (ed.), *The Radical Right* (Garden City, N.Y.: Doubleday, 1963), pp. 313–378; Sears, 1969, *op. cit.*]. Yet with racial nationalism the situation seems to be reversed: relatively strong support for many of the basic ideological components of black power, but generally unfavorable attitudes toward its advocates. The issue of separatism is the one that most clearly divides the thinking of the militant leaders from that of conventional black politicians.

[13]See K. E. Taeuber and A. F. Taeuber, "The Negro Population in the United States," in J. P. Davis (ed.), *The American Negro Reference Book* (Englewood Cliffs, N.J.: Prentice-Hall, 1966), and D. O. Sears and J. B. McConahay, "Racial Socialization, Comparison Levels, and the Watts Riot," *Journal of Social Issues,* in press, for discussions of demographic changes in the black community and some of their political consequences.

[14]For details on the several scales discussed in this section, see Sears and McConahay, "Politics of Discontent," *op. cit.* The age effects in this section are tested with two degrees of freedom, since age was trichotomized, and the education effects are tested with three degrees of freedom, since four levels of education were used. For the general procedure, see B. J. Winer, *Statistical Principles in Experimental Design* (New York: McGraw-Hill, 1962).

[15]For example, see J. W. Prothro and C. W. Grigg, "Fundamental Principles of Democracy; Bases of Agreement and Disagreement," *Journal of Politics,* 1960, 22, pp. 276–294; Stouffer, *op. cit.*; McClosky, *op. cit.*; J. Dennis, "Support for the Party System by the Mass Public," *American Political Science Review,* 1966, 60, pp. 600–615; and S. M. Lipset, *Political Man* (Garden City, N.Y.: Doubleday, 1960), among others.

[16]The lesser partisanship of the young has been also characteristic of whites. Whether this simply represents the immaturity of youth or genuine generational differences is not yet clear. See Sears, 1969, *op. cit.*

[17]For age, $F = 16.85$, $2/508$ $df,$ $p < .001$; $F = 3.80$, $2/515$ $df,$ $p < .025$; $F = 4.67$, $2/517$ $df, p < .025$, respectively, and for education, $F < 13.15$, $3/508$ $df,$ $p < .001$; $F = 11.65$, $3/515$ $df, p < .001$; and $F = 6.39$, $3/517$ $df, p < .001$, respectively.

[18]See L. W. Milbrath, *Political Participation* (Chicago: Rand McNally, 1965); and Sears, 1969, *op. cit.*

[19]For one thing, the rioting was mainly done by young blacks. See Sears and McConahay, "Riot Participation," *op. cit.,* National Advisory Commission, *op. cit.* Even so, one can speculate about the remoteness of the young and less educated whites from the white political Establishment; some have ascribed the popularity of Eugene McCarthy and Ronald Reagan, respectively, to their appeals to these two left-out groups.

Chapter 9

POLITICAL TRUST AND
RACIAL IDEOLOGY

Joel D. Aberbach
Jack L. Walker

I. INTRODUCTION

No government yet established has had the loyalty and trust of all its citizens. Regardless of the popularity of its leaders or how careful they are in soliciting opinions and encouraging participation in the process of policy-making, there are always those who see inequalities and injustices in the society and harbor suspicions of the government's motives and intentions. Resentment and distrust are elements of disaffection and the first step toward resistance. Therefore, even the most dictatorial governments have usually striven to increase their credibility and popularity. For democratic governments, however, the problem of combating distrust and encouraging voluntary acceptance of its institutions and decisions is a paramount concern. One of democratic theory's distinctive characteristics is its strong emphasis on voluntary consent, both as a basis of political obligation and as a central attribute of citizenship. The concern expressed by democratic thinkers about the elements of due process and the protection of opportunities for widespread participation is directed toward the creation of citizens who voluntarily accept the society's goals; "the demand for consent is the demand that the govern-

Reprinted from *The American Political Science Review,* 64 (December, 1970), pp. 1199–1219, by permission of the authors and publisher. Footnotes and tables have been renumbered; some footnotes have been deleted.

The principal grant which supported this study came from the National Institute of Mental Health. Additional support also came from the Horace H. Rackham Faculty Research Fund and the Institute of Public Policy Studies, The University of Michigan. Thanks are due to Steven L. Coombs and William A. Gamson who read and criticized an earlier version of this paper and to James D. Chesney and Douglas B. Neal who assisted in the data analysis.

ment must be more than self-appointed and must, in some significant way, be the chosen instrument through which the body politic and community acts. . . ."[1]

Democracy's guiding ideal is the substitution of mutual understanding and agreement for coerciveness and arbitrary authority in all phases of social and political life. The existence of distrustful citizens who are convinced that the government serves the interests of a few rather than the interests of all is a barrier to the realization of the democratic ideal. In Sabine's words: "full understanding cannot be reached except on the basis of mutual respect and with a mutual acknowledgment of good faith and the acceptance of the principle that the purpose of understanding is to protect all valid interests."[2] Leaders in a representative democracy cannot be successful until they have gained the trust of the citizens; this is even more important in American society where racial and ethnic minorities are actively searching for a new, more dignified role as political equals.

Besides its important normative implications, the level of trust in government also is an important determinant of political change. The rise and fall in the number of distrustful citizens over time is a sensitive barometer of social conflicts and tensions. When any sizable group becomes distrustful and begins to make demands, the government is prompted to reallocate its resources or change its institutions to accommodate these new pressures. If the political system is flexible and adaptive enough, needed adjustments can be made without any consequent outbreak of violence, but if distrustful groups are denied access to decision-makers, or if institutions are too rigid to change, destructive conflict and a breakdown in the social order are possible. Under the right political conditions, distrustful groups, which exist in all societies, may produce the kind of creative tensions needed to prompt social change, but under other conditions, these same tensions may lead to either violent disruption or indiscriminate and cruel repression. A society's leaders may either strive to meet the demands of the distrustful group, or instead, endeavor to violate and attack the group, making it a scapegoat for the resentment and hostility of the majority. Rising distrust is often a stimulant to social change, but its consequences depend on the response it provokes from leaders and other elements of the society.

The level of trust in government strongly influences the kind of policies and strategies available to political leaders. As Gamson has argued, when the level of trust is high, "the authorities are able to make new commitments on the basis of it and, if successful, increase such support even more. When it is low and declining, authorities may find it difficult to meet existing commitments and to govern effectively."[3] Levels of trust and allegiance differ greatly among countries and these differences determine both the number of options open to the government and the relative danger of political fragmentation.[4] The distribution of trust among different social groups in the society also may have an important effect on the relative success of different governmental policies, and a sensitive awareness of its importance should allow a political leader to adopt more successful strategies of persuasion.

Widespread trust in government is recognized by students of both normative and empirical questions as the foundation for democratic order. This paper presents a comparative analysis of political trust in the black and white communities of Detroit, Michigan—a city which has a history of racial conflict and experienced major civil disturbances in 1943 and 1967. We discuss: (1) the concept of political trust; (2) the levels of trust in both racial communities; (3) the principal social and political sources of trustful and distrustful attitudes; (4) the contrast between the correlates and nature of political distrust in the black and white communities; (5) the behavioral consequences of distrust; and (6) the racial ideologies linked to political trust in both communities.

II. A REVIEW OF THE LITERATURE

Given the widely acknowledged importance of political trust in maintaining political stability or promoting change[5] it is surprising that empirical research on the origins and consequences of trust is so scarce. In addition, the small body of literature which does exist raises more questions than it answers. Studies contradict each other as conceptual and measurement problems abound. Sometimes political trust is clearly related to social status[6] and sometimes not.[7] Often it is correlated with feelings of political efficacy,[8] but not always.[9] In most instances it is strongly related to measures of trust in other people,[10] but again, not always.[11]

At least some of this confusion is due to the fact that the reported research has taken place in different settings. We know that levels of trust vary according to what Litt has called the "political milieu" in which distrust "may be acquired as a *community norm,* a part of the political acculturation process in the city's daily routine."[12] Not only can the political milieu influence the level of trust, but the relationships between variables are not always the same in each setting. For example, in Litt's comparative study of a middle class neighborhood in Boston and a comparable area in adjoining Brookline there is no relationship between feelings of political trust and political efficacy in Boston and yet there is a strong relationship in Brookline. The explanation offered is that in Boston, a city noted for blatant corruption in its political life, "community-wide suspicions of 'base practices' may go hand in hand with a belief that the professional practitioner of politics will still turn an attentive ear to the plaints of his constituents,"[13] while in Brookline, a community with a history of clean government, those who are distrustful are fully convinced that political leaders will not be responsive to their requests. In Brookline the citizens' distrust can be traced to personality variables, while in Boston the political milieu is the dominant factor.[14]

A study of distrust at the federal level raised similar issues. Stokes, using data from the Survey Research Center's 1958 national election study, found a correlation between feelings of political efficacy and political trust. He hypothesized that under certain conditions one could find subjective powerlessness linked with a positive attitude toward government, but "in the context of democratic values, feelings of powerlessness toward public authority tend to create feelings of hostility toward the authority."[15] While Stokes reported a relationship between political trust and efficacy similar to that found among Litt's Brookline residents, his national sample resembled Litt's Boston respondents in that social status variables were at best weakly correlated with trust.

The setting of the research apparently is important in determining both the level of distrust and the relationship between it and other variables. If we are to explain successfully the origins and consequences of distrust, therefore, we must systematically introduce into our measures factors associated with the political settings of the population. To do so we must deal with conceptual problems which are intimately tied to problems of measurement. The concept of political distrust is defined by Stokes as a "basic evaluative orientation toward the . . . government."[16] However, items in many of the scales designed to measure political distrust often involve simple clichés about the quality of politics and politicians with little or no indication as to the governments or figures involved. McClosky, who employs such items in his measure, is quite concerned about their validity and therefore about the interpretation of his results. "It is," he says, "impossible in the present context to determine the extent to which scores contained in these tables signify genuine frustration and political disillusionment and the extent to which they represent familiar and largely ritualistic responses."[17] This is not to deny that some element of dissaffection may be tapped by questions of this kind, but one can only guess at how much. We cannot tell which politicians the subject is reminded of, or the relative importance of most of the images conjured up by the statements. The goal of scholars in the field is to get below this surface veneer to tap deeper hostility.

To do this it would seem vitally important that the subject be stimulated to think about some more focused symbol than "politicians"[18] and that the items not be phrased in simple agree-disagree form. This will not completely avoid the problem of imperfect measurement due to ritualistic responses, but it should mitigate it somewhat by making the statement of disaffection more meaningful to the subject.

Stokes' scale is a model of what we seek here. Before the items are presented to the respondent he is told: "Now I'd like to talk about some of the different ideas people have about the government in Washington and see how you feel about them. These opinions don't refer to any single branch of government in general."[19] A series of items (see below for examples) follows which are not in agree-disagree form and which are reversed so that the positive alternative is not presented first in each case. These questions measure whether the respondent believes that the government generally does the right things, and whether it serves the public interest. The format is designed to cut down response-set problems and, in this case, focus the respondents' attention on the collective workings of an identifiable set of political arrangements and institutions.

As Gamson says, "it is possible for individuals simultaneously to feel high confidence in political institutions and alienation towards those who man them."[20] In fact, according to Gamson, it is important to find out whether political trust is generalized—that is, in the simplest case, whether people dissatisfied with a given decision or set of decisions first begin to distrust the authorities, then perhaps the institutions and procedures of the regime, and finally become so disenchanted with the political community itself that they wish to separate themselves from the community. Where trust is high a negative decision may be bearable because of a belief in the integrity of the authorities and the legitimacy of the procedures employed. Where trust is low, negative outputs may be unbearable and lead to an intensification of distrust or separatist feelings. If several sets of authorities prove unsatisfactory, citizens are likely to "conclude that the institutions themselves may be the source of bias, and 'throwing the rascals out' will have little effect if indeed it is even possible."[21] The existence of high levels of trust allows authorities to make commitments which build more trust and weather situations in which citizens are unhappy about governmental outputs. A distrustful citizenry, however, is suspicious of every perceived governmental move, impatient for results and prone to deeper and more extreme levels of distrust. Ultimately, this process may lead to acts which undermine the political system.

III. THE ORIGINS AND CONSEQUENCES OF POLITICAL TRUST

There are two general approaches to explaining political trust employed in the existing literature. Gamson, for example, emphasizes political factors. The content of decisions and the reactions they provoke are seen as the basic sources of political trust and distrust. Other scholars stress personality factors which are basically independent of political considerations as explanatory variables. They believe that: "If one cannot trust other people generally, one can certainly not trust those under the temptation of and with the powers which come with public office. Trust in elected officials is seen to be only a more specific instance of trust in mankind."[22]

Litt has introduced the idea that both political and personality variables are potentially important as explanatory factors. The relative importance of each class of variables, however, depends on the political environment or "milieu" prevailing in the community being examined. Stokes draws attention to the importance of generalized political expectations born of widely held democratic values as influences on political trust. Individuals may be influenced in their thinking by a local government's reputation for political corruption, and this seems to affect the relative influence of personality factors in explaining the existing degree of political trust. Trustful attitudes are also determined, however, by general public expectations about the nature of democratic governments, and a government's general record of performance in certain policy areas.

We do not suppose that levels of political trust are immutable. We conceive, instead, of a process in which this basic orientation toward the system[23] slowly changes as individuals are subjected to outside influences. In Gamson's model, for example, the individual's level of distrust is based on his judgement of the content of political outputs important to him and the procedures used to reach decisions. These judgements cumulate through time and are affected by cures from his experiences with government and his group allegiances. For a person with a high level of trust, a bad decision may be seen as an understandable, if unfortunate, mistake which does not call the political system's legitimacy into serious question. For a person with a moderate level of trust, however, the same bad decision is more likely to serve as proof of fundamental faults in the political system and may precipitate a rapid decrease in political trust. For the already distrustful person, the bad decision is merely further proof that the system is evil and may move him to some extreme, perhaps violent, protest.

There are numerous feedback loops in the complex process which generates or maintains trust. For example, satisfactory outputs stimulate trust, but trust itself predisposes a person to view outputs positively. The same process operates when we view trust or distrust as an element leading to radical ideologies or behavior. A distrustful person, for example, should be more disposed to take part in violent activities or to endorse radical interpretations of social ills than a trusting one, but his behavior or endorsement reinforces his distrust or tends to lower his previous level of trust.

We will need extensive time-series data to study this developmental process in detail and to determine precisely the levels of trust and the structural conditions which are sufficient to maintain a stable system or to inhibit the generalization of distrust. We are currently gathering data which we hope will carry us in this direction.[24] Many important questions, however, can be answered simply using data collected at one point in time, although this limits us to inferences about feedback loops and to primary reliance on summary measures (overall assessments gauged at one point in time) of people's satisfaction with their status in life and their political achievements.

IV. THE DATA

Our data come from a survey of the residents of Detroit, Michigan, completed in the fall of 1967. A total of 855 respondents were interviewed (394 whites and 461 blacks). In all cases whites were interviewed by whites, and blacks by blacks. The total N came from a community random sample of 539 (344 whites and 195 blacks) and a special random supplement of 316 (50 whites and 266 blacks) drawn from the areas where rioting took place in July 1967.[25] When we discuss the attitude patterns in the communities we will use the random sample data. However, since there are few meaningful differences between the distributions and relationships in the random and riot-supplement samples, we have employed the total N in the analysis so that a larger number of cases are available when controls are instituted.

V. LEVELS OF POLITICAL TRUST: A RACIAL COMPARISON

We defined political trust, following Stokes' lead, as a basic evaluative orientation toward government. Our measure of trust is a revised version of his. The following questions were asked at various points in the questionnaire.[26]

>   1. How much do you think you can trust the government in Washington to do what is right: just about always, most of the time, some of the time, or almost never?
>   2. Would you say that the government in Washington is pretty much run for the benefit of a few big interests or that it is run for the benefit of all the people?
>   3. How much do you feel that having elections makes the government in Washington pay attention to what the people think: a good deal, some, or not very much?
>   4. How much do you think we can trust the government in Detroit to do what is right: just about always, most of the time, some of the time, or almost never?
>   5. How much do you feel having elections makes the government in Detroit pay attention to what the people think: a good deal, some, or not very much?

In the minds of Detroit residents there is a generalized sense of trust in the federal and local governments.[27] While trust in the Washington government on the individual items is always higher than trust in the Detroit government, the differences are slight. Detroit city government is relatively well run, nonpartisan, and generally not in such ill repute as the governments of cities like Boston or Newark.[28] This is apparent in Table 1 where we compare the levels of political trust exhibited by blacks in Newark and Detroit. It is clear that Litt is correct and the particular political setting is an important determinant of the level of trust. Since this is so, in the Detroit case we are fortunate to have an adequate distribution of responses to the attitude items so that we can examine the relationship between political trust and a general personality variable like trust in people which many scholars believe is the foundation of political trust under ordinary circumstances.

When we compare the political trust of blacks and whites (Table 2) we find that the blacks are less trusting. This holds for all of the individual items as well as the index as a whole. This actually represents a change in the usual pattern, as blacks have always had at least the same distribution as whites on answers to these political trust questions.[29] No survey data exist concerning levels of trust which prevailed at earlier times, but through the years the federal government and local governments in much of the North, for all their shortcomings, have been the black man's friend in an otherwise hostile environment. The federal government, especially, won him his freedom, gave him the best treatment he received in his bleakest days in the South, provided relief in the Depression and in the difficult periods which have followed, and has

Table 1
Trust in Detroit and Newark Governments for Riot Area
Black Males: 18-35*

Item: How much do you think you can trust the government in (Newark/Detroit) to do what is right: just about always, most of the time, some of the time, or none of the time?

	Trust City Government				
	Just about always	*Most of the time*	*Some of the time*	*None of the time*	
Newark (N = 232)	2%	9	50	38	= 100%
Detroit (N = 71)	10%	21	51	18	= 100%

*The figures for Newark are recomputed from the table in the *Report of the National Advisory Commission on Civil Disorders* (New York: Bantam Books, 1968), p. 178. This survey, conducted for the Commission by Nathan Caplan of the University of Michigan, covered only males 15 to 35 living in the riot zone and we drew comparable respondents from our sample to facilitate comparison.

Table 2
Political Trust in the Detroit Black and White Communities

	Political Trust Index		
	Low *0–1*	*2*	*High* *3–4*
Black random sample (N = 186) $\bar{x}$ = 1.66*	52	13	35	= 100%
White Random sample (N = 327) $\bar{x}$ = 2.13*	33	24	43	= 100%

*The mean in the Black Riot Area Sample (N = 341) is 1.67 and 1.66 in the Total Black Sample (N = 461).

The mean in the White Riot Area Sample (N = 75) is 2.12 and 2.11 in the Total White Sample (N = 394).

done the most to secure him his rights and protect him during his struggle for equality.[30] In addition, the government in Washington has been the symbol of the American Negro's intense identification with and "faith in the American Dream."[31] Now, at least in cities like Detroit, this sense of trust is being undermined as many black people are beginning to reject their traditional ties with paternalistic friends and allies, and are striking out at the more subtle forms of discrimination and deprivation found in the North. These expressions of distrust, as we shall see in more detail below, are accompanied by a militant racial ideology and an expressed willingness to resort to almost any means necessary to achieve their goals.

VI. EXPLAINING POLITICAL TRUST

A. As a Function of Trust in People

As we have mentioned, one commonly held hypothesis about the origins of political trust is that it is "only a more specific instance of trust in mankind"[32] — which is a personality factor basically independent of political considerations. Our survey contained a standard version of the Rosenberg Trust-in-People measure[33] which should provide an excellent means of testing the relationship between interpersonal trust and political trust. Given the similarities in the concepts *and* the measures, in fact, anything short of a strong relationship would raise serious questions about the hypothesis and one would expect "personality" variables other than trust in people to show even weaker direct effects on political trust.

The relationship between the indicators of trust in people and political trust is positive but weak. Rank-order correlation coefficients (Gamma) between the two are .17 for blacks and .16 for whites.[34] Clearly, political trust is more than a mere specific instance of trust in mankind. A strong relationship between interpersonal trust and political trust would hold ominous implications for American race relations given the low level of trust in people which most studies have discovered among blacks. In our data, for example, over 50 percent of the whites but less than 30 percent of the blacks have high scores on our trust-in-people scale. The pattern of these differences hold with education controlled and was the same in the Michigan Survey Research Center's 1964 national survey where similar questions were asked.[35]

B. As a Function of Social Background Factors

A simple and plausible explanation of variation in political trust is that the socially advantaged are more trusting than the disadvantaged because they possess the status and the skills which bring them societal rewards and honors, while the disadvantaged achieve relatively little, and as a result, have little faith either in their fellow men or their government.[36] Our data forces us to reject this simple explanation. There is virtually no relationship between indicators of social advantages, such as education, occupation and income, and political trust.[37] If such factors have an effect, it is indirect.

There are other background factors, however, which have a greater influence on political trust. Individuals who were born in the South are somewhat more trustful than those born in the North[38] and people who have active affiliations with churches (i.e., are members of churches or church-related groups) are more trusting than those who are inactive.[39] These relationships are not strong, but reflect important acculturation patterns; persons born in the North more readily adopt a "worldly" cynicism about government, and individuals who have broken away from the traditional moorings of the church are also less likely to believe that government represents a benevolent authority. Our measures of this acculturation process are crude and indirect at best. In future studies we intend to create more explicit measures of this form of modernization which will enable us to ascertain more exactly the strength of its impact on political trust.

C. As a Function of Political Expectations

Since political trust does not seem to be merely a reflection of basic personality traits, or a simple product of social background, we turn to political factors in search of a more satisfactory explanation. As a person gains experience in the political realm, he slowly builds an assessment of himself as a political actor and develops his ideas about the fairness of the political process and the utility of its outputs. These evaluations are summaries both of his actual experiences and his expectations. They are answers to a series of questions:

1. Am I, or can I be, influential?
2. Do governmental outputs make a difference in my life—are they beneficial?
3. Do I, or will I, receive equal treatment if I have a grievance about governmental decisions?

Each answer is an element in the political equation suggested by Gamson where political trust is a function of an individual's cumulative assessment of the procedures and outputs of the political process.[40] Also, if Stokes is correct, in a system infused with the democratic ethos, perceived influence is as important as the quality and justice of the outputs themselves in determining political trust.[41]

Obviously, political expectations are a complex function both of factors in an individual's personality and his assessment of a political situation. We cannot hope to sort out these elements in the attitudes we use as predictors, but we assume that political evaluations have strong foundations in the cumulative political experiences of an individual or group. In the process model we are developing, political experiences and expectations have a more immediate effect on political trust than personality factors, and are themselves conditioned by a respondent's level of trust. Because of these feedback relationships, we would expect individuals' political experiences and expectations and their feelings of political trust to be strongly associated. We do not assume that all governmental decisions will affect political trust, but we are struck by Gamson's idea that "disaffection begins to be generalized when an undesirable outcome is seen as a member of a class of decisions with similar results."[42]

In order to investigate these relationships we have utilized measures of our respondents' sense of political competence, their beliefs about the importance of the actions taken by government, and their expectations concerning the kind of reception they would receive at a government office. (The questions employed and the methods used in constructing indices are listed in the footnotes to Table 3.) A look at Table 3 will show that each of the political indicators is much more strongly related to political trust than was our measure of trust in people. These are substantial relationships, indicating the power of a political explanation. Controlling for education does not change the basic picture in two of the three cases, even though a variable like political competence is strongly related to education. However, the effect of education on the gamma between trust and expectations of equal treatment is worth further discussion.

First of all, a feeling that one would receive worse treatment than other people in attempting to solve a problem at a government office is more strongly related to political trust for whites than for blacks. Naturally, there are more blacks who expect unequal treatment (35 percent versus 12 percent of the whites), but if we correctly gauge the intensity of emotion reflected in answers to this question in our survey, white respondents who believe they would receive a harder time at a government office are even angrier than blacks with similar expectations. Many of the whites are evidently convinced that blacks receive special treatment and are given favors without deserving them. One typical white respondent said he would be given unequal treatment

> because the white people are discriminated [against]. If you have a home and are working and you have pride, they just don't come to your assistance. One who has no will power or pride, they'll give you assistance.[43]

Table 3
Correlations (Gamma) Between Political Expectations
and Political Trust, by Race and Education

Political experiences and expectations	Blacks			Whites		
	Zero-order	Low[a] educa-tion	High[a] educa-tion	Zero-order	Low[a] educa-tion	High[a] educa-tion
Political competence[b]	.40	.37	.45	.32	.30	.44
Impact of governmental actions[c]	.40	.42	.43	.32	.34	.21
Expectations of equal treatment[d]	.26	.32	.13	.42	.51	.33
(N) =	(461)	(322)	(122)	(394)	(254)	(124)

[a]Respondents in the low education group include all individuals who have completed high school, while those in the high education group have, at minimum, gone beyond high school to either special training or college. These definitions of low and high education are retained throughout the paper. The Ns for each group are also the same. We chose education as a status indicator and dichotomized the sample in order to preserve the maximum number of cases for the analysis.

[b]The following items were used in the political competence index:
1. How much political power do you think people like you have? A great deal, some, not very much, or none?
2. Suppose a law were being considered by the Congress in Washington that you considered very unjust or harmful. What do you think you could do about it?
   2a. If you made an effort to change this law, how likely is it that you would succeed: very likely, somewhat likely, or not very likely?
3. Suppose a law were being considered by the common council that you considered very unjust or harmful. What do you think you could do about it?
   3a. If you made an effort to change this law, how likely is it that you would succeed: very likely, somewhat likely, or not very likely?

[c]How much difference do you think it makes to people like yourself what the government in Washington does? A good deal, some, or not very much?

[d]Suppose that there was some question that you had to take to a government office – for example, a tax question, a welfare allotment, or a housing regulation. Do you think that most likely you would be given a harder time than other people, would be treated about the same as anyone else, or would be treated a little better than most people.

All variables are coded so that positive experiences and expectations receive high scores.

For the minority of whites with such extreme views (especially those in the lower education group), the emerging assertiveness of blacks is clearly a factor of the utmost importance in determining their level of political trust.

Expectations of treatment in a government office is of less direct importance for blacks, especially the upper educated group. This is not because all upper status blacks expect equal treatment (25 percent do not), but results from the fact that there is a relatively flat distribution of political trust scores across categories of our expectations-of-equal-treatment measure. One possible explanation, which is supported by data we will now present, is that distrust among upper status blacks does not arise so much from actual or expected discrimination as from empathy for others in the black community who experience these insults in worse form. The stronger relationship for lower education blacks indicates a more direct effect of expected discrimination on trust for this group, but even here the effect is weaker than for whites. Something more than blatant personal mistreatment underlies black political distrust.

D. As a Function of Feelings of Deprivation

There is a large literature concerning the relationship between psychological deprivation and political unrest (defined as violence or propensity to engage in violent behavior)[44] and a developing literature, using aggregate data, which speculates about the relationship between deprivation and feelings that the government is not legitimate.[45] One of the best psychological measures of deprivation now available is the Cantril Self-Anchoring Scale which indicates the discrepancy between an individual's definition of the "best possible life" for him and his past, present, or future situations.[46] After each respondent gives a definition of the life "he would most like to lead" in his own words, he is shown a picture of a ladder with ten rungs and asked to imagine that the top rung represents the best possible life which he has just described. He is then asked to rank, in comparison with his ideal, his present life, his life five years ago, and what he expects his life to be like five years in the future. A person's position on these scales is a function of his own definition of the best possible state of affairs. His standards may be determined by class or race models, or expectations created by the mass media, but no simple objective indicator of achievement like income or occupation will be an adequate substitute for this psychological measure.[47]

We use these measures of deprivation as indicators, based on standards meaningful to each individual, of a deep-rooted dissatisfaction or expectation of dissatisfaction which may be blamed on government. They are conceptually and empirically independent of the *political*-expectations indices employed in the previous section since a person may be deeply dissatisfied with the general course of his life, but feel politically powerful, believe he receives equal treatment from government and feel that governmental outputs have a beneficial impact. In other words, the two sets of indicators are related, but do not have the same psychological significance for the individual, and each has an independent effect on political trust.[48]

We employed two sets of self-anchoring scales in our surveys: One was the standard "best possible life" question explained in note 46 and a second sought the respondents' definitions of the "best possible race relations" as a base for selecting rungs on a ladder running from 0 to 10.[49] Both whites and blacks gave a wide variety of definitions of the "best possible life" in response to that question, with almost none of them directly involving race relations. While whites were much more satisfied with their past and present lives, both racial groups are strongly optimistic about the future.[50] When we turn to race relations we find very substantial differences in the patterns of answers. Blacks talk almost exclusively in terms of total integration, better personal relationships with whites, the disappearance of color consciousness, and respect and dignity for all, while more than 30 percent of the whites spontaneously endorse segregation or separation of some kind. In addition, many more whites than blacks are pessimistic about the future in this area[51] with the correlation between expressed separationist feelings and whites scores on the future ladder at (Gamma) .40.[52] The white community, not the black, is divided over the desirability of integration and whites are more depressed than blacks about the prospects for future race relations in Detroit.

This fact is reflected in Table 4 which indicates how much more potent a predictor of political trust the present and especially the future race relations ladders[53] are for whites than for blacks. The situation is

Table 4
Correlations (Gamma) Between Ladder Positions on Self-anchoring Scales and Political Trust, by Race and Education

Scales*	Blacks Zero-order	Low education	High education	Whites Zero-order	Low education	High education
"Best possible life" ladders						
Past life	.18	.27	−.12	.02	.06	.03
Present life	.31	.39	.05	.20	.23	.20
Future life	.30	.38	−.11	.15	.14	.13
"Best possible race relations" ladders						
Past race relations	.16	.22	.04	−.04	−.07	.00
Present race relations	.13	.23	−.17	.26	.29	.17
Future race relations	.10	.17	−.11	.37	.40	.29

*The ladders were trichotomized as follows: 1-3 = 0; 4-6 = 1; 7-10 = 2. (This is the division used by Cantril, *The Pattern of Human Concern* [New Brunswick: Rutgers University Press, 1965], p. 257.) Therefore, a positive coefficient indicates that the higher a person's score on the various ladders, the higher his trust in government.

reversed when we look at the "best possible life" ladders. Here the correlations are higher for the black sample. In addition, for whites, controlling for education has only mild effects on the relationship between the ladders and trust (the high education group is somewhat more homogenous on the ladders than the low education group), but it substantially increases the correlations in the low education black group. The signs are actually reversed in four of six cases for the high education black group where those who are dissatisfied are actually more trusting than those who are satisfied.

If we look back at the discussion of the correlation in Table 3 between expectations of equal treatment and political trust we recognize certain similarities to the relationships we are now describing; in both cases a racial question is a better predictor of trust in the white community, and in both cases the upper education black group is quite different from the lower education black group. In summary:

> 1. Blacks are less likely than whites to lose faith in the government when they expect discriminatory treatment in a government office or when they see failures in achieving the pattern of race relations they favor. For high education blacks there are even cases when the relationship between the race relations ladders and political trust is negative.
> 2. Lower status blacks tend to be very bitter about government when they fail to achieve their personal goals in life while higher status blacks do not.
> 3. While higher status black people are somewhat more satisfied and less discriminated against than lower status blacks, this is not enough to account for the differences in relationships found here since there is a fairly uniform level of trust no matter how poorly the higher status person expects to be treated or how deprived he feels. In fact, the deprived high education black person is likely to be a little more trusting than those in the same group who are relatively satisfied.

The data for the white community are relatively easy to interpret: racial issues, especially those involving integration and governmental treatment of blacks become so important that they have superseded considerations of personal achievement, especially for the lower status group. Some of this may be due to the fact that our survey was conducted soon after a major disturbance, but large numbers of whites are clearly upset about the future of race relations and some actually feel discriminated against because of their race.[54] Government officials are faced with an increasingly angry, bitter and frightened group of white people who feel persecuted and unrepresented.[55] These feelings are undermining their basic trust in government and making them much more sympathetic to political candidates who call for repression of the blacks in the name of law and order.

A more complex process is at work in the black community. In Table 5 we see that the indicators of reported discrimination are differentially related to political trust for the lower and upper education segments of the black sample. Experiences of discrimination in obtaining housing or on the job are associated with distrust for the lower education group, but not the upper education group. Even police mistreatment, the most volatile issue in Detroit's black community, is much more strongly related to political distrust in the lower education segment of the population. (This is not because only lower status blacks experience mis-

Table 5

Correlations (Gamma) Between (A) Personal Experiences of Discrimination and (B) Recognition of Serious Community Problems and Political Trust for Blacks, by Education

	Zero-order	Low education	High education
(A) *Personal experiences*			
Personal experiences of discrimination index (Police excepted)[a]	−.15	−.18	.00
Personal experiences of police mistreatment[b]	−.43	−.57	−.21
(B) *Recognition of serious community problems*			
Crowded conditions	.02	.05	−.22
Poor education	−.01	.00	−.21
The way the police act	−.21	−.21	−.24

[a]This is a simple additive index of personal experiences of discrimination in Detroit in obtaining housing, in the schools, from a landlord, or in obtaining, holding or advancing on a job.

[b]This is an index of reports of police mistreatment experienced by the person himself.

A negative coefficient indicates that the more a person has been discriminated against, mistreated, or recognizes a community problem as serious, the lower his trust in government.

treatment, since about 15 percent of each group report some form of bad experience.) However, when the issue is simply whether a community problem is recognized as important or not, the relationship between recognition and distrust is stronger in the upper education group. Their distrust, unlike that of the lower education respondents, may not be rooted so much in concerns about *personal* experiences of expectations, nor even in considerations of larger and more abstract feelings about the conditions of race relations in Detroit, but in *empathy*—a feeling of identification with the black political and social community which includes persons from all social classes. This is part of a group identification gaining momentum in the middle class which identifies the fortunes of the black community, rather than prospects of the individual, as the key in evaluating decisions and institutions.[56] This could be the reason that our ladder measures of personal achievement are so successful as predictors for the lower education group and yet so unsuccessful for the upper education group. If some upper status blacks are identifying with others in the community who are persecuted, we would expect segments of both the lower and upper status groups to share a racial ideology of protest which is related to feelings of political trust. We will test this proposition in the next section.

VII. POLITICAL TRUST AND RACIAL IDEOLOGY

Our data give clear evidence of a developing racial ideology in Detroit's black community.[57] The elements of this belief system include a favorable interpretation of black power, the choice of militant black leaders as representatives of one's own point of view on race relations and a revolutionary interpretation of the meaning or significance of the 1967 disturbances. Scholars studying other cities have reached similar conclusions.[58] This ideology is not a manifestation of growing sentiments for separation,[59] but of a militantly expressed ideology of protest which demands quick and effective action to better conditions for *all* black people. Unfortunately, it is opposed by an equally militant ideology held by a large segment of the white community which demands racial separation and the curtailment of programs designed to aid disadvantaged blacks. These are the kinds of emotional issues which destroy trust in government and undermine the normal constraints on intemperate or even violent political behavior.

We will now examine the relationship between elements of these belief systems and political trust. Here, even more than in the previous section on explanations of political trust, we are dealing with a process in which a set of beliefs influences the level of trust which in turn influences or deepens the beliefs; the man who sees the 1967 riot as a justified reaction to social injustice is more likely to develop or sustain distrust of the government, but, in a cumulative spiral, this distrust strengthens his belief in the justification of the riot as a reaction to oppression. Since we are measuring these phenomena at a single point in time we cannot give our process model an adequate empirical test. Before progress can be made in verifying and refining our model, data on the same individuals must be collected on several different occasions.

Bearing in mind the restrictions placed on our efforts by the nature of our data, we turn first to our black respondents (Table 6) and see that each of the elements we have measured in the developing racial ideology is related to political trust. Blacks who label the 1967 disturbances as a

Table 6
Correlations (Gamma) Between Militant Ideology and Political Trust
for Blacks, by Education

	Zero-order	*Low education*	*High education*
Favorable interpretation of "black power"[a]	−.39	−.39	−.37
Favorable explanation of the July, 1967, disturbance[b]	−.22	−.20	−.25
Leader best representing the respondents views on relations between the races[c]	−.23	−.19	−.32

[a]Favorable interpretations of black power (given a high score on this index) consist almost exclusively of notions about a "fair share" for blacks or "racial unity" in the black community as a tactic in bettering conditions. See Aberbach and Walker, *op. cit.,* for an extensive discussion of this.

[b]This is an index in which a high score indicates a revolutionary label for the disturbance and a belief that those who took part did so not because they were riffraff or criminals, but because they had been mistreated by society.

[c]Respondents selected, without any cues from the interviewer, the leader who "best represented" their views on relations between the races. The selections were then scored from militant black leaders (high) through to conservative white leaders. See Aberbach and Walker, *op. cit.* (1970), p. 385, for distributions.

revolutionary protest against mistreatment, favorably interpret the black power slogan, or select a militant as the leader best representing their views on relations between the races, are also likely to distrust the government. These sentiments are not a function of social status and, as we can see, the relationships are as strong or stronger for the upper educated black group as for blacks with lower levels of educational achievement. We should emphasize that these relationships are quite strong when we take into account the fact that the elements in the black ideology are all measured with open-ended survey questions. It is possible, therefore, to speak as we did before of a *black political commu-*

nity, crossing social class lines, marked by a developing racial ideology focused on militancy and pride and connected with a strong distrust of government. This growing solidarity is a political phenomenon of the utmost importance for a minority community which needs to mobilize the skills of its growing middle class.

Turning now to the white community, we again find that racial variables are of great importance as predictors of trust, only here views on integration versus separation and spending public money to improve conditions in the ghetto are key factors in determining the level of trust. Whites are almost evenly divided on these issues (about 50 percent of our white sample favor integration and approximately the same percentage endorse spending more money).[60] Such an overwhelming majority of blacks (over 90 percent) favor both, however, that analysis of the correlates on these questions is not very fruitful.

The racial issue and the means of dealing with it inspire great emotion in the white community and threaten to undermine trust in the government for a substantial segment of the population. As Table 7 demonstrates, separationists and those opposed to spending more money to improve ghetto conditions are decidedly more distrustful of government than integrationists and those willing to spend more money. The

Table 7
Correlations (Gamma) Between Attitudes on Integration, Public
Expenditures and Political Trust for Whites, by Education

	Zero-order	Low education	High education
Integration[a]	.28	.29	.28
More money for improve-ments[b]	.35	.31	.39

[a]This is a summary index of responses to items calling for the endorsement or rejection of a general policy of integration or separation, school integration and the description of the "best possible race relations" coded according to the degree of integration or separation endorsed. We used the word separation in preference to segregation to insure that black respondents could comfortably endorse this alternative, only 2% did so.

[b]The following close-ended question was asked in the middle of our section on the riot and conditions in the black community: "Do you feel that more money or less money should be spent on trying to improve conditions?"

relationships hold for those with high levels of educational achievement as well as those with lower levels of education. In addition, attitudes on integration and scores on the race relations ladders have independent effects on the level of trust,[61] so that, for example, integrationists who are dissatisfied with the current or emerging course of race relations are more distrustful of the government than those who are satisfied, and they are also more distrustful than satisfied or optimistic segregationists. It is easy to envision situations in which events or governmental policies and pronouncements embitter both segregationists and integrationists, thereby dealing a double blow to the level of political trust in the white community.

VIII. POLITICAL DISTRUST AND POLITICAL BEHAVIOR

Distrust of the government creates a tension in the polity which can build for some time, but ultimately seeks release. Among other things, people can revolt, engage in limited displays of violence like riots, demonstrate, or support candidates for elective office who give voice to their fears and frustrations. The mode of expression depends on the depth of the discontent, traditions of violence in the society, loyal coercive forces available to the government, and the availability of free. electoral processes.[62] At this point many distrustful blacks have taken to the streets and distrustful whites troop to the polls to vote for so-called "law and order" candidates.

We asked respondents whether they could "imagine any situation" in which they would take part in a disturbance like the one Detroit had in July of 1967 and we also conducted a mock mayoral election in which the choice lay between the incumbent mayor (Jerome Cavanaugh) and a very vocal member of the Detroit Common Council (Mary Beck) who had been courting backlash support. Since very few whites could envisage taking part in a disturbance, of the 1967 variety at least, and few blacks would ever vote for Miss Beck, we could only employ each indicator for one racial group. This is simply a matter of convenience. We certainly do not wish to imply that blacks would never vote for extremist candidates or that whites would never engage in violence.

As Table 8 indicates, distrustful whites are indeed strongly in favor of Miss Beck and distrustful blacks are better able to imagine situations in which they would riot. Distrust clearly stimulates a willingness to engage in violence or favorably predisposes people toward voting for extremist candidates. Moreover, high levels of trust serve to dampen the behavioral impact of adverse experiences while low levels of trust lead to volatile situations in which each insult increases the probability of extreme behavior. In statistical terms, political distrust and adverse experiences interact.

A classic example of this interaction can be seen in the Detroit black community where political distrust and reported experiences of

Table 8
Political Distrust and Potential Political Behavior for Blacks and Whites

	Blacks			*Whites*		
				If the election for mayor of Detroit were held tomorrow and the candidates were		
Political trust	Can you imagine a situation in which you would riot?*			Jerome Cavanaugh and Mary Beck, who would you vote for?		
	Yes or maybe	*No*	*(N)*	*Beck*	*Cavanaugh*	*(N)*
Low 0	54	46	(129)	74	25	(42)
1	35	65	(86)	42	58	(36)
2	35	65	(94)	52	48	(60)
3	21	79	(75)	39	61	(46)
High 4	17	83	(59)	26	74	(69)
	Gamma = .40			Gamma = .35		
			(Percentages are across.)			

*The word "riot" was not actually used. Respondents were asked early in the interviews to give their own label to the events of July, 1967, and this term was used throughout by the interviewer.

discrimination interact to inspire willingness to engage in a civil disturbance (See Table 9). When trust is low, experiences of discrimination have a very powerful effect on a person's ability to imagine a situation in which he could take part in a civil disturbance, but high trust seems to serve as a dike which blunts somewhat the political effects of these experiences. Persons who are low in trust seem to interpret each experience of discrimination as further proof that the political system is evil and must be dealt with by any means, while those who are trusting have a less severe reaction to these experiences. High levels of trust are resources which governments can use to gain time in order to correct

Table 9
Experiences of Discrimination and Willingness to Take Part in a Civil Disturbance by Level of Political Trust for Blacks*

Trust	Low (0–1)			High (2–4)		
Reported experiences of discrimination	Can you imagine a situation in which you would riot?					
	Yes or maybe	*No*	*(N)*	*Yes or maybe*	*No*	*(N)*
Few (0–1)	30	70	(122)	22	78	(139)
Medium (2)	60	40	(31)	30	70	(37)
Many (3–4)	71	29	(61)	36	64	(44)
	Gamma = −.65			Gamma = −.26		
			(Percentages are across.)			

*This is a simple additive index of reports of personal experiences of discrimination in Detroit in obtaining housing, in the schools, from a landlord, or in obtaining, holding, or advancing on a job.

wrongs in the society. When trust is low injustices have a stronger and more immediate impact since the reservoir of good will has been destroyed. . . .

X. POLICY IMPLICATIONS

Emerging from our analysis are the outlines of an ominous confrontation between the races. The growing sense of solidarity and racial identification among blacks is being matched by rising, increasingly bitter resentment among elements of the white community. More often than in past decades, the anger and resentment of both sides is being translated from generalized racial hostility into focused political demands for specific programs or policies from agencies of both local and national government. These developing tensions may precipitate the kinds of social changes being called for by blacks, but they could lead to an altogether different result. If both black and white citizens lose sufficient confidence in the essential trustworthiness of the government, the society may reach its political "tipping-point," constraints on intemperate or even violent protest may completely disappear, and the stage will be set either for large-scale anti-democratic efforts at change by blacks and/or massive attempts at reaction and repression by whites.

The government's success in avoiding a complete break-down in race relations depends, to a significant degree, on its success in building political trust. Declining trust can be a stimulant to social change. The direction or nature of the changes, however, will be determined by the reactions of the government or the rest of society to the demands of distrustful groups. If public officials are able to build or maintain high levels of trust, a broader range of policy options are opened for consideration and governments can more easily risk short term opposition from some groups in the hope of achieving an important long term result. When trust is low, however, groups are unlikely to give the government the benefit of the doubt and may begin to call for immediate fulfillment of their demands. A dangerous process of competitive mobilization may begin. In Gamson's words: "The presentation of demands by one group stimulates their presentation by others. Thus, it is possible for the loss of trust to encourage a 'deflationary' spiral akin to a run on the bank."[63] The level of trust, in other words, determines the amount of patience or forbearance citizens can be expected to exercise. Since the problems of finding an equitable and peaceful new basis for racial harmony cannot be quickly solved, governments must have time to deal with them successfully. By building trust, governments may buy the time they need.

The level of political trust existing at any time is the result of a

156   J. D. Aberbach & J. L. Walker

complex process involving interactions with many variables. It is a changing reflection of a society's politically relevant conflicts and tensions. When trust is high, officials are in a better position to make commitments or adopt controversial policies aimed at the solution of difficult problems. Since high levels of trust are an important resource which cushions the impact of programs some groups find intensely objectionable, whenever substantial segments of the population begin to grow distrustful, it is important for the government to act before the level of trust drops to the point where the resources to solve societal problems and rebuild trust cannot be mustered. When distrust is growing leaders are faced with the delicate problem of making policies which reach the sources of dissatisfaction at a time when any action is likely to make some group angry—often even some of those among their traditional political constituencies. This is a high political price which leaders seek to avoid, thereby making the problem worse for themselves and often much worse for their successors. It is difficult to devise policies which can solve social problems, and still more difficult to build coalitions which can enact these policies and support their enforcement. The problem is doubly difficult when political trust is low. . . .

NOTES

[1] Joseph Tussman, *Obligation and the Body Politic* (New York: Oxford University Press, 1960), p. 23.

[2] George Sabine, "The Two Democratic Traditions," *The Philosophical Review,* 61 (1952), p. 471.

[3] William A. Gamson, *Power and Discontent* (Homewood, Ill.: Dorsey, 1968), pp. 45–46.

[4] Gabriel A. Almond and Sidney Verba, *The Civic Culture: Political Attitudes and Democracy in Five Nations* (Princeton: Princeton University Press, 1963), p. 490.

[5] Gamson's work, *op. cit.,* builds on the concerns of Parsons and Easton. See, especially, Talcott Parsons, "Some Reflections on the Place of Force in Social Process" in Harry Eckstein (ed.), *Internal War* (New York: Free Press, 1964), pp. 33–70, and David Easton, *A Systems Analysis of Political Life* (New York: Wiley, 1965).

[6] Robert E. Agger, Marshall N. Goldstein and Stanley A. Pearl, "Political Cynicism: Measurement and Meaning," *The Journal of Politics,* 23 (1961), 477–506 and Herbert McClosky, "Consensus and Ideology in American Politics," *American Political Science Review* (1964), 361–383.

[7] Donald E. Stokes, "Popular Evaluations of Government: An Empirical Assessment," in Harlan Cleveland and Harold D. Lasswell (eds.), *Ethics and*

Bigness: Scientific, Academic, Religious, Political and Military (New York: Harper, 1962), pp. 61–73; and Joel D. Aberbach, *Alienation and Race* (unpublished Ph.D. Dissertation, Yale University, 1967), especially pp. 102–126 and 206–208.

[8]Stokes, *op. cit.,* p. 68; Agger, *op. cit.,* p. 494; and Edgar Litt, "Political Cynicism and Political Futility," *The Journal of Politics,* 23 (1963), p. 321, Table 5.

[9]Litt, *op. cit.,* p. 320, Table 2.

[10]See Morris Rosenberg, "Misanthropy and Political Ideology," *American Sociological Review,* 21 (1956), 600–695.

[11]Litt, *op. cit.,* p. 320, Table 1.

[12]*Ibid,* p. 319.

[13]*Ibid,* p. 320.

[14]*Ibid.,* pp. 317. Litt finds that the "degree of personal trust, unrelated to political cynicism in Boston, is directly related to the expression of cynical comments about politicians in the suburban community."

[15]Stokes, *op. cit.,* p. 67.

[16]*Ibid.,* p. 64.

[17]McClosky, *op. cit.,* p. 370.

[18]See Aberbach, *op. cit.,* pp. 25–42 for a detailed discussion of the importance of specifying the focus in measuring disaffection and pp. 46–56 for a critique of the political trust literature using this perspective. A briefer discussion can be found in Joel D. Aberbach, "Alienation and Political Behavior," *American Political Science Review,* 63 (1969), pp. 86–90. See, also, Kenneth Keniston, *The Uncommitted: Alienated Youth in American Society* (New York: Harcourt, Brace & World, 1965), pp. 453–455.

[19]Inter-University Consortium for Political Research (ICPR), *1966 Election Study* (Ann Arbor, 1968), p. 129.

[20]Gamson, *op. cit.,* p. 49.

[21]*Ibid.,* p. 51. Gamson suggests a series of conditions which discourage the generalization of political distrust. Among them are the disaggregation of large issues into smaller ones, an emphasis on the ad hoc nature of decisions (so that citizens do not see in negative decisions the application of general rules or principles), and a structural situation in which memberships of groups with varying goals and experiences overlap.

[22]Robert E. Lane, *Political Life* (Glencoe: Free Press, 1959), p. 164.

[23]M. Kent Jennings and Richard G. Niemi discuss political trust in these terms on p. 177 of their article on "The Transmission of Political Values from Parent to Child," *American Political Science Review,* 62 (1968), 169–184.

[24]This paper is based on data gathered in 1967 in Detroit. In 1968 we re-interviewed a random subsample of the original sample (N = 295) and we will interview a larger number of respondents in 1970, many of them for the third time. Our study will also include interviews done in 1967 and 1970 with administrators in the Detroit city government and with business, civic and labor leaders who are members of the New Detroit Committee.

[25]Riot areas were defined by a location map of fires considered riot-related by the Detroit Fire Department.

[26]The wording of these questions is drawn from Survey Research Center questionnaires. Preliminary statements of the kind cited above were included. See ICPR, *op. cit.,* pp. 129–132.

[27]A single political trust index was constructed. The items formed a clear dimension when data from the study were factor-analyzed. The factor analyses (varimax rotation) were performed on the whole data-set and separately for blacks and whites. Questions on Detroit and Washington are equally weighted so that the index runs from 0 to 4.

[28]For confirmation of this view see: Edward C. Banfield, *Big City Politics* (New York: Random House, 1965), pp. 51–65; and David Greenstone, *Report on the Politics of Detroit* (Joint Center for Urban Studies of the Massachusetts Institute of Technology and Harvard University, 1961), Chapter 2.

[29]See Stokes, *op. cit.*, pp. 61–73 and Aberbach (1967), *op. cit.*, pp. 119–126.

[30]For example, see William Brink and Louis Harris, *The Negro Revolution in America* (New York: Simon and Schuster, 1964), pp. 131 and 232–233 on Negro attitudes towards various political institutions and figures.

[31]Louis E. Lomax, *The Negro Revolt* (New York: Harper and Row, 1962), p. 250; and also see Gunnar Myrdal, *An American Dilemma* (New York: Harper and Row, 1944), pp. 3–5, 880 and 1007 on the Negro as an "exaggerated American."

[32]Lane, *op. cit.,* p. 164.

[33]See Rosenberg, *op. cit.* The version we used consists of two of the three questions regularly asked by SRC in their surveys. They are:

1. Generally speaking, would you say that most people can be trusted or that you can't be too careful in dealing with people?

2. Do you think that most people would try to take advantage of you if they got a chance or would they try to be fair?

[34]See Aberbach, *op. cit.* (1969), pp. 92–93 for somewhat similar findings for whites using 1964 SRC national sample data.

[35]Aberbach, *op. cit.* (1967), pp. 104–114.

[36]The notion of a "theory of social disadvantages" as a general explanation for attitudes of estrangement is developed at length by Marvin E. Olsen, "Political Assimilation, Social Opportunities, and Political Alienation" (unpublished Ph.D. Dissertation, The University of Michigan, 1965).

[37]For example, the correlation (Gamma) between education and political trust is .08 for blacks and .03 for whites.

[38]The correlation (Gamma) between regional birthplace and political trust is .14 for blacks and .13 for whites.

[39]The correlation (Gamma) between active affiliation with a church and political trust is .24 for blacks and .15 for whites.

[40]Gamson, *op. cit.*, p. 51.

[41]Stokes, *op. cit.,* p. 67: "When the individual's sense of political efficacy is compared with his positive or negative attitude toward government, it is apparent that a sense of ineffectiveness is coupled with feelings of hostility. This relation is more than a tautology. In other cultures or other historical eras a sense of ineffectiveness might well be associated with a positive feeling. In the context of democratic values, feelings of powerlessness toward public authority tend to create feelings of hostility toward that authority."

[42]Gamson, *op. cit.*, p. 51.

[43]This quote is from one of the respondents included in our 1968 panel. The 1967 questionnaire did not probe answers to the close-ended question on equal treatment in a government office. After examining the 1967 interview protocols,

we believed that whites who felt they would receive unequal treatment often ascribed this to reverse discrimination and we used the 1968 interviews to confirm this hypothesis.

A poll by the Gallup organization reported in *Newsweek* (October 6, 1969) gives evidence of somewhat similar feelings among "a substantial minority of whites" that "the black man already has the advantage." (p. 45).

[44]For examples of analyses employing aggregate data see Ivo K. Feierabend, Rosalind L. Feierabend, and Betty A. Nesvold, "Social Change and Political Violence: Cross-National Patterns" and James C. Davies, "The J-Curve of Rising and Declining Satisfactions as a Cause of Some Great Revolutions and a Contained Rebellion," pp. 632–688 and 690–731 respectively in Hugh D. Graham and Ted R. Gurr (eds.), *The History of Violence in America* (New York: Bantam, 1969). An example of the use of psychological data is Don R. Bowen, Elinor Bowen, Sheldon Gawiser and Louis H. Masotti, "Deprivation, Mobility and Orientation Toward Protest of the Urban Poor," pp. 174–187 in Louis H. Masotti and Don R. Bowen (eds.), *Riots and Rebellion: Civil Violence in the Urban Community* (Beverly Hills: Sage Publications, 1968).

[45]A particularly interesting analysis of this type which is used to speculate about urban unrest in the United States is found in Ted Gurr, "Urban Disorder: Perspective from the Comparative Study of Civil Strife," pp. 51–69 in Masotti and Bowen, *op. cit.* More details on the measures used in Gurr's study can be found in Ted Gurr, "A Causal Model of Civil Strife: A Comparative Analysis," *American Political Science Review,* 62 (1968), 1104–1125.

[46]See Hadley C. Cantril, *The Pattern of Human Concerns* (New Brunswick: Rutgers University Press, 1965). Our respondents were given the following set of questions:

Now could you briefly tell me what would be the best possible life for you? In other words, how would you describe the life you would most like to lead, the most perfect life as you see it? (Show R card with a Ladder.)

Now suppose that the top of the ladder represents the best possible life for you, the one you just described, and the bottom represents the worst possible life for you.

"Present Life"A.   Where on the ladder do you feel you personally stand at the present time?

"Past Life"   B.   Where on the ladder would you say you stood five years ago?

"Future Life" C.   Where on the ladder do you think you will be five years from now?

[47]In our study, for example, income is correlated (Gamma) .29 for whites and .23 for blacks with position on the "present life" ladder. Income is thus a meaningful predictor, but these are far short of simple one-to-one relationships.

[48]This proposition was tested for each racial group by a multiple regression analysis in which the measures of trust in people, the background factors, political experiences and expectations, and the ladders were used as predictors of political trust. The political variables and the relevant ladders each had an independent effect on trust with all of the other variables controlled. Multiple R's were .52 for the blacks and .49 for the whites.

[49]See footnote 46 above for the wording on the "best possible life" ques-

tions. The "best possible race relations" items were in the same form with the following sentences as the initial stimulus:

Here in Detroit, as in many places, different races of people are living together in the same communities. Now I would like for you to think about the very best way that Negroes and white people could live in the same place together. In other words, what would be the very best kind of race relations, the most perfect you could imagine?

This item was adapted from that used by Donald R. Matthews and James W. Prothro, *Negroes and the New Southern Politics* (New York: Harcourt, Brace and World, 1966), pp. 285–294, 513–514.

[50]Income and job advancement were desired by 28% of the blacks and 16% of the whites, good health or family life by 22% of the blacks and 20% of the whites and personal property (homes, cars, etc.) by 15% of the blacks and 11% of the whites. The major difference was that 13% of the whites (as opposed to 3% of the blacks) said the life they were now living was the best possible and 23% of the whites, compared with 9% of the blacks, mentioned peace and tranquility.

% Scoring High (7–10) on "Best Possible Life" Ladders, by Race

	Past Life	Present Life	Future Life
Blacks	13%	23%	64%
Whites	49%	47%	66%

We will present more complete descriptions and analysis of the answers to the "best possible life" question in Joel D. Aberbach and Jack L. Walker, *Race and the Urban Community* (Boston: Little Brown, forthcoming).

[51]Our "Best Possible Race Relations" ladders yielded the following results:

% Scoring High (7–10) on "Best Possible Race Relations" Ladders, by Race

	Past Race Relations	Present Race Relations	Future Race Relations
Blacks	10%	22%	61%
Whites	39%.	23%	40%

[52]The correlation (Gamma) is .09 for blacks because there is virtual unanimity in the black community on integration. See Joel D. Aberbach and Jack L. Walker, "The Meanings of Black Power: A Comparison of White and Black Interpretations of a Political Slogan," *American Political Science Review*, 64 (1970), p. 383.

[53]Ted Gurr stresses the importance of "anticipated interference with human goals" in his analysis of discontent. He says that,

analysis of the sources of relative deprivation should take account of both actual and anticipated interference with human goals, as well as of interference with value positions both sought and achieved. Formulations of frustration in terms of the "want: get ratio," which refers only to a discrepancy between sought values and actual attainment, are too simplistic. Man lives mentally in the near future as much as in the present. Actual or anticipated interference with what he has, and with the act of striving itself, are all volatile sources of discontent.

See p. 254 of Ted Gurr, "Psychological Factors in Civil Violence," *World Politics,* 20 (1968), 245–278.

[54]We have already seen above that there are some whites who believe that they would receive unequal treatment at a government office because of their race. Even more astounding, however, is the fact that in our 1968 survey of a random subsample of the original (1967) sample 46% of the whites believed that if they were black they would be either making advances toward their goals in life or advancing more rapidly toward their goals. This compares to 57% giving similar answers in the black community. Unfortunately, this question was not on our 1967 questionnaire.

[55]More than half of the white respondents in our sample could not name any national or local leader who represented their views on race relations and whites actually scored lower than blacks on our measure of subjective political competence. See our discussion of these points in Joel D. Aberbach and Jack L. Walker, "The Meanings of Black Power: A Comparison of White and Black Interpretations of a Political Slogan," a discussion paper issued by the Institute of Public Policy Studies, The University of Michigan, 1968, pp. 27–34.

[56]Lupsha has discussed the same basic phenomenon: "Anger can occur without one's being frustrated or deprived. One can learn that certain events, or violations of one's rights and values, should be responded to with hostility. One can be angry and aggressive because one's values or sense of justice (a learned phenomenon) have been affronted, without any blocking of the individual's goal-directed activity, or awareness of any personal "want-get ratio" deprivation, or any personal feelings of "anticipated frustration." One can be angry and aggressive simply because one believes the behaviors of the situation are wrong or illegitimate." See p. 288 of Peter A. Lupsha, "On Theories of Urban Violence," *Urban Affairs Quarterly* (1969), 273–296.

[57]Aberbach and Walker, *op. cit.* (1970), pp. 379–386.

[58]See, for example, T. M. Tomlinson, "The Development of a Riot Ideology among Urban Negroes," *American Behavioral Scientist* (1968), 27–31.

[59]Less than 2 percent of our black sample endorsed the idea of the separation of the races. This is not surprising in light of the history of the concept integration as a symbol of equality in the black community. We used the word separation in our questions in order to overcome the obvious connotations of segregation, but few of our respondents were attracted by the term and almost none used it spontaneously in their definitions of the "best possible race relations." Even among intellectuals, most of the debate about race relations revolved around various forms of social pluralism as opposed to assimilation. One of the major goals of our panel study is to examine the ways in which people modify their ideals about desirable forms of race relations and community goals

through time. See Aberbach and Walker, *op. cit.* (1970), p. 383, especially footnote 49.

[60]The correlation (Gamma) between the two is .49 for whites. The exact distributions by race on spending public money are as follows:

Spend More Money to Improve Conditions

	More	Same	Less	DK, NA	
Blacks	94%	4	1	1	= 100%
Whites	50%	28	19	3	= 100%

[61]For example, the correlation (Gamma) between political trust and scores on the future race relations ladder is .36 for segregationists and .27 for integrationists. It is .37 for the entire white sample.

[62]Gurr, "Urban Disorder: Perspectives from the Comparative Study of Civil Strife," *op. cit.* See Aberbach, *op. cit.* (1969) for an extended discussion of political distrust and political behavior.

[63]Gamson, *op. cit.*, p. 45.

PART THREE

Policy Outputs and Black Political Support

The policy outputs of the political system are a central consideration, particularly in the development of specific support. The concept of specific support suggests that if blacks succeed in obtaining desired policy decisions, their behavior and attitudes toward the government should become more favorable. As has been suggested earlier, variations in black support levels for local and national governments may result from differences in the demand satisfaction derived from the governmental units.

If evaluations of the performance of political authorities, or less specifically the government, become extremely low, drastic steps may be taken in an attempt to achieve demand satisfaction by showing the extent of current disaffection. Whether policy dissatisfaction be a cause or a rationalization, riot participants have often mentioned public policies in explaining riots. Police mistreatment, racial discrimination, and inadequate job opportunities have been cited as major considerations leading to violent outbursts. The need for specific support is especially critical when diffuse support is already low.

Until quite recently, there was scant likelihood that blacks could succeed in obtaining favorable policy decisions. In the South, where most blacks lived, almost all of them had been denied the franchise.[1] In most parts of the North blacks were too few or too scattered to be an important component in successful political coalitions.

In recent years, it can be argued, blacks have reached the threshold at which they can become effective in shaping public policy. Reapportionment in accord with the Supreme Court's one-man, one-vote edict coupled with the urban concentration of blacks has produced a growing number of constituencies, North and South, in which blacks have won public office. Moreover, in the 11 states that comprised the Confederacy the registration of 2 million voters in the wake of the Civil Rights Acts of 1957, 1960, 1964, and the Voting Rights Act of 1965 has been instrumental in the election of candidates of both races. Latest figures show 1,769 elected black officials in the country of whom 665 are in the South.[2] Also, a number of white office holders at all levels have received their margin of victory from black voters.[3]

Despite these gains, blacks have won control of relatively few city or county governments; black office holders remain a small minority in state and national legislatures, bureaucracies, and judiciaries. Nonetheless, blacks, as well as sympathetic whites who have come into office with margins of victory provided by black votes, are often expected by their black supporters to improve conditions. A question that may become increasingly critical is whether black votes are translated into desired policies. A negative answer may produce less trust in political authorities and the regime.

Available evidence suggests that blacks have enjoyed greater success in achieving a more equitable distribution of public goods and services than in altering practices of racial discrimination. Keech, when studying Durham, North Carolina, and Tuskeegee, Alabama, found that once large numbers of blacks began participating in Tuskeegee the more brutal tactics used by police to enforce segregation disappeared. Also, in southern districts in which blacks have become an important factor in electoral outcomes there is a greater likelihood that the ghettoes will have regular garbage pickup, paved streets, running water, and a share of the new public construction.[4] Another positive consequence of black voting may be at least a token number of public jobs for blacks. It does not seem, however, that segregation in public or private facilities diminishes at the local level with a rise in black voters. Of course, it may be that the federal initiative that has typically been prerequisite to breaching racial barriers would not have been undertaken had not the votes of blacks and sympathetic whites become important to various decision makers at the national level.

At the state level in the South, the extent of black voter registration seems to be related to the type of racial appeals made by successful gubernatorial candidates.[5] During the 1950s most southern governors (10 out of 13) made blatant segregationist appeals during their campaigns. This trend reached a peak in the quadrennium 1958–61. Militantly racist stands became less common in the 1960s with seven of the 13 governors who were elected between 1966 and 1969 either urging limited compliance with federal civil rights laws or at least refusing to make race a campaign issue. Improvements (from the standpoint of poor blacks) in economic policies are less often mentioned in the campaigns of future governors. Earl Black notes that

it must be emphasized that the decline of segregationist orato-
ry, where it has occurred, has not been accompanied by much
specific attention to the socio-economic needs of black southerners. Progress in civil rights, as measured by the campaign
rhetoric of white politicians, has been more verbal than substantive.[6]

Although change has been less than might be hoped, it should not be
dismissed altogether. "In view of the tenacity of southern racial norms,
the emergence of *non-segregationist* [governors] is a development of
considerable significance."[7]

In Part Three we present two articles dealing with black influence
on national policy outputs. The first selection, by Harlan Hahn and Joe
Feagin, focuses on urban riots by blacks as a technique of demand input.
Data the authors present show some differences in black-white mass
perceptions and black mass-white elite perceptions concerning the
causes and cures of riots. Survey data they report show that while
blacks tended to attribute the riots to unsatisfactory policy outputs,
whites most frequently saw outside agitators or hoodlums as fomenting
the unrest. A sample of congressmen gave responses more consonant
with those of the white than the black mass samples when asked to
evaluate a number of factors often mentioned as having set the scene for
the riots. Of particular interest is the consistency with which congressmen deny that congressional policy decisions (for example, lack of
federal support for various welfare and training programs) were causal
factors. Similar patterns emerged when the three samples were probed
as to possible remedies for riots. Ghetto residents cited the need for
improvements in various policy areas while the congressmen suggested
vague palliatives and/or supported mobilizing greater force with which
to deal with rioters and other law breakers.

The significance of these findings is that even a form of demand
input that threatens the very stability of the political system failed to
convey the wishes of a significant segment of the black population to
congressmen. Thus, neither peaceful attempts at influence—the
inefficiency of which seemingly was a cause of riots—nor violent protest
seem able to introduce sorely felt black demands into the policy arena.
This suggests that blacks have still not become a critical component in
the electoral coalitions of the vast majority of congressmen. Or, perhaps,
even concerned congressmen have inadequate communications ties with
their black constituents. Obviously, while riots attract attention, they are
an inefficient means of securing favorable policy decisions.

In the second article in Part Three Wolman and Thomas deal with the impact of black influence on policy making in the areas of education and housing. After extensive interviewing of policy makers in these areas, the authors "found an absence of black access and effective black influence at critical stages in the [policy] process." Few blacks were in the policy elite and black groups were only infrequently in the forefront of organizations perceived as involved in shaping housing and education policy. While some policy makers did recognize the absence of black participants and sought to fill this void, indirect representation was judged inadequate.

Taken together the articles in this part describe serious difficulties encountered by blacks both in presenting policy demands and in securing outputs. Their dissatisfaction with the status quo is not heard by many of those in a position to correct the situation. If they seek to work through the accepted channels, they may fail because of 1) a scarcity of blacks or black supporters in policy-shaping positions, 2) an absence of coherent programs formulated by black organizations, 3) a lack of skilled black lobbyists and of requisite resources, or 4) the resources of black groups being concentrated on local rather than national problems.

In addition to organizational deficiencies, certain system characteristics mitigate against blacks' achievement of favorable policies. Our political system is weighted against change, especially when those who demand change are a relatively powerless minority, comprising 10 percent of the public. As we have argued elsewhere, the American political system tends to respond to policy demands incrementally, even in crisis situations.[8] The separation of powers between branches and levels of government, the typical electoral security of incumbents, crowded court dockets, largely autonomous bureaucrats, the seniority system in Congress, and other features of American government constitute a series of hurdles that impedes the realization of black policy goals. Even when action is taken by a legislative or executive agency, the product may be largely symbolic, intended to placate members of the decision-makers' reference groups while altering the status quo only marginally. The Civil Rights Act of 1957 and the Supreme Court decision holding separate but equal schools unconstitutional exemplify instances in which federal actions, at least initially, produced little change.

Another obstacle is the difference between black and white perceptions of the amount of change achieved thus far. Many whites feel that blacks have been given complete equality of opportunity and that anything more would be unwarranted preferential treatment. Blacks whose lives may have changed little as a result of the civil rights laws and court decisions believe that much remains to be done before the disparity in black and white standards of living is eliminated. As evidence, in 1966, 70 percent of a nationwide sample of whites thought blacks were trying to secure changes too quickly. The opposing view was held by blacks, 43 percent of whom thought progress had come too slowly; only 4 percent of blacks judged it too fast.[9] Two years later a 20-percentage point difference existed between the proportion of whites and the proportion of blacks who thought progress in civil rights should come at an accelerated pace.[10] As further evidence that white support for black demands was declining, the proportion of whites thinking marches and protests were an acceptable means of securing civil rights for blacks declined from 53 to 35 percent between 1963 and 1966.[11]

As the expectations of militant blacks are increasing geometrically and patience is declining, piecemeal responses by decision makers may prove wholly inadequate. The consequence may well be that political support, especially among young ghetto blacks, will drop at an accelerating rate.

It seems likely that during the seventies black policy demands will focus on the attainment of economic equality rather than social equality. In a recent article Form and Huber report that blacks

> realize that the system is neither working for their benefit nor working according to their interpretation of democratic ideology. Therefore, pressure for equality – economic, political, and social – becomes a central concern of their ideology.[12]

Seventy-three percent of the poor blacks in the Form and Huber sample saw little equality of opportunity, as compared with 24 percent of the middle income whites and 2 percent of the wealthy whites. With white cognizance of the inequality perceived by blacks being so low, it is problematic whether the government will act to improve the situation of millions of poor blacks.

SUMMARY

To the extent that political support is conditioned by system performance, the outlook is not promising. Black demands, whether articulated through accepted techniques or through violence, have met with little success. The perceptions of blacks and whites as to the causes and cures of black unrest differ greatly with the result that perceptions about the extensiveness of change are at variance. Because of the political handicaps of blacks, the obstacles to change in our political system, and the paucity of support among whites for black goals, it seems questionable whether policy decisions that will engender specific support are likely.

NOTES

[1]For a full discussion of black disfranchisement and the difficulties in reversing this practice, see Harrell R. Rodgers, Jr., and Charles S. Bullock, III, *Law and Social Change: Civil Rights Laws and Their Consequences* (New York: McGraw-Hill, 1972), Chapter 2.

[2]*Congressional Quarterly Weekly Report* (December 11, 1970): 2951.

[3]For some notable examples, see Rodgers and Bullock, *Law and Social Change,* Chapter 2.

[4]William R. Keech, *The Impact of Negro Voting* (Chicago: Rand McNally, 1966); Hugh D. Price, "The Negro and Florida Politics, 1944–1954," *Journal of Politics,* 17 (May, 1955): 198–220; U.S. Commission on Civil Rights, *Voting, 1961* (Washington, D.C.: U.S. Government Printing Office, 1961), p. 187.

[5]Earl Black, "Southern Governors and Political Change: Campaign Stances on Racial Segregation and Economic Development, 1950–1969," *Journal of Politics,* 33 (August, 1971): 703–34.

[6]Black, "Southern Governors and Political Change": 731.

[7]Black, "Southern Governors and Political Change": 711.

[8]Rodgers and Bullock, *Law and Social Change,* Chapter 9.

[9]William Brink and Louis Harris, *Black and White* (New York: Simon and Schuster, 1967), pp. 220 and 258.

[10]Data collected by Louis Harris in 1968, reported in Hazel Erskine, "The Polls: Speed of Racial Integration," *Public Opinion Quarterly,* 32 (Fall, 1968): 523.

[11]Brink and Harris, *Black and White,* p. 222.

[12]William Form and Joan Huber, "Income, Race, and the Ideology of Political Efficacy," *Journal of Politics,* 33 (August, 1971): 688.

Chapter 10

RANK-AND-FILE VERSUS CONGRESSIONAL PERCEPTIONS OF GHETTO RIOTS

Harlan Hahn
Joe R. Feagin

The numerous ghetto riots which erupted in the sixties raised anew the critical issue of the ability of democratic institutions to respond to the needs of a deprived and disaffected minority. As yet, the disorders have not become an organized movement to overturn the existing political structure. The characteristic features of the riots, their confinement to ghetto neighborhoods, the lack of specific targets other than local merchants and police, the relative absence of conflict between black and white civilians, the absence of wide support in the general population, have distinguished them from more violent forms of political upheaval such as revolutions.

While the ghetto riots did not represent an organized attempt to wrest control from existing political authorities, few would argue that they lacked a political purpose. After centuries of frustrating experience with the traditional avenues of political expression, many black Americans displayed their dissatisfaction by adopting a type of protest that could not be ignored. Evidence of dissatisfaction with traditional political mechanisms can be found in the famous Kerner Report, which concluded that the "ineffectiveness of the political structure and grievance mechanisms" was a major complaint in many ghettos. Furthermore, the rioters themselves, according to 1967 Newark and Detroit surveys, were more disaffected with the government and more convinced that anger against politicians was a major cause of the riot than were non-involved ghetto residents; yet these same rioters were actually better informed on political matters than were the non-involved.[2] After

Reprinted from the *Social Science Quarterly,* 51 (September, 1970), pp. 361–73, by permission of the authors and publisher.

169

the failure of other avenues for expressing dissent, such as voting, petitioning government officials, and nonviolent demonstrations, rioting may well have become a desperate method of communicating ghetto frustration to the outside public.[3]

If one can indeed perceive the riots as a form of political protest, then an important question arises: What were the political effects of the riots? A comprehensive answer to this broad question would doubtless fill several volumes. The main purpose of this paper is to examine one particular segment of the governmental process, the U.S. Congress, to determine its response to the 1964–1967 ghetto riots; this will be done by contrasting Congressional perceptions with the perspectives of black and white rank-and-file citizens. Specifically, differences in perspectives on the causes of, and cures for, ghetto riots will be examined.

THE DATA

Data for this study were obtained primarily from two sources: (1) a survey conducted by the senior author of the black residents of Detroit's Twelfth Street area shortly after the 1967 riot there; (2) a unique survey of U.S. Senators and Representatives conducted by Congressional Quarterly, Inc., in the summer of 1967. The Detroit data will be supplemented, where appropriate, with data from similar post-riot surveys in other black ghettos, particularly the Bedford-Stuyvesant ghetto of New York City (1964).[4] The Detroit survey data were obtained from a modified probability sample of black ghetto residents interviewed by professional black interviewers; the Congressional data were obtained from a mail questionnaire survey that yielded replies from about half of all Senators and Representatives, almost all of whom were white.

RANK-AND-FILE VIEWS ON RIOT CAUSES

A convincing argument might be made that the persons in the best position to assess the causes of urban violence were the residents of the ghetto areas in which riots have erupted. The perspectives of Detroit's Twelfth Street ghetto residents, after the 1967 riot there, can be seen in Table 1. The overwhelming majority (86 percent) of these black respondents singled out discrimination and deprivation as the main "reasons" for the riot, as key factors in the generation of ghetto tensions lying behind riots. Hostility toward the police and discontent over police brutality ranked second in their list of causes. Only one in seven men-

Table 1
Ghetto Resident Evaluations of Riot Causes*
(Detroit, 1967)

	Percentage of Respondents *(N = 270)*
Precipitating incident (Raid on "blind pig" social club)	8
Reaction to other riots; related to other riots	3
Hostility to police; police brutality	24
Protest discrimination: deprivation	86
Animosity toward whites; revenge	12
Agitation, organized by militants	8
Delinquents, criminals, hoodlums	15
Miscellaneous and vague responses	22
Don't know	14

*Question: "What were the two or three main reasons for the trouble?"

tioned criminals or delinquents; and a very small fraction cited agitators or militants as main reasons for the trouble.[5] Of the socioeconomic conditions which have spawned violence, these Detroit respondents emphasized employment problems as the most important; when they were asked whether unemployment, bad housing, or poor police practices was "most likely to produce trouble," more than 60 percent chose unemployment as the principle cause of civil disorders.

These findings have been confirmed by other surveys of rank-and-file ghetto residents made in riot areas. In a 1964 Bedford-Stuyvesant survey a similar ranking of riot causes was found. A majority viewed the riot there as a protest against the police, discrimination, or deprivation; only a handful saw the activities of agitators or delinquents as the "real cause" of the riot.[6] A Kraft poll after the 1965 Watts riot found that over half of the blacks interviewed mentioned economic problems; one-fifth, racial humiliation; one-quarter, prior police actions; one-sixth, present police actions, as the "real cause" of the violence in Watts. Again, only a small percentage (8 percent) referred to hoodlums or agitators.[7] The importance of long-standing ghetto complaints was made clear in a UCLA survey, also based on interviews with Watts ghetto residents after the riot there. The survey found that two-thirds of the Watts residents said that long-term grievances, such as economic deprivation and mistreatment by whites, caused the riot; only one in ten cited criminals, agitators, or extremists.[8]

The pattern of responses found in the riot area surveys was borne out by a much more extensive survey of ghetto residents in 15 major cities, including non-riot cities, conducted by the University of Michigan Survey Research Center.[9] Early in 1968, nearly 3,000 black ghetto residents were asked about the purpose and causes of urban riots. A majority viewed the disorders as "mainly a protest by Negroes against unfair conditions." When asked specifically about the main cause of the disturbances, the respondents emphasized discrimination (49 percent), unemployment (23 percent), and bad housing (23 percent). Only one in ten cited "looters or other undesirables," while one in twenty mentioned militants or radicals as a main cause.[10]

The attitudes of ghetto residents whose lives have been touched by riots provide a sharp contrast to the prevailing opinions of rank-and-file white Americans. In a nationwide poll conducted shortly after the 1967 riots, Harris asked white adults to specify in their own words the "two or three main reasons" for the disorders. By far the most frequent replies fell into the category of "outside agitation." While 45 percent of the whites interviewed spontaneously cited agitators, much smaller proportions mentioned such things as prejudice (16 percent) and poverty (14 percent), ranking a poor second and third, respectively, on the white list of causes.[11] Moreover, in the 1968 University of Michigan survey, 3,000 white urbanites in 15 major cities were asked a question about the main cause of ghetto riots. Leading the list of causes cited by white males in that sample were "looters and other undesirables" (34 percent) and "black power or other radicals" (26 percent).[12]

Even many of the predominantly white occupational groups in daily contact with black urbanites seem inclined to blame riots primarily on agitators, militants, or criminals. One important survey of three such groups with extensive ghetto contacts found that samples of policemen (75 percent white), merchants (70 percent white), and employers (100 percent white) placed the greatest emphasis on "criminal elements" and "nationalists and militants" in assessing the main reasons for urban disorders. They also tended, more so than the predominantly black occupational groups also interviewed, to play down the importance of police brutality in their appraisals of theories of riot causation. In contrast, the predominantly black occupational groups interviewed in the same project (educators, social workers, political workers) were more sympathetic to the rank-and-file Negro point of view. Overwhelming majorities of these occupational groups attributed the riots to "unheard Negro complaints;" deviants, whether criminals or militants, received relatively little emphasis in their evaluations of riot causes.[13]

Agitators, especially "Communist" and "outside" agitators, criminals, delinquents, and hoodlums — these are the main reason that riots have occurred, as seen by large proportions of the white population.[14]

Conditions in the ghetto are spontaneously mentioned less frequently. Rank-and-file black Americans, assessing the same riots, have a substantially different ranking of causes, with conditions of discrimination and deprivation leading their lists, and with agitators and delinquents ranking near the bottom. Thus, recent opinion surveys dealing with riots provide clear evidence of the black-white polarization of rank-and-file perspectives in American society.[15]

CONGRESSIONAL PERSPECTIVES ON RIOT CAUSES

Such a polarization of public attitudes poses a serious dilemma for Congressmen and other public officials. Which of the publics, the blacks or the whites, are they to listen to? With which view should they agree? Large-scale urban disorders obviously cannot be overlooked. For most Congressmen, the white community within which they were socialized has long been a primary reference group in regard to racial matters. Given this, one would expect the orientation of a predominantly white Congress to follow that of the white public. Yet, if the disorders have been a successful means of communicating ghetto problems to white leaders, one might expect the attitudes of Congressmen to parallel the sentiments of black ghetto residents.

An unusual opportunity to examine legislative perceptions of urban riot causes was provided by a Congressional Quarterly poll of Senators and Representatives, who were asked, "What importance would you attribute to the following factors mentioned by various persons as playing a significant role in the build-up to the riots?" Table 2 records the percentage of Congressmen, by region and party, that viewed each of the 13 factors as being "of great importance" as a cause of riots.[16]

The causes in the table are listed in rank order of the importance attached to them by the Congressmen. The cause most frequently cited as of great importance was "joblessness and idleness, especially among young Negroes." Unfortunately, the phrasing of this item joined the term "idleness" with the somewhat different notion of "joblessness." Two different perceptions of the job situation were probably present in the replies: (1) an individualistic view that regarded self-generated lack of initiative or motivation as primary, and (2) an alternative perspective that emphasized structurally-generated unemployment. That an individualistic perspective lay behind many Congressional comments seems likely, since this item received more emphasis than other statements that placed the blame unequivocally on social conditions or white indifference.

Table 2
Congressional Evaluations of Riot Causes (1967)[a]

		Percentage replying "of great importance"[b]			
	N	All Congress-men	North-ern Demo-crats	South-ern Demo-crats	Repub-licans
Joblessness and idleness, especially among young Negroes	(259)	68	87	54	62
Lack of responsibility among Negroes	(257)	47	33	55	55
Outside Negro agitators	(259)	46	17	62	59
Neglect of social and economic problems by state and local governments	(241)	41	69	31	27
Irresponsible news media coverage of riots	(254)	39	33	55	36
Supreme Court crime decisions	(256)	33	5	56	41
Poor administration of existing federal programs in these areas	(254)	31	18	23	43
Poor police-community relations	(252)	27	44	28	15
White indifference to Negro needs	(254)	26	51	21	10
Insufficient federal aid in such areas as education, job training, anti-poverty, housing, etc.	(250)	26	58	12	8
Irresponsible training techniques in Community Action Programs	(237)	22	13	25	28
Communist agitation	(241)	20	8	38	20
Negro resentment against Congressional inaction or restrictions on Great Society legislation and House exclusion of Adam Clayton Powell	(248)	5	7	6	4

[a]Data presented with permission of Congressional Quarterly, Inc.
[b]Question: "What importance would you attribute to the following factors mentioned by various persons as playing a significant role in the build-up to the riots?"

The tendency of Congressmen to rely upon social stereotypes and to reflect the views of the white constituency was illustrated most dramatically by the second and third ranked causes. More than half of the southern Democrats and Republicans, as well as a third of the northern Democrats, stressed a "lack of responsibility among Negroes"; and nearly half of all the Congressmen believed that "outside Negro agitators" were of great importance in the build-up of the riots. This general emphasis corresponded with the prevailing opinions of rank-and-file white Americans who, in the surveys cited previously, have most often blamed irresponsible agitators and criminal elements for ghetto riots. This is in stark contrast to the de-emphasis which such theories of riot causation have received among rank-and-file black Americans. For example, only 8 percent of our Detroit sample cited "agitation" as a main cause of the riot there, while just 15 percent mentioned "delinquents" or "criminals." This conspicuous lack of emphasis on agitators and criminals has been characteristic of other post-riot surveys of black ghetto residents.

These Congressmen also exhibited a strong tendency to blame the riots on political institutions other than the federal government itself. The public agencies that drew the most criticism were "state and local governments," cited by 41 percent for their "neglect of social and economic problems." Causes that reflected adversely upon Congress such as "insufficient federal aid" were rated rather low on the list. Significantly, the factor that was selected *least* often by members of Congress was "Negro resentment against Congressional inaction or restrictions on Great Society legislation." Only one Congressman in 20 felt this factor was of great importance as an underlying cause of the riots.

Congressional evaluations of certain causes varied significantly by party and region. The three causes most frequently cited by northern Democrats—joblessness and idleness among young Negroes, neglect of social and economic problems by state and local governments, and insufficient federal aid—were more or less related to social and economic conditions affecting ghetto residents. These causative factors were given much less emphasis by southern Democrats. Southerners placed the greatest emphasis on outside Negro agitators, Supreme Court crime decisions, irresponsible news media coverage, and a lack of responsibility among Negroes as causes of great importance. A cause that would be regarded as very significant by ghetto residents—white indifference to Negro needs—was viewed as of great importance by half of the northern Democrats, but by only one-fifth of the southern Democrats, and by only one tenth of the Republicans.

RANK-AND-FILE VIEWS ON RIOT PREVENTION

Given the divergent views of black ghetto residents and the predominantly white Congressional sample on the causal factors in the development of ghetto riots, one might well predict differing perspectives on riot prevention. Although numerous ghetto residents have volunteered the response that riots were difficult to avoid, many have not hesitated to suggest possible remedies for riots. The post-riot survey in Detroit posed the question as follows: "Before it started, did you think the trouble could have been avoided or did you feel it had to happen sooner or later anyway?" Fifty-eight percent of the Detroit respondents initially said that the riot was bound to happen sooner or later, while 27 percent felt that it could have been avoided. In follow-up questions, persons in the Twelfth Street area sample were asked why it had to happen, or how it could have been avoided.

Responses to both open-ended questions from the Detroit survey have been combined in Table 3, which reports the proportion of respondents in Detroit that suggested, explicitly or implicitly, various remedies for the riots.[17] It can be seen from examining the table that many people

Table 3
Ghetto Resident Remedies for Riots (Detroit, 1967)*

	Percentage of respondents (N = 270)
Improve police practices	22
More discussions, negotiations with white leaders	2
Give black people equal rights	27
End job discrimination	15
Improve housing in the area	8
Provide more education, social welfare services	11
Keep criminals, looters at home	17
Could not have been avoided under the circumstances	20
Miscellaneous	11
Don't know	14

*See text for questions.

who initially replied that the riot had to happen later touched on possible remedies that might be developed to prevent future urban disorders. The largest proportion of respondents gave answers such as "give black people equal rights." Most stressed the need to improve ghetto conditions and/or to end discrimination as the major means of avoiding the riot, while over one fifth stressed the need for improved police practices. Less than one fifth of these ghetto residents suggested tougher social control measures in regard to deviants and criminals.

Other post-riot surveys have found ghetto residents stressing the need to eradicate oppressive ghetto conditions in order to prevent riots, a logical recommendation given the theories of riot causation which they support. The aforementioned 1964 Bedford-Stuyvesant survey asked "How do you think the trouble could have been avoided?" Articulate in their replies, the largest proportion placed the responsibility for riot prevention directly on the white establishment. Most emphasized the need to alleviate ghetto conditions, to improve police practices, to eliminate discrimination, and to increase black-white communication as the primary means of avoiding disorders. Proposals to suppress local ghetto residents, including juvenile delinquents and criminals, were mentioned by a very small minority (8 percent). Moreover, few respondents were fatalistic; the overwhelming majority felt that "had certain persons acted differently or had certain intolerable conditions been altered, there would not have been a riot."[18]

A survey after the Watts riot in Los Angeles produced a similar ranking of riot avoidance suggestions. A Kraft poll asked black residents of the area about actions that could have prevented the riot there. In reply, nearly one third focused on police brutality and malpractice issues, one third mentioned the need for increased economic assistance, and one third called for an end to racial discrimination. Again, relatively small proportions mentioned tougher law enforcement (16 percent) or the need for greater respect for the law (10 percent).[19] Moreover, this focus on underlying social and economic conditions was also found in the extensive University of Michigan survey of ghetto residents in 15 major cities. Inspecting their data on proposals to reduce the likelihood of riots, the researchers note that over half of the black urbanites spontaneously recommended the "improvement of social and economic conditions as the first solution, with more and better jobs the most frequently offered specific recommendation."[20]

Although the riots represented intense demands for social and political reforms, they failed to yield the desired response from most rank-and-file white Americans. In their fifteen-city survey Campbell and Schuman found that whites assigned top priority to more police control as the "most important thing the city government . . . could do to keep a disturbance like the one in Detroit from breaking out here." Social and economic reforms received less emphasis in the spontaneous white replies to this open-ended question.[21] Lack of spontaneous and enthusiastic support for social and economic reform was apparently based on white failure to recognize the intensity of Negro feelings about ghetto problems. For example, Campbell and Schuman report some data indicating that, when you specifically call it to their attention and talk in terms of long-term goals, a majority of whites will give some support to "trying harder" to improve the conditions of black urbanites, though many will still couple that with tighter police control. Campbell and Schuman make the interesting suggestion that the fundamental difference between rank-and-file blacks and whites may be more one of "salience and focus of attention" than of absolute opposition on the part of whites.[22]

This ability to play down the significance of ghetto conditions and the need for immediate far-reaching reforms was also reflected in the Rossi study of the perspectives of three predominantly white occupational groups with extensive ghetto contacts. In reply to a question, "How well are Negroes treated in (your city)?" three quarters of the police interviewed denied the existence of racial discrimination; similar proportions of the merchants and employers interviewed also denied the existence of racial inequality in their cities.[23] Given these views of white "experts" on the ghetto, it is not surprising that rank-and-file whites do not emphasize the need for crash programs to deal with discrimination and ghetto conditions. The polarization between white and black citizens on these issues, therefore, raised the problem of whether or not Congressmen would exclusively represent the white constituency in framing solutions and enacting legislation to avoid further violence.

CONGRESSIONAL PERSPECTIVES ON RIOT PREVENTION

Table 4 presents Congressional evaluations of ten proposals to prevent the recurrence of rioting. While the largest proportion yielded to the propensity to delegate vague responsibilities to state and local officials, thereby again transferring responsibility from the federal level to other governmental levels, sizeable proportions also stressed a moralistic reliance on "traditional church and family values" as well as a program of "private sector involvement." Majorities felt "greater penalties for rioters" and "larger, better-paid police forces" to be of great importance in preventing riots. "Greater expenditures for police anti-riot training" were frequently emphasized. Significantly, suggestions for expanded federal economic programs, such as a "Marshall plan" for the cities and "increased federal aid," ranked near the bottom of the list. Most Congressmen were apparently willing to rely heavily on traditional social control mechanisms to prevent future riots, particularly the reassertion of traditional moral and religious values and tougher police action. There was less emphasis on remedies focusing on ghetto conditions; where such remedies received substantial support they seemed to be vaguely-

Table 4
Congressional Evaluations of Remedies for Riots (1967)[a]

	N	*Percentage replying "of great importance"*[b]			
		All Congress-men	*North-ern Demo-crats*	*South-ern Demo-crats*	*Repub-licans*
Greater state and local efforts (unspecified)	(257)	74	86	66	68
Emphasis on traditional church and family values	(254)	73	54	85	80
Private sector involvement through such devices as public low-income area development corporations	(235)	66	69	44	74
Greater penalties for rioters and those who incite to rioting	(249)	61	44	77	65
Larger, better-paid police forces	(263)	54	49	64	52
Greater expenditures for police anti-riot training	(258)	42	43	38	43
Legislation to avoid Supreme Court decisions relating to arrest, interrogation of prisoners, etc.	(252)	33	7	46	47
A massive "Marshall Plan" for the cities using federal funds	(239)	26	60	14	4
Gun control legislation	(243)	23	49	18	6
Increased federal aid for urban problems . . . through block grants to the states	(231)	17	11	6	27

[a] By permission of Congressional Quarterly, Inc.
[b] Question: "What importance would you attach to each of the following proposals to prevent recurrences of the rioting?"

defined local government programs or private plans rather than massive efforts by the federal government to deal with urban problems.

Although northern Democrats were more likely than other legislators to stress economic assistance, particularly an urban "Marshall Plan," many of them shared the sentiments of their colleagues from the South and from the opposition party regarding traditional moral values, as well as law enforcement tactics. However, legislation designed to void Supreme Court crime decisions received little support among northern Democrats. As reflected in this survey, the general mood of Congress seemed to represent a desire to avoid major social reform or—at best—to escape the responsibility for preventing future riots by delegating it to other public and private agencies.

CONCLUSION

Riots in black ghettos have so far produced few major disruptions in traditional political procedures or perceptions. The grievances of ghetto citizens who have experienced violence have been clearly and powerfully expressed. Black urbanites interviewed after the critical riots in Detroit, Watts, and elsewhere have attributed the disorders to underlying social and economic conditions; moreover, they have placed a predominant emphasis on anti-discrimination and economic assistance programs as specific governmental remedies to prevent future disturbances.

Despite the fact that these ghetto revolts demonstrated extensive dissatisfaction, they have failed to stimulate significant new attempts by the outside white society to understand ghetto problems or to undertake large-scale ameliorative action. In fact, the violence seems to have promoted a growing polarization between rank-and-file white and black Americans. Unlike most of their black counterparts, white citizens have reacted to the disorders by blaming them primarily on militants, agitators, and criminals and by emphasizing increased police control measures to avert them in the future.

The conflicting perspectives of black and white voters have posed an important dilemma for elected representatives. Congressmen might have adopted the perspective of black urbanites on discrimination and the oppressive character of ghetto conditions, supporting the remedial recommendations of those directly affected by such conditions; yet, to adequately represent the views of the white majority, they might have felt compelled to take a diametrically opposite position. Although northern Democrats were more sensitive to socioeconomic problems than other legislators, the prevailing Congressional views on riot causes and remedies seemed closer to that of the white community than to that of black ghettos. Prevailing Congressional sentiment contained a pronounced individualistic and moralistic strain that placed an emphasis on Negro idleness, lack of responsibility, and agitators in assessing the causes of riots, and that pinned hopes for the future on a renewed emphasis on traditional moral values, plus a heavy dose of tougher law enforcement and a vaguely-conceived program of private sector involvement in low-income areas. A minority of the Congressmen emphasized the pervasive role of white indifference and discrimination in laying the groundwork for riots and stressed their own (federal) responsibility for grappling with ghetto conditions with tools equal to the task, such as a massive "Marshall Plan" for the cities.

The polarization not only between black and white Americans at the grass roots level but also between ghetto residents and influential policy-makers hints at a bleak prospect for the future. The perennial problem of a visible and disaffected minority within a system of representation based upon majoritarian principles has been raised in a radical new form; and it apparently has been resolved again in favor of the majority. Even in the face of extreme threats to the societal fabric, the majority of Congressmen have continued to neglect the sentiments of black ghetto residents and to provide almost exclusive representation for the white community.

NOTES

[1] The authors wish to express their appreciation to Congressional Quarterly, Inc., for permission to re-analyze and incorporate some of their data in this paper and to the University of Michigan for the support which made the Detroit survey possible.

[2] *Report of the National Advisory Commission on Civil Disorders* (Washington, D.C.: Government Printing Office, 1968), pp. 76–82.

[3] Since this was originally written, other analysts have emphasized the political inplications of the ghetto revolts. See Jerome H. Skolnick, *The Politics of Protest* (New York: Simon and Schuster, 1969).

[4] For a description of the Bedford-Stuyvesant sample, see Joe R. Feagin, "Social Sources of Support for Violence and Nonviolence in a Negro Ghetto," *Social Problems*, 15 (Spring, 1968), pp. 432–441. The sampling procedure in the Detroit survey was as follows: All blocks in the Twelfth Street neighborhood were stratified on the basis of a socioeconomic status index derived from the value of owner-occupied dwelling units, mean rent, and substandard units (according to the 1960 housing census). Respondents were selected randomly within each stratum; quota assignments in each block were based on age and race. The Detroit sample included 270 Negroes and 37 whites, roughly proportionate to the racial characteristics of the neighborhood; only the data for the black respondents are discussed in this paper.

[5] The "miscellaneous" category in the Detroit study also included 5 percent of the respondents who cited complaints against government officials as a primary reason for the riots.

[6] Joe R. Feagin and Paul B. Sheatsley, "Ghetto Resident Appraisals of a Riot," *Public Opinion Quarterly*, 32 (Fall, 1968), p. 354.

[7] John R. Kraft, Inc., "The Attitudes of Negroes in Various Cities" in *Federal Role in Urban Affairs*, Part 6, Hearings before the Subcommittee on Executive Reorganization of the Committee on Government Operations, U.S. Senate, 89th Congress, 2nd Session, September 1, 1966, pp. 1387–1388.

[8] T. M. Tomlinson and David O. Sears, *Negro Attitudes Toward the Riot* (Los Angeles: UCLA Institute of Government and Public Affairs, 1967), p. 13.

[9] Angus Campbell and Howard Schuman, "Racial Attitudes in Fifteen American Cities" in *Supplemental Studies for the National Advisory Commission on Civil Disorders* (Washington, D.C.: Government Printing Office, 1968), pp. 47–48. These percentages are for the Negro males in the sample, since total figures are not presented; however, the pattern for females is quite similar.

[10]One study of black participants in the Newark and Detroit riots concluded similarly that: "The survey data support the blocked-opportunity theory. One is led to conclude that the continued exclusion of Negroes from American economic and social life is the fundamental cause of riots." Nathan S. Caplan and Jeffrey M. Paige, "A Study of Ghetto Rioters," *Scientific American*, 219 (Aug., 1968), p. 21.

[11]The proportion of Negroes spontaneously citing agitation as a main cause was only 10 percent. *Newsweek*, Aug. 21, 1967, pp. 18-19.

[12]Campbell and Schuman, "Racial Attitudes," p. 48. These percentages are for males in the white sample, since total figures are not presented. The pattern for white females is roughly similar, although they place greater emphasis on discrimination.

[13]Peter H. Rossi, *et. al.,* "Between White and Black: The Faces of American Institutions in the Ghetto" in *Supplemental Studies for the National Advisory Commission on Civil Disorders* (Washington, D.C.: Government Printing Office, 1968), pp. 96-97.

[14]For a brief explanation of the American tendency to view causes of social crises in individualistic terms, see Feagin and Sheatsley, "Ghetto Resident Appraisals," p. 362.

[15]Compare David O. Sears and T. M. Tomlinson, "Riot Ideology in Los Angeles: A Study of Negro Attitudes," *Social Science Quarterly*, 49 (Dec., 1968), pp. 485-503.

[16]Unlike the ghetto surveys, the CQ poll did not use open-ended questions. Percentages are based on the number of Congressmen responding to a given fixed-response item, a number which varies; inclusion of "no answer" Congressmen reduces the percentages somewhat but does not significantly alter the ranking. Proportions of Congressmen replying "of some importance" or "insignificant" have been omitted from the tables but can be calculated by subtracting the tabulated figures from 100 percent. The raw numbers from which the percentages were calculated were taken from *Congressional Quarterly Weekly Report*, No. 36, Sept. 8, 1967, p. 1738.

[17]Those who said that the Detroit riot was inevitable because "it had happened in other cities" and those who guessed "it was planned" have been classified among those who felt the riot "could not have been avoided under the circumstances."

[18]Feagin and Sheatsley, "Ghetto Resident Appraisals," p. 360.

[19]Kraft, "The Attitudes of Negroes," p. 1401.

[20]Campbell and Schuman, "Racial Attitudes," p. 48.

[21]Only the first responses are tabulated. *Ibid.*

[22]*Ibid.,* p. 37. These data suggest that there is, at least potentially, significant white support for concrete social and economic reforms, should these be emphasized and implemented by progressive political leaders. The failure to implement the necessary reforms in the midst of racial crisis would seem due more to the failure of political leadership than to any other single factor. Compare the argument in Skolnick, *Politics of Protest*, pp. 208-209.

[23]Rossi, *et al.,* "Between White and Black," p. 88. In contrast, overwhelming majorities of the social service groups interviewed in the same study (but 50 percent or more Negro in composition) acknowledged the existence of racial discrimination.

Chapter 11

BLACK INTERESTS, BLACK GROUPS, AND BLACK INFLUENCE IN THE FEDERAL POLICY PROCESS: THE CASES OF HOUSING AND EDUCATION

Harold L. Wolman
Norman C. Thomas

Few would disagree that American politics is characterized by bargaining, negotiation, compromise, and mutual accommodation. But some have argued that these characteristics, rather than indicating consent as Dahl has suggested, indicate instead that dissent is being suppressed and that the political system is stable *because* of that suppression. Thus, Jack Walker has remarked that

> one of the chief characteristics of our political system has been its success in suppressing and controlling internal conflict. But the avoidance of conflict, the suppression of strife, is not necessarily the creation of satisfaction or consensus. The citizens may remain quiescent, the political system might retain its stability, but significant differences of opinion remain, numerous conflicts are unresolved and many desires go unfulfilled.[1]

Walker and others dispute the assumption[2] that the absence of articulated demands signifies consent. Rather, they believe that the absence of articulated demands reflects the fact that not all interests are expressed

Reprinted from *The Journal of Politics,* 32 (November, 1970), pp. 875–97, by permission of the authors and publisher.

The authors acknowledge financial support for this research from the Institute of Public Administration of the University of Michigan, the National Woodrow Wilson Fellowship Foundation, and the Relm Foundation. They also thank Allan Kornberg for helpful suggestions regarding certain sections of the paper.

through organized groups and that not all organized groups have effective access to centers of decision making.[3]

All interests do not become translated into group demands, it is argued, because certain segments of the population lack the resources for effective group participation. Studies of participation have shown that lower-class people in particular, possessing little education and low political efficacy, are less likely to join groups than are their middle- and upper-class counterparts.[4] As a result, according to critics like E. E. Schattschneider, the interests of the lower classes are much less likely to be articulated through groups. Schattschneider concludes, "The flaw in the pluralist heaven is that the heavenly chorus sings with a strong upper-class accent."[5]

Moreover, the critics contend, decision makers are likely to be much less receptive to certain types of groups, particularly those that put stress on the social system by pushing for change. The decision makers do not dispassionately weigh the relative forces of the contending groups and then register a decision. In many cases the decision makers can determine who has effective access on the basis of their own values. The "mobilization of bias"[6] by political decision-making institutions plays a major role in determining which groups are heard and which are not.

The "Negro revolt" of the past decade provides an important and appropriate setting for an investigation of the relevance of some of the criticisms that have been made of the pluralist description of American politics. To the extent that black Americans do share common interests, how successful have they been in achieving effective access to federal decision makers and in helping to shape national policy to conform with those interests? The "Poor People's Campaign" of 1968 provided a dramatic indication that black participation in federal policy processes has not been satisfactory in the view of many black groups and their leaders.

Studies that we conducted during 1967–68, independently but in close contact with each other, of the process of formulating national policies in the areas of housing and education, have provided us with evidence that black participation in national policy processes is not as effective or as extensive as the pluralist description suggests it should be. (We are assuming the existence of relatively greater unmet demands, i.e., felt needs, among black Americans than among the rest of the population.) Specifically, we examined the federal policy-making processes to discover which groups had access and where, and at what points in the policy process that access occurred. We found an absence of black access and effective black participation at crucial stages in the

process. It is our purpose in this paper to present that evidence, to suggest explanations for it, and to assess its significance in relation to the pluralist description of American politics.

METHODOLOGY

In studying national policy making in housing and education we employed the conceptual framework of a policy system. The policy systems, as we defined them, included key individuals located in the bureaucracy (the departments of Housing and Urban Development and Health, Education and Welfare and their principal operating agencies in the areas of housing and education), Congress (the relevant legislative and appropriations committees), organized clientele or special interest groups in each policy area, and persons whom we have designated as "public-interest representatives" (influential persons in related professions, in the general community, or affiliated with general or non-clientele interest groups). We distinguished between clientele-group representatives and public-interest representatives because the former have a sustained professional concern over the policy areas through an organization created for that purpose while the latter are involved either as individuals or as members of groups with a broader focus, e.g., labor unions or business associations. The members of the two policy systems were quite similar in terms of their institutional affiliations, positions, or resource bases. (See Table 1.)

Table 1

Membership in the Housing and Education Policy Systems
by Institution/Position/Resource Base

	Housing	*Education*
Congress: members	19	18
Congress: staff	7	7
Bureaucracy	14	18
Executive Office of the President	8	6
Clintele groups	12	16
Public interest representatives	8	10
Total	68	77

We identified the members of the two policy systems through techniques that combined elements of the positional and reputational approaches.[7] Initially we compiled a list of potential members of each policy system. We identified these persons on the basis of their formal positions of authority, e.g., chairman of a congressional committee or a high-ranking departmental or agency official; on the basis of a reputation among informed observers and other potential participants as influential participants in the policy process; or on the basis of their appearance as contributors of inputs to the policy system through such vehicles as testifying before congressional committees or service on presidential task forces and other major advisory bodies. The lists contained 165 persons of potential influence in housing and 175 in education.

The next step involved interviews with persons possessing substantial knowledge of federal programs in housing and education. These persons, 25 in housing and 24 in education, included congressional staff members, bureaucrats, lobbyists, and journalists. We asked them to examine the list of persons with potential influence and check those whom they considered to be most important with respect to the states of the policy process: innovation and formulation, legislative consideration, appropriation, and implementation. Their responses, along with other information obtained through more general background investigations, provided the basis for reducing the lists to a total of 68 persons in housing and 77 in education.

At the final stage of data gathering, we conducted interviews with 62 members of the housing and 71 members of the education policy systems. The interview instruments employed primarily open-end questions. We asked similar, but not identical, questions in the two areas regarding the representation and access of various groups in the different stages of the policy process. Because our interview procedures were eclectic, as elite studies tend to be, the data are non-quantitative and our analysis is conducted in qualitative terms. Where we do discuss data, it is not precisely comparable between the two policy areas. Our decision to present these findings regarding black nonparticipation in advance of complete reports on the policy systems we studied is prompted by our belief that they are of considerable immediate social and political relevance.

BLACK GROUPS AND PARTICIPATION IN POLICY MAKING

How do groups representing black interests attempt to influence public policy at the national level? Do they take advantage of the multiplicity of access points available in the education and housing policy processes? To answer these questions, we first considered the major black groups on the assumption that each represented interests held by some portion of the black community.

Historically, the NAACP has been the black organization most active in attempting to influence public policy. The principal thrust of the NAACP's efforts has been towards achieving integration, particularly in the area of education. It has employed litigation as the principal means to this end.[8] But the NAACP has neither engaged in any form of long-range policy planning for education nor made organized efforts to influence federal policy at the innovative or formulative stages.

A substantial amount of litigation is also initiated by the Legal Defense and Education Fund, a legally independent organization associated with the NAACP.[9] It has been concerned primarily with the enforcement of Title VI of the Civil Rights Act of 1964 which requires state and local governments to comply with federal desegregation guidelines in order to participate in various federally funded programs.

The NAACP's concentration on educational integration has rendered it nearly quiescent in other areas. From 1963 to 1968 it had no particular housing program and no staff member to deal with matters of housing policy—an area that is surely one of major concern to members of the black community.[10] Prior to 1963, the NAACP's housing program, as might be expected, was concerned mostly with segregation in the housing market.[11]

The NAACP, through its lobbyist Clarence Mitchell, does make efforts to influence policy at the legislative consideration stage. Mitchell often directs his efforts through the vehicle of the Leadership Conference of Civil Rights, an umbrella group consisting of 112 organizations whose purpose is to "advance the cause of civil rights through the enactment of legislation."[12] The Conference acts primarily as a coordinator; its influence derives from the resources possessed by its most important constituents groups—the NAACP, the Industrial Union Division of the AFL-CIO, and the National Council of Churches.

The Leadership Conference is primarily concerned with securing the passage of civil-rights laws such as the Civil Rights Act of 1964 and the Voting Rights Act of 1965. The Conference—and Mitchell in particular—is credited with playing a major role in the passing of the federal open-housing law in 1968.[13] The Leadership Conference's major efforts, however, have been directed towards civil rights legislation in the strict sense; its involvement in other areas of concern to black people—such as education and housing—is on an ad hoc basis, usually to meet an overt threat related to civil rights.[14] Like the NAACP, the Leadership Conference has been almost completely uninvolved in housing legislation. Generally, in areas other than civil rights, the Conference's involvement in the policy process does not occur soon enough to influence substantially the shape of the final product.[15] Rather, it reacts to threats and emergencies. Of course, more extensive or clever lobbying on the part of the Leadership Conference and other civil-rights organizations would not alone be sufficient to produce changes in housing and education policies favorable to the black community. Such changes require expanded black participation at all stages of the policy process, to say nothing of substantially increased support among members of the white majority.

The National Urban League is involved in operational programs, particularly in housing at the local level, but it makes no major effort as an organization to affect national policy other than through *pro forma* testimony before congressional committees. Like the Legal Defense and Educational Fund, it is forbidden to lobby because of its tax-exempt status. Even so, Whitney Young, the Urban League's Executive Director, is very active personally in the innovation and formulation stage of the housing policy-making process. Young emphasized desegretating the housing market and providing governmental resources to private enterprise so that the supply of low- and moderate-income housing may be increased. It seems clear that Young's influence is due to his reputation and his personality — and particularly to the high respect that President Johnson held for him — rather than to the resources of the Urban League.

The Congress of Racial Equality (CORE) has made little attempt to influence policy at the national level, although its leaders have, from time to time, testified before congressional committees. Neither has it developed a coherent national program for either housing or education. CORE's position, as reflected in congressional testimony, has emphasized the following: the need to provide the resources from which private enterprise can increase the supply of low-income housing; the desirability of establishing housing co-ops; and the necessity for black control of decision-making processes at the local level. The Student Non-violent Co-ordinating Committee (SNCC) makes no attempt either to influence policy or to formulate a program at the national level other than to say that "the U.S. Government ought to give massive amounts of money directly to black communities with no strings attached."[16]

The Southern Christian Leadership Conference does not lobby in the normal sense of the word, but the late Dr. Martin Luther King, Jr., frequently used public confrontation to gain access to the mass media in order to influence decision makers in the legislative-consideration stage through moral suasion. King employed this strategy most successfully on civil rights issues that were publicly perceived as "moral" issues.[17]

In summary, black groups have directed most of their efforts to influence national policies on issues involving civil rights. These have been largely formal and visible activities, e.g., lobbying and litigation, that occur fairly late in the policy process, particularly at the stages of legislative consideration and implementation. At those stages certain actions can be prevented and marginal changes in policy outputs affected, but the major thrust of policies cannot substantially be altered, for they have been shaped in the earlier innovative and formulative stages when the basic agenda is set.

BLACK GROUPS AND ACCESS TO THE POLICY-MAKING ELITE

The pattern of black participation in the policy-making process is quite similar in housing and education. Very few blacks were found in the policy-making elites that we studied. In housing there were only two black members of the elite, including, of course, Robert Weaver who, as the first Secretary of Housing and Urban Development, was also the first black member of the Cabinet. While not the major concern of this paper, the nature and significance of Weaver's involvement in the housing policy system is a matter of some controversy. On the one hand, there are those, including some of our respondents, who believed that he exercised a steady, persuasive influence from his key position and that his influence was of considerable value to the black community. On the other hand, his critics, who included not a few black leaders, some journalistic commentators, and a number of our respondents, depreciated his impact on two counts: that he was an inept administrator and an ineffectual politician, and that he thought and acted like a white person. We can only note but not settle the debate. In the education policy system, only one black participant was involved and he was associated with organized labor.

But did the organized groups representing black interests have effective access to members of the policy-making elite? The evidence indicated that they did not. We asked the members of the education policy system: "What are the two or three groups or forces outside the government that have the most impact on federal policy involving elementary and secondary education?" and "higher education?" Not one of the 71 respondents cited a civil rights organization or any other element in the black community. Among those groups that they frequently cited, however, were the National Education Association, the Council of Chief State School Officers, and the American Council on Education, the National Association of State Universities and Land Grant Colleges, the American Association of Junior Colleges, major philanthropic foundations, and the Roman Catholic Church. We also asked the education respondents, "Outside your immediate office, who are the ten people whom you see most frequently, formally or informally, with respect to matters that involve federal educational policy?" None of the 71 respondents cited a representative of a civil rights organization or any other black leader as a person whom they consulted. This is fairly impressive negative evidence of the absence of black access to the national educational policy-making elite. Members of the policy-making elite had neither reference groups nor personal contacts in the black community.

We obtained at least some positive evidence of the same phenomenon by asking 59 of the respondents:[18] "Do you feel that all relevant and concerned groups have adequate opportunity to express their views concerning federal educational policies?" Thirty-six of those who responded to the question believed that certain groups did not have adequate access to the policy process in education. These groups included four distinct categories: the Negro-urban poor; various educational interests, including vocational education, independent schools, and private liberal-arts colleges; teachers, students, and parents; and state and local education officials. A smaller but sizable number — 20 of the 59 respondents — expressed the opinion that no groups with relevant interests in Federal educational policies lacked adequate access, and the remaining three responses could not be categorized.

Of particular interest here are the 13 respondents citing the Negro urban poor as lacking adequate access. Typical responses in this category were those of a bureau chief in the U.S. Office of education: "Negroes do not have an adequate opportunity to express their views. Not only are the civil rights groups not represented in the policy process, but the Negro man on the street is not either."[19] And, a lobbyist for an education clientele group: "The civil rights groups and others who can speak for the poor do not get involved in shaping educational policy."[20] It should be noted, however, that while the Negro urban poor are cited more than any other group, there was by no means a widespread sentiment among the respondents that any identifiable group was seriously underrepresented. Yet a substantial uneasiness was apparent over the representativeness of the education policy process as a whole.

Some explanations of these phenomena are suggested by examining the location of the respondents in the policy process. Only one of 16 congressionally affiliated respondents in comparison with two of 18 bureaucrats and eight of 25 persons located outside the federal government were of the opinion that the Negro-urban poor lacked adequate access. These differences are substantial if not striking. It is possible that for members of Congress and their staffs, the Negro urban poor are not a meaningful constituency. Indeed, they are but a recently invented constituency with relevance for persons outside the federal government and, to a lesser degree, for bureaucrats. It is also probable that the presence of highly visible black lobbying on Capitol Hill kept most congressional respondents from citing the black community or its organizations as groups lacking effective access.

It is necessary to give some interpretation of the fact that one-third of the respondents did not consider that any groups lacked effective access to the policy process. Outsiders and congressional personnel expressed approximately the same level (30 percent) of satisfaction with the availability of access. The bureaucrats, however, were considerably more inclined to believe that the process was open to all who cared to enter it. (Eight of 18, or 44 percent, expressed this opinion.)

Perhaps the bureaucrats conceive of their role as providing easy access, of being open and available to all, and consequently they are somewhat reluctant to acknowledge that certain groups do not have adequate access. Although congressional personnel indicated little concern over the adequacy of black access, they did cite other groups that experience difficulties in this regard. Among them were state and local education officials, who were mentioned by four of the 16 congressional affiliates, and teachers, students, and parents, who were cited by three. The outsiders, however, did believe that blacks have access problems — eight of 25 respondents held this view. Also, a sizable number of the outsiders, six of 25, were of the opinion that professional interests in education lacked adequate access. Possibly congressional personnel and outsiders are more aware of the difficulties various groups encounter in securing access than bureaucrats are. A number of the respondents who expressed the belief that no groups lacked access pointed out that groups differ greatly in the use made of access. As an HEW executive commented, "To say that groups have access is one thing, but all of them don't have an equal chance to affect policy."[21]

It is difficult to reach a clear and confident interpretation of these responses. On the one hand, it is notable that more of the respondents cited the Negro urban poor as lacking adequate access than any other group. On the other hand, it is impressive that so few mentioned the lack of access for black groups. We can conclude that there is some concern over the lack of black access (expressed by one in five respondents) and substantial concern over the adequacy of access for *all* relevant groups including the blacks (expressed by three in five). We can offer no evidence of the attitudes of black people toward the success or failure of their own efforts to obtain access to the policy process.

In housing, the pattern of responses was substantially the same. Members of the housing policy system were asked how often over the course of a year they communicated with the 16 interest groups identified as participants. The more moderate black organizations, the NAACP and the Urban League, ranked seventh in frequency of the policy-makers' contacts while the more militant groups, SNCC and CORE, ranked sixteenth, with many decision makers almost never communicating with them.[22]

In sum, the responses indicate that black access to the policy-making elites is limited in terms of the reference groups and personal contacts with the influential policy makers and that a sizable, but not substantial, number of those who are influential believe that black people lack adequate access to the process.

VIRTUAL AND INDIRECT REPRESENTATION

Although our findings strongly indicate that black groups on the whole do not possess effective access to the major centers of decision making in the domestic policy-making process, it does not follow that black interests are ignored by the policy-making elite. Indeed, members of the elite themselves may share these interests. Thus, when housing decision makers were questioned about their agreement with the policy positions of the four major black organizations, 34 of the 42 who responded either generally agreed or agreed very strongly with the NAACP or Urban League, while 13 answered similarly for SNCC and CORE. Interestingly enough, 26 indicated that they did not know what SNCC's or CORE's policy positions were, tending to verify our previous observation that neither group makes much effort to achieve access. As a black official in HUD commented, "I am not aware, except in great generalities, what the housing programs and policies of CORE, SNCC, and SCLC are or might be."[23]

More specifically, certain units within the executive branch were institutionally structured and certain officials took it upon themselves to represent the interests of the black community — or at least some of the interests of some parts of the black community. In HUD, the Office of Community Development and the Office of Equal Opportunity, both headed by blacks, provided such representation, particularly in the implementation stage. Neither of these units, however, was a major center of policy making. Within HEW the Commissioner of Education and the Special Assistant to the Secretary for Civil Rights assumed a special responsibility for the interests of black people. At the time of this inquiry, the commissioner was a white man while the Civil Rights Assistant was a black woman. The commissioner's record as a champion of civil rights had earned him the antipathy of most Southern congress-men. The Civil Rights Assistant was concerned primarily with Title VI compliance and she did not participate in the overall development of educational policies except as they related to civil rights matters. The U.S. Office of Education (USOE) also maintained an Office of Programs for the Disadvantaged which had the responsibility of receiving and processing suggestions and complaints from poor people about the oper-ation of federal education programs.

Federal institutions outside the main policy system also represent-ed some black interests. Demands from these institutions acted as inputs to the policy-making system from within the Administration. The Office of Economic Opportunity (OEO) in particular argued the case for black interests, although much more effectively in education than in housing. In education, the OEO administered two programs, Head Start (later transferred to USOE) and Upward Bound, oriented towards helping black children overcome cultural, economic, and educational obstacles. Through these programs, OEO was able to influence other programs that affect black children.

Probably the most important form of indirect representation of black interests came from demands on the policy-making elite made by certain nongovernmental groups such as the Urban Coalition, the Na-tional Council of Churches, and the AFL-CIO. Of these groups, organ-ized labor has clearly been the most important. Despite the fact that many rank-and-file unionists did not appear to support black-oriented policies, labor leadership consistently pushed for legislation favorable to moderate black interests. The fight to pass a federal open housing law in 1968 is a prime example. According to a survey of the AFL-CIO membership conducted by the Joseph Kraft polling organization in January 1967, a majority of the membership opposed labor's stand in favor of the federal law.[24] Yet a year later, labor lobbyists were in the forefront of the fight to pass the legislation.

Labor, or at least its leaders, apparently has fairly explicit working relations with the black civil rights groups. According to an AFL-CIO lobbyist, "We often draw the attention of civil rights groups to problems in pending legislation, like the changes in Title III (of the Elementary and Secondary Education Act) last year."[25] And, as a member of the National Urban League's staff observed, "Labor is the biggest lobby in town. I consider them experts. When something comes up I need help on, I go to them."[26]

There are a number of other ways in which black "representation" is achieved in the policy process. Perhaps the most important in the minds of the policy-making elite, which tends to believe that there *should* be black representation, is the practice of consulting a few well-known black leaders or enlisting them in formal and highly visible advisory capacities. One respondent called this "the Whitney Young approach" in reference to the frequent inclusions of the prestigious Executive Director of the Urban League on advisory councils, public commissions, and other study groups. The other aspect of this form of black representation is consultation with intellectuals and experts, e.g., educators, urbanologists, etc. who tend to be affiliated with universities, foundations, and research institutes. The comment of an official in the Executive Office of the President reflects the thinking behind this approach, which appeared to be fairly widespread in the Executive branch:

> The interests of urban Negroes are effectively and well represented. We have consulted people like Kenneth Clark and Wilson Riles. We have also had the views of white educators and experts on the problems of the disadvantaged child. Anything that comes in from the civil rights is also a part of our thinking.[27]

Although black interests are not excluded from any of the stages of the policy-making process, serious deficiencies do exist in efforts at interest articulation through indirect representation. The most obvious is that groups or institutions attempting to represent black interests are often restrained by their own constituencies from fully representing those interests. Thus, although labor may support open housing, the building-trade unions strongly oppose efforts to allow Negro residents to work on housing rehabilitation projects in their neighborhoods, since this requires using non-union labor. As a black observer remarked, "The Negro has fared pretty well through labor. But, despite their speeches, the old AFL craft and guild unions will shaft you every chance they get."[28]

More important, however, is the question of which black interests get articulated through indirect representation. Obviously the black community is not monolithic; various segments within it do have interests that differ, and in some cases quite markedly.[29] In the extreme case are large numbers of blacks who view integration as a major and important policy goal while a smaller but highly articulate number of blacks espouse racial separation. It is quite apparent that the black interests articulated through indirect representation are those that are popularly termed moderate. The more militant interests only come to the attention of the decision makers, if at all, through the mass media, which have recently focused much attention on militant black spokesmen. Thus, black interests that focus on integration and on relatively traditional governmental efforts to alleviate and ultimately to eliminate black poverty receive the bulk of indirect representation. But some of the interests represented by organizations such as SNCC remain largely unarticulated in the policy-making system. The top federal policy priority of SNCC – that large sums of federal money be given to the black communities with no strings attached – was expressed neither by the decision-making elite nor by any of the groups that had access to that elite.

Finally, at this point in history, the very existence of indirect representation – regardless of how adequate that representation may be – is unacceptable to many blacks. No matter how noble the intentions of liberal white groups, blacks frequently perceive white efforts to aid the black cause as paternalistic and patronizing. Blacks tend to regard such efforts as a continuation of the master-subordinate relation implicit in the history of race relations in America. Whites may unwittingly reflect this relation even as they seek to improve racial harmony. These remarks of a white participant in the work of a major education advisory committee illustrated the type of liberal white attitude that is so offensive to many blacks:

> We have not actively consulted with civil rights groups or with people from the Negro community. We have not had to do so. Our own members are intimately aware of the problems connected with ghetto education and with the needs of Negro children. One of them is a Negro. So, we feel that we know what Negro parents want for their children.[30]

ANALYSIS

Both pluralists and most of their critics have assumed that rational men who hold common interests will organize into groups in order to achieve their goals. Mancur Olson has recently argued, however, that exactly the opposite is true.[31] The rational individual will not make the sacrifices – such as time, energy, money – necessary to join a large voluntary group. He reasons that his participation will not make any measurable difference in the group's accomplishments, yet he will benefit from the group's accomplishments whether he is a member or not.[32] Successful groups are, by Olson's persuasive logic, necessarily small groups or groups that are "fortunate enough to have an independent source of selective incentives."[33] Thus, in order to receive the AMA journal, which keeps them informed on recent advances in medicine, doctors must belong to the American Medical Association. Unfortunately black groups offer no similar incentives to provide an effective means of coercing black people to join and contribute to them.

The consequent lack of resources has meant that black groups have had to make hard choices about where to concentrate their energies. Because almost all of the black groups at the national level are no more than coalitions of local groups,[34] there is a natural reluctance to expend already scarce resources at the national level. Instead, efforts have been concentrated on influencing policies at the local level where the problems and processes may be less complex, and where the payoffs will, in all probability, be more tangible and visible.

The emerging ideology of black power, shared to some extent by nearly all black groups, reinforces the tendency to focus on local politics. Local activity is consistent with an emphasis on direct citizen participation, which seems to form an integral part of the ideology. In addition, the more militant version of the ideology holds that it is pointless to work with or through a "racist white power structure" at the federal level. As a leading Washington, D.C., black militant put it, "On the basis of past experience, I would say that it would not do us much good if we did try to influence federal policy. Once a position is identified with us, the chances of its ever being adopted are very slim."[35] Or as a SNCC worker commented more pithily, "It's irrelevant, the U.S. government isn't going to do a damn thing for black folks. So there's no use even talking about it."[36]

The lack of special incentives and the concentration of effort at the local level means that black groups suffer from a severe lack of resources when they do attempt to influence policy at the national level. Many of the groups with which black groups compete do possess selective incentives. In education such groups include the professional education associations and the Catholic Church; in housing they include a variety of professional groups such as the National Association of Real Estate Boards and the National Association of Housing and Redevelopment officials, as well as organized labor. As one black observer lamented, "The staffs of the civil rights organizations are too small, and they aren't technical enough. The National Urban League has a staff of six. Any 'first-rate' lobby has way more than that."[37]

Indeed, the lack of technical expertise among black groups has been a major problem. On the whole, black organizations have not been able to develop coherent programs in either housing or education. As a black official in HUD commented:

> By and large most civil rights leaders and staffs are really babes in the woods so far as policy is concerned. We recently had a meeting of all civil rights groups for the purpose of getting advice on how to implement the new fair housing law. Our bureaucrats had thought of much more active things than these groups had. What they basically said

was "we don't believe HUD will really enforce it." But *they* really had no ideas what to do. In fact they asked to hear what the bureaucrats had said. I said "No. What we want is fresh ideas from you."[38]

In a sense, however, it is hardly surprising that blacks have not made a more extensive effort to develop national programs in housing and education. In education in particular white experts are divided and uncertain over how the federal government can most effectively improve the situation of black children. As a university-based educational leader in the field of teacher training remarked, "One reason why Negroes may not have tried to influence national policy is that they, like the rest of us, really do not know what to do. Title I (of the Elementary and Secondary Education Act) is the best that white educators have come up with and it is hardly a big success."[39] We have ample diagnoses of the ailments, but little capacity — white or black — to prescribe remedies.

Probably a more serious lack has been the inability of black groups to develop more lobbyists of the quality of Clarence Mitchell. As a labor lobbyist remarked, "Negro groups make so little effort to learn Washington and to learn how to operate in Congress. The great lack in Negro organizations is for effective lobbyists, but it's hard to get people like Mitchell."[40] The reason for this lack may be that the kind of temperament characteristic of a good lobbyist is not readily found in members of most black groups and particularly not in militant ones. "Lobbying emphasizes compromise, accommodation, patience," one lobbyist explained. Most black groups, however, have emphasized a highly moral and emotional approach better aimed at the mass public than at the policy-making elite. For whatever reasons, however, there is widespread agreement that most black groups do not have a good understanding of the operations of the policy process. One black observer commented, "The civil rights groups have a total ignorance of how important appropriations and administrative guidelines are. They just don't understand the process."[41]

In addition, black groups face a number of specific problems in securing access simply because they are black groups. The concentration of black people in the urban North and the rural South limits the willingness of many congressmen to pay them much heed since they are not major factors in their constituencies. Another problem is that relatively few black leaders have sufficient personal prestige or professional status to guarantee their inclusion, formally or informally, at the innovative and formulative stages. Aside from Whitney Young in housing and Kenneth Clark in education and a handful of others of similar stature, few blacks are actively consulted by the White House, the agencies, or the key congressional leaders. Nor do they have easy access to influential policy makers in those places. Finally, it may be that access is severely restricted by certain members of the elite who do not view some of the black groups—particularly the more militant ones—as legitimate participants in the political process.

SUMMARY AND IMPLICATIONS

The major reason for the ineffectiveness of black participation appears to be a severe lack of resources and a decision to concentrate most activity at the level of local communities. The result is that the few efforts made by black groups to influence national policy suffer from insufficient expertise, with respect to both the complexities of policy and the workings of the policy process. Black participation and representation occurs primarily in the legislative-consideration and the implementation stages of the policy process. Black organizations and leaders have made little attempt to influence policy development at the innovative and formulative stage where meaningful choices between long-range alternatives are for the most part made.

The policy goals that black groups have pursued have been short run, direct, and highly visible: principally to attack overt racial discrimination and to promote integration. Only recently have black groups begun to direct their efforts towards problems of black poverty rather than towards the lack of legal equality. Most black participation has been aimed at the courts and Congress through litigation and legislative lobbying.

Black interests are represented indirectly in the policy-making process through a variety of mechanisms. Probably the most important of these is that certain members of the decision-making elite may already share some attitudes of some black groups. Outside the elite, organized labor has often represented black interests to decision makers. But indirect representation is often incomplete and ineffective, and many blacks perceive it to be a demeaning survival of the paternal master-slave relation between blacks and whites.

It appears that the pluralist description of the American political system is not entirely adequate. Our research has shown that black interests and black groups do not, on the whole, possess effective access to the centers of decision making in federal education and housing policy. This lack of influence is not, however, due primarily to the causes that most critics of pluralism have suggested. Contrary to their analyses, channels of access do appear to be relatively open and most decision makers seem willing to listen to any groups who use them. The extremely limited use of the channels by groups with the most manifest set of unmet demands reveals a flaw in the pluralist analysis. As Mancur Olson has pointed out, the main assumption of the pluralists—that rational men sharing interests will form groups in order to accomplish their ends—is defective. This applies not only to the black community, but to other interests as well—for example, housewives, students, commuters or, more generally, consumers, as opposed to producers, of goods and services.

Furthermore, there are defects in the pluralist assumption that the response of the decision-making elite will normally be satisfactory. Without examining specific policy outcomes, it seems obvious that the response of federal policy makers to black demands, whether they are articulated by marginal black participation or indirect white representation, is inadequate. This inadequacy is reflected in continued social and economic discrimination against black Americans and in the rise of the black-power movement. Indeed, Dahl notes the "spirit of alienation and despair" that affects black ghetto dwellers and suggests that it is associated with the emergence of civil disorders.[42] To us this constitutes recognition, *albeit en passant,* that *pluralism is not producing the social stability that ought to accompany the incremental change and mutual adjustment that, according to Dahl, are its byproducts.*[43]

It is quite possible that the American political system may be able to proceed on the basis of incremental change and mutual adjustment because the interests that are not easily susceptible to mutual adjustment, such as those of the blacks, are not effectively included in the process of political decision making. If this is the case then it ought to be recognized that the process exacts a price: as the political system responds incrementally, the social system experiences severe instability.

Alternatively, it may well be that violence is more a response to the beginning of elite recognition of mass demands. That is, that the initial substantive responses of the system (in the form of some satisfactory outcomes) to groups that hitherto have elicited little or no response may result sequentially in: (a) a degree of initial gratification; (b) the expectation of continued and more meaningful responses; (c) pressure for such responses; and (d) to the extent that such responses are not forthcoming, disappointment, anger, frustration, and ultimately violence directed at the system and institutions that seemingly have failed. While pluralism "worked" according to theory in its initial responses to black demands, i.e., favorable judicial action, the subsequent course of events was quite different. Initial successes through litigation were followed by extensive organized efforts to end legal and political discrimination. The campaign, which was marked by the sit-ins and the 1963 March on Washington, culminated in the passage of the Civil Rights Act of 1964. This successful effort in turn gave rise to black expectations that public policies leading to the rapid achievement of full social and economic equality would be adopted. When the political system proved incapable of meeting these expectations, which may have been heightened by the black power movement, violence resulted. The fact that urban violence is often centered in the black community is undoubtedly the product of many complex systemic factors that are beyond the scope of this paper. It is quite possible, however, that one of those factors may have been limited black participation in the federal policy process.

These seemingly antithetical interpretations can perhaps best be reconciled by the proposition that substantial disadvantaged groups in American society do not possess "the capacity and opportunity to influence some officials somewhere in the political system to obtain at least some of their goals"[44] and that when they finally do begin to achieve elite recognition of their demands *instability and conflict rather than satisfaction* are a probable result. On that basis, we urge caution against the belief that disadvantaged groups such as the blacks can be drawn into active participation in the system, at the mass or elite levels, without incurring social costs. The pluralist description has implied that this can be done. We believe that a more realistic expectation is in order.

In addition, we suggest that extensive efforts should be made to secure more effective and meaningful involvement of black interests and black leaders in all aspects of the federal policy process. It is appropriate to do so on the basis of democratic ideals alone; it also makes eminent sense as a possible means of strengthening the black community's support for the social and political systems. The civil rights movement did not result in extensive involvement by black groups in the federal policy process in housing or education. It is apparent that the policy makers are aware of the need to represent the blacks and the poor, but that they are uncertain about what can and should be done. The dilemma of the decision makers extends not only to the process of representation of interests, but also to the substance of what should be done for the disadvantaged who are themselves unable to develop viable suggestions. Deliberately expanded black participation in the federal policy process will not solve these problems, but it should be an important step towards overcoming the lack of leadership, disorganization, and resultant frustration that now characterize black involvement in the pluralist system.

Finally, we must conclude with a disclaimer. This paper is not primarily an attack on pluralism nor is it a definitive examination of black involvement in the policy-making behavior of the national elite. It is a call for reassessment of some pluralist assumptions and an urgent plea for more research on the processes by which people with shared interests organize into groups and gain access to political decision makers.

NOTES

[1]Jack L. Walker, "A Critique of the Elitist Theory of Democracy," *American Political Science Review,* 60 (June 1966), 291. For a rebuttal of Walker and other critics see Peter Y. Medding. " 'Elitist' Democracy: An Unsuccessful Critique of a Misunderstood Theory," *Journal of Politics,* 31 (August 1969), 641-644.

[2]See Bernard Berelson, Paul F. Lazarsfeld and William McPhee, *Voting* (Chicago: University of Chicago Press, 1954). ch. 14; Seymour M. Lipset, Introduction to Roberto Michels, *Political Parties* (New York: Collier Books, 1962), 14-16; and W. H. Morris-Jones, "In Defence of Apathy: Some Doubts on the Duty to Vote," *Political Studies,* 2 (February 1954), 25-37.

[3]Also, see Paul H. Conn, "Social Pluralism and Democratic Representation" (paper presented at the 1968 annual meeting of the American Political Science Association, Washington, D.C., September, 1968), 13-14, 17.

[4]Robert Lane, *Political Life* (New York: The Free Press, 1959); and Conn, "Social Pluralism."

[5]E. E. Schattschneider, *The Semi-Sovereign People* (New York: Holt, Rinehart and Winston, 1960), 35.

[6]See Peter Bachrach and Morton Baratz, "The Two Faces of Power," *American Political Science Review,* 56 (December 1962), 950.

[7]Our approach is similar to, but less complex than, that outlined by Kenneth J. Gergen, "Assessing the Leverage Points in the Process of Policy Formation," in *The Study of Policy Formation,* ed. by Raymond A. Bauer and K. J. Gergen (New York: The Free Press, 1968), 182-203. Undoubtedly the precision of our procedures could have been increased if we had had the opportunity to read Gergen's discussion before conducting our studies. Nevertheless, we believe that both we and Gergen recognize the same problems in the identification of persons of influence, that we have the same basic objectives, and that our techniques yield similar results.

[8]In its recent suits, the NAACP has concentrated on attacking de facto segregation outside the South. In addition to litigation, it has convened conferences of educational experts to discuss, among other things, what federal programs can do for black children.

[9]Its efforts have involved litigation, which most recently has attacked freedom-of-choice plans in Southern school districts, and monitoring administrative implementation of programs in education and other areas.

[10]In early 1968 it did hire a staff member versed in housing to develop a housing program for the NAACP and to influence the implementation of housing policy through direct contacts with HUD.

[11]The director, Jack Ward, left to head the National Committee Against Discrimination in Housing, a small group that attempts to influence public policy

at the stages of formulation and legislative consideration, primarily by writing research monographs that it distributes to decision makers. One of these monographs, "How the Federal Government Builds Ghettos," was credited by several respondents with having had a significant effect on HUD.

¹²Interview with a Leadership Conference lobbyist, April 1968. In most cases our respondents asked that their anonymity be preserved. Consequently we have identified them only in terms of their location and function in the policy process. Wherever possible we have identified them by name.

¹³See "Open-Housing Law Credited to Mitchell's Lobbying," *Congressional Quarterly Weekly Report,* April 26, 1968, 931–934.

¹⁴In 1967, for example, Mitchell was involved in the passage of the Elementary and Secondary Education Act Amendments with respect to two issues. He joined in a successful attempt to have the Senate kill the House-passed Foundation Amendment, which would have complicated enforcement procedures under Title VI of the Civil Rights Act of 1964. He also worked unsuccessfully against the Green Amendment which transferred responsibility for the administration of Title III of the Elementary and Secondary Education Act from the United States Office of Education to state departments of education. See the testimony of Mitchell with respect to these issues before the Senate Education Subcommittees. U.S. Congress, Senate, Labor and Public Welfare Subcommittee on Education, *Hearings on Education Legislation,* 1967, part 6, 90th Cong., 1st sess. (Washington, D.C.: Government Printing Office, 1967), 2235–2245.

¹⁵According to a conference spokesman, the organization is aware of its emphasis on civil rights, considers it a deficiency at this point, and is moving to become more involved in the areas of education, housing, and poverty.

¹⁶Interview with spokesman for SNCC, June 1968.

¹⁷The Poor People's Campaign of 1968 attempted to transfer this technique to issues of public policy not generally perceived as moral issues. The Campaign sought to influence all stages of the policy-making process through visits to high-ranking administrators and key congressmen, but the Campaign's demands were not well articulated. As one observer commented, "The Campaign was a failure. They cried out in pain: 'We want jobs and incomes. We are crying out. You are the technicians. You devise the programs.' But that was a level so foreign to congressmen that nothing happened." Because the demands were poorly articulated, the Campaign was "bought off" easily. Thus, as its major accomplishment, it claimed passage of the 1968 housing legislation despite the fact that enactment was never in doubt even before the Campaign. This is not to say that the Campaign was a failure. It did accomplish some changes in the Food Stamp program that would have not occurred otherwise and, more important, through the publicity it received, it may have helped to shift public attitudes in the long run.

¹⁸Because we used an interview schedule consisting of 14 open-end questions covering a wide range of subjects, it was not always possible to ask all of the questions in the course of each interview. Consequently an accidental bias of indeterminate direction results from the failure to ask the question of 12 members of the policy-making elite.

¹⁹Interview, June 1969.

²⁰Interview, March 1968.

²¹Interview, January 1968.

[22]Nothing in these data indicates, of course, the degree of support that any black organization enjoyed in the black community. We make no assumptions regarding the level of that support, nor is it relevant to the fact that the more moderate organizations, the NAACP and the Urban League, enjoy greater support among members of the housing policy system than the more militant groups, SNCC and CORE.

[23]Interview, February 1968.

[24]Emmanuel Gutman, "Social Attitudes of Trade Unionists," *Dissent,* 15 (January-February 1968), 12.

[25]Interview, February 1968.

[26]Interview, January 1968.

[27]Interview, March 1968.

[28]Interview, January 1968.

[29]For a discussion of values held by the black community, see Gary T. Marx, *Protest and Prejudice: A Study of Belief in the Black Community* (New York: Harper and Row, 1967); and William Brink and Louis Harris, *Black and White* (New York: Simon & Schuster, 1966).

[30]Interview, April 1968.

[31]Mancur Olson, Jr., *The Logic of Collective Action* (New York: Schocken Books, 1968).

[32]The bitter fight organized labor has conducted against state "Right-to-Work" laws is based exactly on this logic. If "Rights-to-Work" laws are allowed, labor argues, non-unionized workers will be able to benefit from union gains without themselves making any contributions such as union dues. There would, in short, be a positive incentive not to join unions.

[33]Olson, *Logic,* 166–167.

[34]Olson's argument appears to hold for groups joining coalitions as well as for individuals joining groups.

[35]Interview, May 1968.

[36]Interview, February 1968.

[37]Interview, March 1968.

[38]Interview, February 1968.

[39]Interview, March 1968.

[40]Interview, February 1968.

[41]Interview, April 1968.

[42]R. A. Dahl, *Pluralist Democracy in the United States* (Chicago: Rand McNally & Co., 1967), 301.

[43]Dahl concluded his initial description of the American political system with the observation that "it appears to be a relatively efficient system for re-enforcing agreement, encouraging moderation, and maintaining social peace in a restless and inmoderate people operating a gigantic, powerful, diversified, and incredibly complex society," R. A. Dahl, *A Preface to Democratic Theory* (Chicago: University of Chicago Press, 1956), 151.

[44]Dahl, *Pluralist Democracy,* 386.